THE SMALL ANIMALS

QUESTION AND ANSWER MANUAL

DAVID ALDERTON

BARRON'S

Contents

First published for United States and Canada
in 2001 by Barron's Educational Series, Inc.

AN ANDROMEDA BOOK

Copyright © 2001 Andromeda Oxford Limited

Planned and produced by
Andromeda Oxford Limited
11–13 The Vineyard, Abingdon,
Oxfordshire, OX14 3PX, England

Edited and designed by Derek Hall & Associates

All inquiries should be addressed to:
Barron's Educational Series, Inc.
250 Wireless Boulevard
Hauppauge, New York 11788
http://www.barronseduc.com

Advisory Editors
DR. DAN RICE (US), DR. JIM COLLINS (UK)

Editor	Derek Hall
Designer	Tony Truscott
Picture Research Manager	Claire Turner
Production Director	Clive Sparling
Publishing Director	Graham Bateman

ISBN 0-7641-5226-2

Library of Congress Card Number: 00-112270

Cover photographs: *front top* Jane Burton, *front
center* Juniors Bildarchiv/R. Kuhn, *back top left*
Juniors Bildarchiv/M. Wegler, *back top right*
AOL, *back bottom* Jane Burton

Film origination by Atcolor, Milan, Italy
Printed by Polygraf Print, Presov, Slovakia

9   8   7   6   5   4   3   2   1

Introduction

Keeping small animals such as rabbits, guinea pigs, and chinchillas as pets is as popular as ever. Once regarded largely as being only a pastime for children, the company of these creatures is now enjoyed by many adults as well. This is reflected by the recent upsurge of interest in house-rabbits, for example, which are often kept in preference to a cat or a dog. Although rabbits are still the most popular of the so-called small animals group of pets, an increasing range of other small mammals is now being kept as household companions. In addition to the more familiar rodents such as mice and gerbils, other animals such as pygmy hedgehogs and sugar gliders are becoming more widely kept and bred. This in turn has led to the coining of the phrase "pocket pets," as a general description of the small mammals which fall into this category today.

Keeping pocket pets is generally straightforward. Furthermore, they do not smell, provided their cages are cleaned regularly, and they are not noisy. Indeed, only the guinea pig is likely to utter sounds regularly, and these are certainly not likely to be disturbing, even in the home. Many of these animals, including guinea pigs, chipmunks, and rabbits, can be housed outdoors if required, even in temperate areas. But these small mammals are so adaptable that even if you have no outdoor space available to house them, they can be kept just as easily in the home.

▶ Mice, gerbils, jirds, and chinchillas must be kept in cages indoors.

▲▶ *Rabbits and chipmunks are among the varieties of small animals that can be kept outside all year.*

It is no coincidence that rabbits and guinea pigs tend to be most widely kept, because they are relatively easy to handle and rarely display any tendency to bite. They are available in a wide range of color varieties and coat types, which enhances the scope of their appeal. This is also true of a number of other popular and freely bred small animals such as hamsters, rats, and mice. This in turn means that there is plenty of scope in terms of breeding these small animals for exhibition purposes, with shows being held on a regular basis. Becoming involved in this area provides a further focus of interest and can develop into a lifelong hobby.

Apart from breeding particular colors, there are also opportunities to work with other breeders to develop and popularize new species as pets. Recent newcomers on the scene include various members of the gerbil group as well as the degu—a South American rodent related to the chinchilla.

This book will help you choose the type of pocket pet which is most suitable for your lifestyle, guiding you through the decision-making process and progressing to explain your pet's requirements in detail. There is also advice about how to deal with illnesses and other emergencies. For the more experienced enthusiast, there is comprehensive coverage of all the different breeds and varieties of popular small animals, making it an indispensable and up-to-date reference manual.

DAVID ALDERTON

What Are Small Animals?

THE SMALL ANIMALS DESCRIBED IN THIS BOOK are all species of mammals. They are grouped within the class Mammalia and are subdivided into various smaller categories known as orders. Mammals have a number of characteristics in common—for example, they can maintain their body temperature independently of their surroundings, they normally have a covering of body fur which serves as insulation, and they suckle their young. The small body volume of many mammals relative to their surface area means that they can lose heat rapidly from their bodies. (This is important to remember when keeping some of the smaller species.)

Almost all the mammals featured in this book belong to two orders. The order Rodentia (rodents) includes mice, rats, gerbils, and guinea pigs. Rabbits, hares, and similar creatures known as pikas, are grouped within the order Lagomorpha.

▼ *The dense coat of the chinchilla helps to protect it from the cold in its Andean homeland. These very attractive and lively rodents appeal to people of all ages.*

For many years, lagomorphs were actually considered to be rodents and indeed share many features with them, such as a similarity in their pattern of dentition—although rabbits also have an additional set of much smaller, secondary incisor teeth.

Teeth and Feeding

The incisors at the front of the mouth are very sharp, enabling rodents not only to crack nuts and other hard-shelled foods but also to gnaw effectively to create safe retreats in buildings or other localities. The incisors of rabbits can easily strip the bark from trees. The shape of these

teeth is critical. The two incisors in the upper jaw are slightly more curved than those in the lower jaw and terminate in a chiseled edge. This is enhanced by the casing of tough enamel on the front of the tooth. It wears down more slowly than the softer dentine at the back, creating a hard, angled, cutting surface.

Rodents and rabbits lack the pointed teeth, known as canines, found in carnivores. Instead, there is a characteristic gap known as the diastema between the incisors and cheek teeth, or molars. Most rodents lack premolars as well, although chipmunks have one premolar tooth on each side of their upper jaws as part of their first set of teeth. The diastema has a functional significance; it allows the cheeks to be pulled in behind the incisors, so that rodents can continue gnawing with their incisors while at the same time chewing selective food items with their molars before swallowing them.

Feeding is a potentially hazardous period for many rodents and lagomorphs, during which they must emerge from the protective environment of their burrows or other retreats. Therefore many are nocturnal. This gives no guarantee of protection, however, since various predators are also well equipped to hunt in darkness. Hamsters have evolved a further adaptation to protect them at this stage, in the form of cheek pouches. These are basically an enlargement of the mouth, extending back as far as the shoulder. Rather than pausing to eat, hamsters quickly fill these pouches with as much food as possible before returning to their burrows to empty them.

▲ *A hamster with cheek pouches full of food. Hamsters sometimes store excess food in their burrows—even amassing quantities of as much as 200lb (91kg).*

● **What happens if one of the incisor teeth is broken?**

... Any damage to the incisor teeth is potentially life-threatening for the creature concerned, especially in the wild. The opposing tooth in the other jaw will continue growing and will not be worn down by gnawing, as happens naturally. As a result, it is likely to develop in such a way that it is impossible for the animal to feed properly. Veterinary assistance will be needed to trim the teeth so that they wear evenly against each other again.

● **What causes misaligned teeth in rabbits?**

The problem of incorrect alignment of the incisor teeth is an inherited condition. Always check a young rabbit's teeth, therefore, before buying it. If it is suffering from non-alignment, you must have the affected teeth clipped back by your veterinarian every eight weeks or so, to ensure that your pet can continue eating properly. Affected individuals should not be used for breeding, because of the possibility of this characteristic being passed to the offspring.

● **Does food ever become stuck in a hamster's pouches?**

This can occur on occasions and may be the result of offering them unsuitable foodstuffs. Veterinary attention may be required to overcome the resulting obstruction.

▼ *The skull of the hamster below shows clearly the characteristic arrangement of the chisel-shaped incisor teeth at the front of the mouth, as well as the diastema separating the incisors from the molar teeth.*

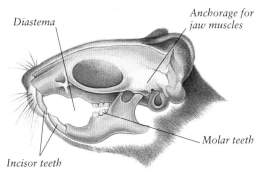

Diastema

Anchorage for jaw muscles

Molar teeth

Incisor teeth

Breeding Rates

A feature commonly regarded as a characteristic of small mammals is their high reproductive rate. However, litter sizes can be quite variable. Within the order Rodentia, for example, members of the myomorph group (such as mice) have large litters. They have a rapid reproductive rate, enabling them to take advantage of favorable environmental conditions. Their numbers can assume plague proportions if unchecked. But in groups such as the caviomorphs (which include the chinchilla), the gestation period is much longer, and fewer young—perhaps only two or three—result from a single pregnancy. This enhances the chances of survival in their native mountainous habitat, where the environmental conditions are harsh yet stable.

Body Adaptations

The coloration of small mammals is usually rather subdued, enabling them to blend into their backgrounds. You can tell much about these animals' environments from their coats. Those originating from desert areas, such as the Syrian hamster, tend to have yellowish coats with whitish underparts. The yellow coloration

▼ *Many rodents are shy, nocturnal creatures that hide away during the day. Large eyes, like those of this hamster (inset), help improve their vision in low light.*

▼ *Some rodents are agile climbers—particularly rats and mice, which rely on their long tails to act as a counterbalance during this activity.*

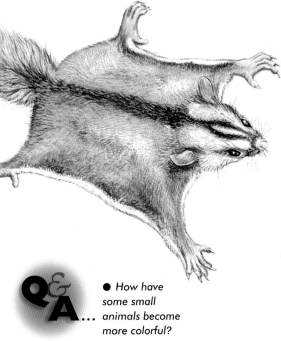

▶ *Sugar gliders are mammals that have evolved special folds of skin on the sides of their bodies, enabling them to glide from tree to tree.*

helps them to blend into the sand to protect them from predators, and the white coloration helps reflect the heat of the sand from their bodies.

Chinchillas, which originate in the Andean region of South America, are faced with the problem of keeping warm in a cold environment. They have larger bodies (to retain heat better) than many rodents and a very dense coat. Instead of a single hair emerging from a hair follicle, chinchillas may have up to 80 hairs arising from a single follicle. This nearly proved to be responsible for their demise, however, since they were hunted almost to extinction for their unique fur—which is so dense that parasites such as fleas cannot become established in it. Rabbits have also been highly valued for their fur, and this feature is still used in the Rabbit Fancy today, where the breeds are divided into fur and fancy categories. Not all small mammals are fur clad, however. The African pygmy hedgehog is covered with spines, which are actually modified hairs.

The presence of a tail is a very variable feature among the small mammals, especially rodents. Rodents that spend their time exclusively on the ground, such as maras and guinea pigs, have no tail, while the stublike tail of hamsters has no functional significance. In contrast, the long tails of gerbils and jerboas are a vital counterbalance, and when combined with their long legs enable them to jump effectively.

This feature is even more pronounced in the sugar glider, which has a heavily furred tail as well as flaps of skin along the sides of its body. These enable this marsupial to glide through the air. Rats and mice are characterized in part by their long, scaly tails. In some species, such as the harvest mouse, the tails are surprisingly prehensile, helping the mice to support their weight and aid their grip as they climb, by curling around stems of grass.

Q & A ...

● **How have some small animals become more colorful?**

The rapid reproductive rate of many species means that the likelihood of an unusual color variant emerging as the result of a mutation is fairly high. Such individuals have certainly occurred in the wild, and by careful breeding in captivity it has been possible to create the wide range of colors that now exists in domestic strains.

● **Why is the tail of my rabbit much paler on the underside?**

The short, fluffy tail of the rabbit is used primarily for communication, especially at mating time. The male, known as the buck, will lift his tail in this way to attract the attention of the female, or doe. This behavior is described as tail flagging.

● **Are any small animals noisy as pets?**

Guinea pigs have a distinctive "oinking" call, particularly when they are excited—awaiting food, for example—but otherwise, you are unlikely to hear many sounds from this group of animals. Rats and mice communicate with each other, but their calls are usually outside our hearing range. However, following damage to their vocal cords, the calls may become audible. Such mice are often described as "whistling mice," because of the resulting sounds. Thumping noises coming from the vicinity of a rabbit hutch at night are the result of the occupant kicking its long hind legs against something, as a means of communicating with other rabbits which may be in the area. This explains why the name "Thumper" is associated with rabbits.

The Responsibilities of Keeping Small Animals

THERE ARE A NUMBER OF QUESTIONS THAT should be addressed before acquiring any small animal. Although the requirements of such creatures are far less demanding than those of a dog, for example, they will still require time spent on their needs every day. Even factors such as coat length are significant, since long-coated varieties will require more frequent grooming than smooth-coated varieties.

The space that must be given over to their accommodation will also influence your choice. Animals such as the mara, and also the larger breeds of rabbit such as the Flemish Giant, require a great deal more space than hamsters and gerbils, for example. Feeding costs are probably less significant when it comes to making a choice, because although you will have to buy some dry food, it is not especially expensive and you can often augment the diet of various small mammals by growing food items in your yard if you have one, or even by allowing your pets to graze on the grass in a run.

Housing costs for rabbits and guinea pigs can

▲ *Smaller animals such as hamsters, mice, and gerbils will require specially purchased accommodation, although it should last throughout the animal's life.*

be reduced if you are able to construct a hutch and run yourself. The housing of some small animals such as chipmunks and sugar gliders is more demanding, though, with a structure not unlike an aviary being required for them.

Lifespan can be another important consideration when choosing a small animal as a pet. Hamsters have a relatively short lifespan, typically not exceeding two years, whereas at the other extreme, chinchillas may often live for over a decade. The average lifespans for each animal group are indicated in the fact files found later in this book.

Handling Small Animals

Ease of handling is also significant, especially when choosing a pet that can be enjoyed by the whole family. Gerbils and similar small rodents do not appreciate being petted for long periods—they may even faint under these circumstances. Hamsters are quite amenable to gentle handling, especially if they become accustomed to being picked up from an early age, but they can sometimes inflict a painful bite with their sharp incisor teeth. The same is true of rats and

▼ *The mara is best housed in a small paddock area. The space you have available is an important consideration when choosing a small animal as a pet.*

mice. Rabbits and guinea pigs are usually unlikely to nip, however. It is important to remember that a large rabbit may be too heavy for young children to pick up easily, and if it is dropped, the rabbit is likely to sustain serious injury.

Pygmy hedgehogs are not recommended for young children, but it is possible to handle these small mammals with care. Breeders often advertize their stock as being "roll free," which means that the hedgehogs are sufficiently tame not to curl up into a ball when handled, so there is less likelihood of being pricked by their spines.

Although it may not be such an obvious consideration, you may want to think about the problems which you could face if your pet escapes at some point. This is not unknown, especially with hamsters which may disappear overnight if the door to their quarters has not been closed securely. It is generally much harder to capture an escaped hamster in the home compared with a rabbit or guinea pig, for example, simply because it can disappear from sight so easily. Gerbils—and especially jerboas—also represent a challenge when loose, since they can leap considerable distances when being pursued around the room.

● *Can I bring home with me a small pet rodent purchased on vacation abroad?*

This is something to investigate with the agricultural department in your country before setting out. You may need to arrange a period of quarantine and also obtain veterinary certification. A few species such as the crested porcupine are incorporated onto the listings of the Convention on International Trade in Endangered Species of Wild Fauna and Flora (CITES), so additional paperwork will be required in these cases. Seek advice on this aspect from the government department which serves as your CITES management authority.

● *I'm interested in exhibiting small animals. With which varieties am I most likely to win?*

You are likely to have a higher percentage of potential exhibition success if you avoid varieties that have specific markings, such as the English breed of rabbit or the Tortoiseshell and White guinea pig, but then so will other breeders! Rarer varieties may offer you the best potential.

▼ *A large rabbit may be too heavy for a young child to handle confidently, and it may be better to choose one of the smaller breeds such as this Netherland Dwarf.*

Choosing a Small Animal

THERE ARE A NUMBER OF POSSIBLE WAYS OF obtaining small animals, and your choice will in part be influenced by the one you are seeking. A good starting point is likely to be your neighborhood pet store. Many stock a range of the more popular small animals, such as hamsters, gerbils, rabbits, and guinea pigs. The choice of colors may be rather limited, and certainly in the case of rabbits, you are unlikely to find a range of breeds for sale. But although the animals for sale

will not be suitable for exhibition because they are unlikely to correspond to judging standards, they can nevertheless make excellent pets.

Apart from ensuring that your new pet is healthy, it is important to start out with a genuinely young animal, so that it can be tamed easily. Pet stores can sometimes be less familiar with the age of their stock than breeders, who will almost certainly have detailed records available showing when their litters were born.

You will probably need to contact a breeder if you are seeking a particularly unusual variety of small animal, or if you are planning to develop a show stud. It can be worthwhile scanning your local newspaper, since breeders may offer their surplus stock here, but a more reliable method of

◀ *Attending shows can provide a useful means of contacting breeders or even obtaining animals. If you are interested in showing your animals in due course, it is important to start out with quality stock.*

▼ *Be sure to check potential purchases carefully, to spot any obvious signs of illness. The general guidelines shown below apply to all small animals. Do not proceed with a purchase if you have any doubts.*

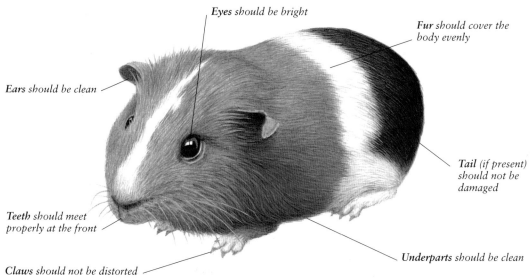

Eyes *should be bright*

Fur *should cover the body evenly*

Ears *should be clean*

Tail *(if present) should not be damaged*

Teeth *should meet properly at the front*

Claws *should not be distorted*

Underparts *should be clean*

making contact will be to obtain details of the national club representing enthusiasts keeping the group of small animals which interests you. This should help put you in contact with breeders in your neighborhood who are likely to have stock available. Some breeders now also have their own web pages. Always telephone first to check that the breeder has suitable stock available and to arrange a convenient time to visit, rather than turning up unannounced.

Be guided by the advice of the breeder. Most are eager to encourage newcomers to the hobby, and will assist not only in terms of selling stock but also in providing help when it comes to advising on the most suitable pairings. You may be lucky enough to end up being offered an older buck which has done well in the past but is now surplus to the breeder's requirements. Such individuals can often give an invaluable boost to a developing new stud.

Checking Out a Potential Purchase

While it is obviously hard to assess fertility, there are a number of points that you will need to check to ensure that your new pet is healthy prior to purchase. Overall condition is clearly very important, and the animal should be sleek and alert and moving readily. The only exception to this rule may be found in hamsters, which tend to be more nocturnal than other pets and so can appear rather dull and sleepy when disturbed during the day. Pay particular attention to the coat, since any underlying areas of baldness or inflamed skin suggest a health problem, particularly in guinea pigs.

Rodents and rabbits are very dependent on the incisor teeth in the front of their mouths, which continue growing throughout their lives. It is vital that these teeth meet properly, so they will wear down correctly.

At the other end of the body, it is important to check the fur around the vent for any sign of staining here that may indicate a digestive disorder. If you are in any doubt, look around the animal's living quarters as well, to check the state of its droppings—which should be firm. Although in some cases diarrhea may be linked with the creature's diet, it can have much more serious causes.

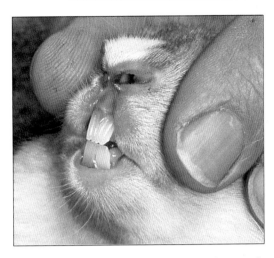

▲ *It is important to check the incisor teeth of any small animal you intend buying. If these are not growing at the correct angle—which can be a congenital problem— the animal will encounter eating difficulties.*

● **When is the best time of year to obtain rabbits?**

... You are likely to find the widest selection of youngsters available in the early summer, because most breeders do not encourage their stock to breed during the cold months of winter. Winter is, however, the time when shows are often taking place, so you can make valuable contacts at this stage or obtain older, breeding stock. Do not put any wintertime purchases outside immediately if they have been accustomed to living indoors.

● *Are there magazines and periodicals catering to the different small animals?*

They are usually covered in general pet-oriented magazines, but for more specific information and contacts, you will need to look in publications that tend to be obtainable only by direct subscription, rather than from news stands. Clubs and societies also frequently produce publications for their members and often have web sites you can visit.

● *Can different small animals be kept together?*

This is not generally recommended, with the possible exception of a guinea pig and one of the smaller breeds of rabbit. Rats and mice will be likely to fight severely if housed together, with the mouse invariably getting the worst. Hamsters are even antisocial with each other. The differing environmental needs of many small animals also mean it is impractical to mix them.

Rabbits

OF ALL THE SMALL ANIMALS KEPT AS PETS, RABBITS ARE THE MOST popular. They look appealing, have gentle natures, and most varieties are fairly hardy and undemanding in terms of their care and housing. There are over 40 different species of rabbits and hares found around the world, but all domesticated rabbits are descended from the European rabbit (*Oryctolagus cuniculus*), an animal which was originally confined to the Iberian Peninsula.

Evidence suggests that after the last ice age ended, some 15,000 years ago, rabbits expanded their range further northward, first crossing the land bridge between mainland Europe and Britain about 5,000 years ago. But their stay here was short-lived initially, since the dense forest vegetation proved to be an unsuitable habitat. It was not until after the Norman Conquest of 1066 that rabbits again reached Britain. Nearly 700 years later the European rabbit was introduced to North America, where it has since flourished in the wild alongside the native species of American rabbits.

There is no doubt that religious teaching helped the domestication process, which has ultimately led to the widespread availability of pet rabbits today, because European monasteries allowed young rabbits to be considered as fish rather than meat. This was highly significant, because it meant that they could be eaten during Lent. There is evidence that rabbits were being kept in French monasteries as early as AD 600, and they were soon taken further afield, to Germany for example, long before wild rabbits were established in this part of the world. Rabbits were also prized for their fur, and records show that large quantities of rabbit pelts were being exported through Europe as early as the 1300s, where they were made into garments.

Widespread interest in keeping rabbits for show purposes began in the 1800s, and has continued to the present day, with many breeds and color varieties now having been created. Rabbits have also become popular as pets and, since the 1980s, more widely accepted as household companions instead of being restricted to an outdoor hutch.

▶ *Their large ears help to make rabbits one of the most instantly recognizable of all small animals, although this feature has been modified in some breeds as the result of domestication.*

The Rabbit's Popularity

IT IS UNCLEAR WHEN THE FIRST COLOR VARIETIES of rabbits arose, but a white rabbit is portrayed in a painting executed by Titian in 1530, entitled "The Madonna with the Rabbit." Today, in addition to white individuals, both black and piebald rabbits sometimes occur in the wild, and even sandy-colored individuals are seen.

Showing rabbits began at a time when there was increasing interest in breeding and stan-dardization of livestock in general. This quest for uniformity is reflected in both the physical appearance or "type" of such rabbits, as well as in their coloration, with these characteristics serving to distinguish the different breeds.

It was also at this stage that one of the most audacious schemes involving the breeding of rabbits was marketed in the United States and helped to trigger widespread interest in keeping these small mammals there for the first time. Although the rabbit family is represented in

▼ *A wild rabbit. Although a range of colors exists in the wild rabbit population, many more color varieties and patterns are to be found in domesticated rabbits.*

● *Has the domestication process caused any changes in rabbits?*

... The most marked difference between wild and domestic rabbits is in the respective sizes of their brains. Studies have revealed that domestic rabbits have a reduction of about 20 percent in their brain capacities, compared with their wild relatives. Since domestic rabbits in the home or yard do not face the constant dangers which they would be confronted with in the wild, the area of the brain used for processing information about their environment is smaller. Other specific changes affecting the length and carriage of the rabbit's ears, as well as its overall size and coloration, have also occurred thanks to domestication.

● *How big can rabbits grow?*

The Angevin rabbits once bred in Belgium could grow to 5ft (1.5m) in length and would weigh up to 33lb (15kg). Although this breed is now sadly extinct, the Flemish Giant, also of Belgian origins, is regarded as the largest breed in the world. Such rabbits may reach 3ft (0.9m) in length and tip the scales at 24lb (11kg).

● *Why are hares not very popular as pets?*

This is almost certainly because of their more nervous and active natures, and possibly their larger size, although they have been kept on occasions.

● *How long does it take to tame a wild rabbit?*

Youngsters will settle quite rapidly, and within a few generations the offspring of wild rabbits will be indistinguishable from domestic rabbits in terms of their friendliness—particularly if they are handled regularly from weaning onward.

● *Have rabbits been domesticated longer than other pets?*

No. In fact, both cats and dogs have a much longer history of domestication than rabbits. But the rapid reproductive rate of the rabbit has helped to ensure that when color or fur mutations occur, these characteristics can be established very quickly in the population. This is true of most pet rodents as well.

▲ *The Flemish Giant is a direct descendent of the Angevin, the largest breed of rabbit ever recorded. Flemish Giants have friendly, placid natures, but they are very bulky to pick up.*

Fact File

Name:	Domestic Rabbit
Scientific name:	*Oryctolagus cuniculus*
Weight:	2.2–22lb (1–10kg)

Compatibility: Does may live together in harmony, but risk of pseudopregnancies is increased. Mature bucks together will fight. Sometimes kept with guinea pigs.

Appeal: Popular as pets and for exhibition. Friendly and will settle well both in the home or in an outdoor hutch.

Diet: Commercially produced rabbit food, pellets, hay, and greenfood plus root vegetables. Also apple.

Health problems: Susceptible to various digestive ailments. Also vulnerable to myxomatosis and VHD viruses.

Breeding tips: Avoid disturbing the doe's nest after she has given birth. Otherwise she may neglect or even attack her offspring.

Pregnancy:	31 days
Typical litter size:	6–8 young
Weaning:	35 days
Lifespan:	6–7 years

North America, none of the native cottontails has been domesticated there. Instead, would-be American rabbit breeders were attracted to the Belgian Hare which, in spite of its name, is a true rabbit—albeit a long-legged one. These rabbits were never really suitable as a commercial meat breed, yet large numbers of farms for Belgian Hares sprang up, with impoverished farmers attracted by the guaranteed purchase of all the rabbits they could produce.

Inevitably, the market finally crashed as supply outstripped demand. But the resulting publicity, combined with the attractive appearance of the Belgian Hare, meant that keeping rabbits, if only for pleasure rather than profit, attracted many ordinary Americans to these likable animals.

The recent trend toward keeping pet rabbits in the home, and the introduction of the description of "house-rabbit" for them, began in the cities of the United States as a direct result of modern urban living. This has led to a resurgence of interest in the larger, so-called "giant breeds" which can attain the size of a small dog. Yet unlike a dog, a house-rabbit does not need to be taken out for walks, nor will it bark or upset the neighbors. Furthermore, unlike owning a cat, there is little possibility of a house-rabbit ending up as a victim of passing traffic on busy roads in the neighborhood.

Keeping Rabbits Outdoors

ORIGINATING FROM A FAIRLY DRY PART OF THE world, rabbits kept outside require accommodation that gives them good protection from the elements, otherwise they are likely to suffer from respiratory illnesses that can be fatal. The basic requirement for housing a rabbit outdoors is a hutch. Most pet stores stock rabbit hutches, or can obtain them to order, so obtaining one should not be difficult. However, there may be significant differences in both the materials used in the construction of the hutch, as well as in the standard of the workmanship. Since hutches are relatively costly to purchase, it is important to check these factors carefully first, and always buy the best quality you can afford.

● *Are rabbits destructive toward their accommodation?*

... This depends partly on the individual, but there is a risk that certain parts of the hutch will be gnawed. Exposed edges of timber are especially vulnerable to a rabbit's teeth, but you can help persuade your pet not to attack its hutch by providing it with special chews to keep its teeth in trim.

● *Not all the hutches I have seen are partitioned. How important is this?*

A partition is important if you intend to keep your rabbit outside. This will provide it with a snug retreat and also ensures that it will feel more secure if a fox or a cat comes close to its quarters.

● *How long should a hutch last?*

With some care and maintenance—in terms of replacing the roofing felt when necessary, for example—the hutch should last for the rabbit's lifetime, and probably longer.

Marine plywood for sides, roof, and floor

▲ *There is a wide range of designs available for housing rabbits today. A combined hutch and run, as shown here, can be an excellent choice. This allows the rabbit more space than a traditional hutch.*

▶ *The main materials needed for constructing a hutch. Do not be tempted to economize on the quality of the materials, or you may find yourself replacing items at an early stage.*

Clout nails

Fixing brackets

Mineralized roofing felt

Stainless steel screws

What Size Hutch?

SMALL HUTCH

length 30in (76cm) x width 24in (60cm)
Suitable for Mini Lop, Netherland Dwarf, Polish, and similar.

MEDIUM HUTCH

length 40in (100cm) x width 24in (60cm)
Suitable for Chinchilla, Dutch, and English.

LARGE HUTCH

length 50in (127cm) x width 24in (60cm)
Suitable for British Giant, Flemish Giant, New Zealand breeds, and similar.

The typical rule is to allow about 155sq in (1000sq cm) of hutch area per 1.1lb (0.5kg) of adult rabbit body weight. The hutch height should be at least 18in (46cm), to allow the rabbit to sit up on its hindquarters.

Building a Hutch

It is quite easy to build a suitable hutch yourself, employing materials that are suitable for outdoor usage. All the necessary components to make a rabbit hutch can be obtained from most lumber stores. It may be possible to have all the components cut to size when you buy them, although you may need to be prepared to do this yourself. If you do have the materials cut when you buy them, be absolutely sure you have all

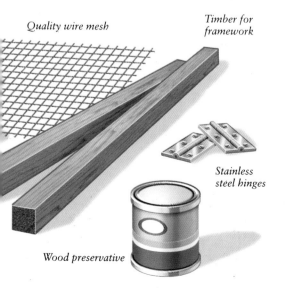

Quality wire mesh

Timber for framework

Stainless steel hinges

Wood preservative

your measurements correct, since a mistake may mean that you have to purchase new items of the correct size. Although plywood can be used on the sides of the hutch as well as for the floor and roof, it will look less attractive on the visible surfaces than tongue-and-groove timber. This timber interlocks snugly and it also reduces the likelihood of drafty gaps occurring, although it is more time consuming to assemble. Tongue-and-groove timber can also be used to make the door of the sheltered area of the hutch. Tongue-and-groove can be more difficult to cut accurately along its length, so design your hutch in such a way that you minimize such cuts.

Design and Materials

The basic materials for constructing a hutch are wood, a safe, non-toxic preservative, some wire mesh, and good-quality roofing felt. You will also need various screws, brackets, nails, and tacks as well as appropriate tools for cutting, joining, and finishing the components. The timber used for the legs of the hutch should be approximately 2in (5cm) square. Timber of the same dimensions should be used for the cross beam supports connecting the legs, as well as for the framework of the hutch itself.

You will also need two shorter pieces of timber to make the vertical supports for the inner partition (see below). The front vertical support is also used as a site for attaching part of the outer door fastenings.

The floor of the hutch should be made from heavy-duty plywood at least 0.5in (12mm) in thickness. (This can prove to be a point of weakness in many hutches, which often start to rot first in this area.) The roof, made from ply of similar thickness to the roof, should slope, to prevent any pooling of water on the top. The sides of the hutch will therefore need to be cut to shape to produce this slope, as will the inside partition running across the center of the hutch. (This partition serves to divide the rabbit's daytime quarters from those where it can rest out of sight.) A sliding door in this partition will enable you to clean the hutch easily, by shutting the rabbit in one part of the hutch while you clean out the other side. The sides and internal partitions can be made from 0.25in (6mm) ply.

Making a Start

It is usually best to prepare the different components inside and then assemble them outside. The first stage, after cutting the timber as necessary, will be to treat all outer wood surfaces with a safe, non-toxic wood preservative. This will increase its lifespan dramatically. Two coats of preservative are recommended, and they must be allowed to dry thoroughly. It is especially important to treat the cut ends of timber, because it is here that rot could start in due course.

◄ Make sure that the hutch has sufficient headroom to enable your rabbit to sit up like this.

The next stage will be to assemble the framework of the hutch in terms of the floor supports and the uprights at the corners—the lower part of which form the legs on which the hutch is supported. It is important that the hutch is supported off the ground, first to prevent the base from becoming wet and second to keep it out of reach of wild rabbits, which might spread diseases such as myxomatosis and parasites such as fleas to a pet rabbit within. The legs should raise the hutch at least 24in (60cm) off the ground for this reason. The floor section should be put in place next, after which the inner partition, dividing the rabbit's daytime and night-time quarters, will need to be fitted. This will join up on the front of the hutch with the vertical support for the two doors which will open outward toward the ends of the hutch from this point.

◄▲ When building a hutch, start by making the basic framework, incorporating the legs, strengthened with corner wedges or brackets (1). Next add the floor and the partition between the two compartments (2).

At this stage, the rest of the construction is probably best accomplished outdoors. Although it is better to screw the framework together for strength, the plywood sides can be nailed in place, as can the roof. It is helpful if the roof is constructed so that it can be lifted off if necessary. The roof must have an overhang of at least 2in (5cm) around the sides for the roofing felt to be attached. This overhang also allows water to be channeled away from the hutch.

While the door of the rabbit's rest quarters is solid timber, the other outer door will need to be made of wire mesh attached to a wooden frame. Use mesh 0.5in (12mm) square for this purpose. This will exclude mice that may be attracted to the rabbit's food and could spread disease if they enter the hutch. Mesh with a 19-gauge strand thickness will be strong enough.

▼ *This semi-exploded view shows the main items that need to be added once the basic framework has been constructed. The main outer door must be covered with mesh and the roof covered with roofing felt.*

● **How can I protect my rabbit from foxes and other predators?**

The door fittings are obviously very important in this regard. Do not rely on simple latches that could be moved by a paw, allowing the door to swing open. Fit proper sliding bolts, or even a hasp and padlock. Like the hinges, these must be kept well oiled to prevent them from rusting and becoming stuck.

● **How should I fix the mesh?**

First cut it carefully to size so that it fits neatly onto the inner frame of the door. Then, with the door lying on a flat, level surface, fix the mesh in place on the inner side of the door with plenty of netting staples, ensuring that there are no loose and potentially dangerous ends of wire protruding. Keep the mesh taut and square to create the best effect. Afterward, you can reinforce it by fixing battening all around the edge.

Roofing felt for covering top of hutch

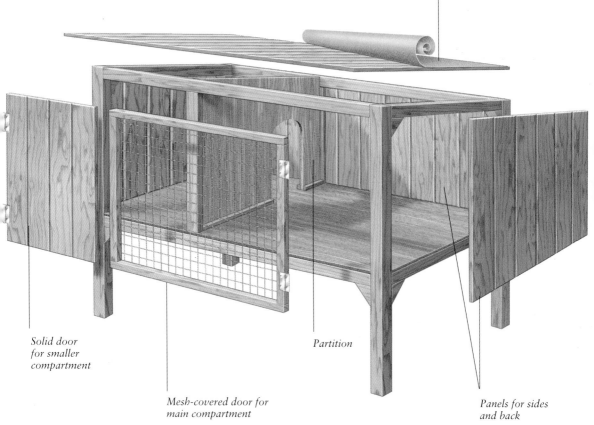

Solid door for smaller compartment

Partition

Mesh-covered door for main compartment

Panels for sides and back

Finishing Off

Cover the top of the hutch with roofing felt. This will ensure that the interior stays dry. Avoid using the cheapest felt, however, because this will often split quite quickly when exposed to the elements. Rain will then be able to penetrate under it, which can trigger rotting of the wood beneath, as well as allowing the water to seep down onto the rabbit's bedding. Green mineralized felt will often create the most attractive appearance. Fold the roofing felt around the edges of the roof overhangs and tack it in place on the underside with special broad-headed nails. Keep the felt as taut as possible, starting on the top edge and pulling it down across the roof. Battening is not normally needed across the roof, but it may be added around the sides to provide extra support to hold the roofing felt in place here. If you need to overlap the felt for any reason, be sure to overlap the bottom layer with the

top, and in this way there should be no risk of rain water running under the felt. As an extra precaution, and also to lessen the likelihood of the felt being ripped in a high wind, you can run special waterproof tape over the edges.

Within the hutch itself, it is a good idea to fit sliding trays to cover the floor area. This will make it much easier to clean out the interior, and also means that the rabbit's urine will not seep directly into the floor of the cage, causing it to become rotten. You can have sheet metal trays made up at a metal fabricators, who can be contacted via the telephone directory. Make sure that the trays have edges which are folded over, and that there are no sharp places that could injure a rabbit. Also, there should be no gaps at the corners where a rabbit could become trapped by one of the nails.

A safer, but less durable option, will be to construct trays using wooden sides and a base made

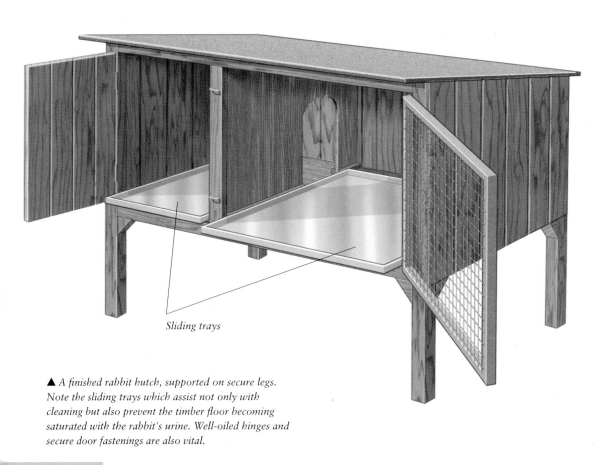

Sliding trays

▲ *A finished rabbit hutch, supported on secure legs. Note the sliding trays which assist not only with cleaning but also prevent the timber floor becoming saturated with the rabbit's urine. Well-oiled hinges and secure door fastenings are also vital.*

of oil-tempered hardboard or thin plywood. The sides must be high enough to retain the bedding, so that when pulled out for cleaning purposes, they can be tipped directly into a rubbish sack. Furthermore, the trays need to fit flush with the sides of the hutch, so there are no significant gaps here, which will otherwise make cleaning the hutch more difficult.

Siting an Outdoor Hutch

● Choose a sheltered, relatively shady spot, out of the direction of prevailing winds. An ideal spot is often against a wall.

● Stand the hutch on blocks or bricks if it does not have legs, to keep it off the ground and avoid dampness.

● Site the hutch quite close to your home if possible, so you can attend to your pet's needs more easily. A position close to your home may also give more protection against unwanted night-time visitors such as foxes or cats.

● An outside light fitted close to the hutch will allow you to attend to your pet more easily when it is dark.

● Avoid positioning the hutch in a conspicuous locality where it is likely to attract thieves or vandals.

▲ *An outdoor hutch should always be positioned in a sheltered, but not dark, locality—such as by a backyard wall as shown here. At the end of the summer, check the hutch over and carry out any repairs before winter.*

● **Should I provide any additional protection for my pet rabbit as winter approaches?**

You can apply a length of clear plastic sheeting, approximately a quarter of the height of the door, along the base of the mesh door, to give extra protection from cold winds at this stage. You must ensure that your pet will still be able to reach its water bottle without difficulty, however.

● *Can I paint the hutch?*

This can be done as an alternative to using a wood preservative, but again you must ensure that all the painted areas of wood are out of reach of your rabbit. Be sure to use a paint that is suitable for exterior timber. If you live in a hot area, then painting the roofing felt white will help to reflect the heat of the sun and helps prolong its life.

● *Our yard slopes, so where would be the best place to site the rabbit's hutch?*

The hutch should be level, so if your yard slopes you may first need to construct a special terrace with bricks and paving slabs to provide a suitable flat surface. Wherever you site the hutch, it should be fairly shady.

Constructing a Run

Rabbits will benefit from the extra space and opportunity to exercise provided by regular access to a run. Depending on where you site the hutch, it may be possible to construct a run around the hutch.

You may even have space for an aviary-type structure, simply placing the hutch within this, so that your pet should be safe here from possible predators. In this case, you simply need to purchase aviary panels, which can be bolted together for this purpose, along with a door unit. The panels will need to be mounted securely on brick footings, however, to prevent them being blown over in the wind.

It will not matter if the floor surface consists mainly of paving slabs or concrete, since these surfaces should help to wear down the rabbit's

▲ *This outdoor run for rabbits has a large opening at one end, making it easy for someone to enter and catch the occupants if required.*

claws and also ensure that your pet will not be able to dig out of the enclosure. Mount the hutch on bricks, if it does not already have legs, to prevent the floor area becoming damp, and provide a ramp which gives the rabbit easy access both into, and out of, the hutch.

If there is space behind the hutch, an entry and exit point can be cut at the back of the hutch, opening onto a ramp leading into the run. A sliding door here, set in channels or on runners, will allow you to confine the rabbit in its hutch when the weather is bad or allow it to be kept outside in safety while you clean out the hutch. The door can be operated from outside the run

quite easily, by attaching a stout piece of wire to it, thus enabling it to be opened or closed on the runners.

Another possible alternative is to have a door held in place with a vertical bolt that can be lowered onto the ramp leading into the run. The drawback of this arrangement, however, is that it can be harder to keep the rabbit in its hutch, since whenever you open the door to the hutch, the rabbit is likely to hop out into the run.

It helps if you can gain access to the run so that you can climb in and catch your pet if necessary. Rabbits soon adjust to a routine, however, and will soon know when they are expected to go back into their hutch if you shut them up for the night at approximately the same time every day. A sliding door at the back of the hutch will again prove easier to operate, rather than one which has to be hinged vertically.

The roof of the run needs to be relatively strong, so you may need to add extra cross beams here to ensure that the wire mesh does not collapse if a passing cat or a fox clambers up. Provided that the run is standing on a secure, level base, there is normally no need to anchor it here, because would-be predators are unlikely to be able to gain access under the sides.

◄ *Always attach a water bottle securely to the side of the run to ensure that your rabbit has fresh drinking water available at all times. Either transfer the bottle from the hutch or invest in a second bottle.*

● **Will our rabbit be safe in our courtyard, or must the enclosure be covered?**

It is advisable to keep your rabbit in a covered enclosure. Even within a courtyard, an animal like a fox or a cat—or possibly even a dog—could gain access. Should your pet be seized by such an animal, then it could die of shock even if the attack itself is not fatal.

● **When should I let my rabbit out into its run?**

Provided that there is protection on the roof and sides of the run, you can let your pet out most days, apart from during very wet or snowy weather. During such conditions it will be better to keep your rabbit confined in its hutch.

● **Our son is confined to a wheelchair, but would like a pet rabbit. What would be the best type of accommodation?**

Choose an aviary-style enclosure, to which your son can gain wheeled access, and where he can have direct contact with his rabbit. By offering pieces of food from the hand, your son should soon be able to tame his rabbit. It should also be possible in this way to encourage the rabbit onto a low platform from where your son can stroke it easily and even hold it.

Keeping Rabbits Indoors

THE TREND TOWARD KEEPING RABBITS IN THE home as pets grew rapidly in the United States during the 1990s, and has since spread to other parts of the world. It has come about partly as a result of changes in the way we live. For people living in apartments or who are out at work all day, keeping a pet rabbit at home is often possible where other pets would not be practical. Dogs, for example, are not suitable for apartments and cannot be left alone for long periods each day, whereas a rabbit will not pine under these circumstances. Rabbits will not disturb neighbors either. Rabbits can also become very friendly, especially when obtained young.

Many people dislike the idea of keeping a cat confined permanently indoors, as may be necessary in apartments or houses close to busy roads, whereas a rabbit will be content in these surroundings. This type of housing arrangement actually provides a better environment in some parts

Q & A...

● *What exactly are house-rabbits? Are they a particular breed?*

No, this is a general name given to rabbits of any type which live in the home. It has become generally accepted to join the two words together—as reflected in the names of societies catering for those keeping rabbits in the home.

● *Is an indoor hutch cheaper to build than outdoor accommodation?*

This should prove to be the case, since you can use lighter materials for the panels and do not need to include the extra cost of timber for the legs or roofing felt. Do not be tempted to economize too much, though. If you use hardboard for panels, for example, you are likely to find that your rabbit will destroy this with its sharp teeth.

▼ *An indoor hutch should be placed within a low-sided box or floor tray to prevent bedding from falling out onto carpets.*

▲ *These young rabbits look appealing sitting on a sofa, but it is advisable not to encourage them onto furniture. They could easily injure themselves if they fell off.*

of the world than outdoor accommodation, which may be too cold for an animal that originates from the warm Mediterranean region.

The growth of interest in keeping rabbits as indoor pets has led to a growing appreciation of the bigger breeds such as the British Giant. Being the size of a small dog, these are often a safer choice than one of the small breeds of rabbit, which are less conspicuous in the home and could hop unexpectedly under your feet.

Allowing a rabbit to run around in the home for long periods each day is a much more natural existence than keeping it cooped up in a hutch, but even so, there will be times when it will be necessary to keep your rabbit confined for its own safety—such as when you are bringing in items through the front door or when you are going out.

Indoor Hutches

The rapidly increasing number of rabbits being kept in the home has led to an expanding range of indoor housing being devised for them. Some are based on the traditional design of hutch, but are more attractively built, since there is no need to worry about weatherproofing. Other designs also include features such as short ramps leading up to the hutch so that the rabbit can come in and out of its accommodation at will (although there will also be doors so that it can be shut in as necessary). There is no need to have hinged doors in this type of hutch, however, since these will occupy space in the room when the hutch is open. Doors that can be pulled up and lifted out when the rabbit is allowed out of its quarters are a better option.

Even so, it is important to ensure that your pet will not be able to force these up by itself and escape when you are not there, so fitting small bolts to the sides of the doors is recommended. It is still a good idea to have only one section of the hutch fitted with a mesh front, however, since rabbits are secretive by nature and will appreciate being able to retreat out of sight on occasions. You should also provide a base for the hutch. This should include a surround constructed from timber battens 1in (2.5cm) square, to reduce the likelihood of bedding falling out onto carpeting. The rabbit's litter tray, lined with wood-based cat litter, can also be placed here.

Finishing Touches

Although there is no need to treat an indoor hutch with a weatherproofing agent, it will look rather unattractive if it is left as bare wood. For this reason, many owners like to paint the hutch so that it matches its surroundings. This can be accomplished by using a non-toxic emulsion paint. Bear in mind that as the rabbit will be allowed out to roam around freely, there is a greater risk that your pet will nibble at the exterior of the hutch, and could poison itself. Providing a range of chews should help to minimize the risk of the hutch being damaged by your rabbit's desire to keep its teeth in trim, but it is still recommended to be cautious in your choice of paint. There is no need to paint the interior of the hutch in any event.

▼ *An indoor pen for a small rabbit. With the door left open, your pet can hop in and out as it chooses. Note that there is room for the rabbit to sit up easily.*

Some owners decorate their rabbit's hutch in a more elaborate fashion, so it looks more like an item of furniture. There are various paint techniques that can be used to achieve this, as well as stencils. Always allow any paint to dry thoroughly before allowing the rabbit access to its new home. It is equally possible to add wooden beading around the doors or elsewhere, or to cut wood into different shapes using a jigsaw and attach these for decorative purposes.

Pens

There are also some commercial alternatives to hutches, the most widely available of which are pens. These are available in a range of various designs and sizes. Pens typically come in the form of a plastic base, which helps to keep the bedding from spilling out over the floor, with a removable mesh section attached to the base by clips. Those held in place with metal, rather than plastic, clips are likely to prove more durable.

▲ *The size of an indoor enclosure must be appropriate to the size of your rabbit. Although this rabbit clearly does not require a large enclosure, not all designs are suitable for the larger rabbit breeds.*

The mesh section may be comprised of a single unit, although there may also be a detachable roof that will allow you to lift your pet out easily. This will help to prevent the rabbit from escaping and should also give it protection from any dogs and cats which may also be sharing your home.

Cleaning these plastic units is very straightforward. All you need to do is detach the entire mesh section and then empty the contents of the plastic base into a garbage bag. It is equally easy to scrub out this bottom section when necessary, allowing it to dry completely before refilling it with bedding material.

The drawback with these units, however, is that you will need to move your rabbit in and out of its enclosure, whereas with a conventional hutch it can come and go as it pleases once the doors have been removed. You will therefore need to offer a further supply of food on a tray in the room, along with a supply of drinking water, if your rabbit is out of its quarters for any length of time.

▶ *You can buy a variety of wooden chews for rabbits. These should distract their attention away from furniture.*

Q&A...

● *Is it necessary to provide my house-rabbit with hay?*

... Yes, this should be provided, because although your rabbit will not need to burrow into the hay in order to keep warm, it will often appreciate being able to hide away here, as well as adding to its fiber intake by eating this bedding.

● *Is it necessary to line both sections of the hutch with some hay?*

No, this will not be necessary. Simply place it within the covered area, or alternatively, up one end of a mesh-topped enclosure, but line the entire floor area with pine and cedar shavings. These are not only absorbent, but also help to control odors, which is especially important in the home.

● *Are floor trays essential?*

These are certainly useful for an indoor hutch, because they will simplify the cleaning process. It will be less messy tipping their contents into a sack, rather than sweeping out the floor of the hutch in the room. Trays are not required for mesh-topped cages, which can be dismantled for cleaning purposes.

Siting an Indoor Hutch

When it comes to siting a hutch in the home, it is important to choose an area where your rabbit will feel secure and will not be exposed to drafts, so avoid a hallway for these reasons. A greenhouse may seem a good choice, but even here there can be problems, because temperatures can soar in summer and drop to very low levels in winter, accompanied by dampness.

These problems will be overcome by choosing a location within the house, but some caution is again necessary, especially if your pet is being housed in an open-topped pen. Never place this directly in front of a window, because the heat generated by the sun's rays on a hot day could easily endanger the rabbit's health. Alongside a wall is likely to be a much safer spot.

You are likely to need to adapt your home to accommodate your new pet, and first, you must decide whether the rabbit will be restricted to one room or will be allowed to wander more widely through the home. In the first instance, however, it is probably sensible to keep your pet confined to one room, so the rabbit comes to recognize this as its territory—which also makes litter training easier.

The major problem that owners of house-rabbits face is their pet's desire to gnaw—which can have fatal consequences if a rabbit bites through a live electric wire. Never leave any cords where rabbits can chew them. Instead, run them out of the rabbit's reach, behind furniture or under carpets, for example. Always take care to unplug cords when they are not required, preferably lifting them up out of the way afterward. Other hazards may also be present in a room—such as

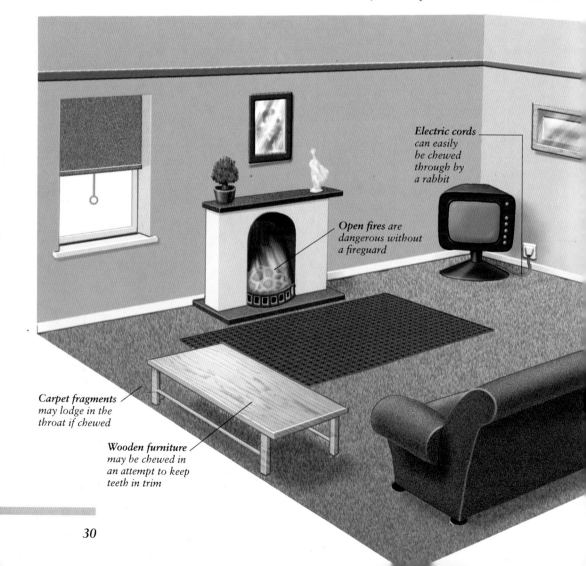

Electric cords can easily be chewed through by a rabbit

Open fires are dangerous without a fireguard

Carpet fragments may lodge in the throat if chewed

Wooden furniture may be chewed in an attempt to keep teeth in trim carpeting, which rabbits often attempt to gnaw, especially if left alone for any length of time. This could prove to be harmful if the fibers are swallowed. This is why it is important to always provide rabbits with an adequate source of roughage in the form of hay, to lessen their instincts to chew unsuitable materials.

If you have a dog or cat in the house, then the rabbit must be kept safely out of its reach. The instinct of a dog is often to hunt rabbits, while cats will also attack small individuals.

A stairguard may be recommended to avoid unwanted excursions upstairs. It is also best not to encourage your rabbit to venture into the kitchen, especially when you are cooking. There is the possibility that it could cause you to trip, with the risk of spilling the boiling contents of a pan onto your pet or yourself.

Q & A

● *Will it be safe to keep our rabbit in our utility room?*

... This is a possibility, provided that the temperature does not fluctuate dramatically—which can be a problem to regulate with appliances such as a drier running. As always, it is vital to ensure that all the cabling is out of reach, and most importantly, the door to the drier and washing machine are kept closed to avoid your rabbit hopping in unnoticed.

● *What should I do if our rabbit grabs hold of a live electric cord?*

Most importantly, switch off and disconnect the appliance first, to safeguard both you and your pet. Then attempt to pry the cord out of its mouth. Should the external plastic covering be damaged, you will need to replace the wiring.

● *Will a rabbit eat our houseplants?*

Yes, this is a distinct possibility, so make sure they are located out of reach. Many, including bulbs and poinsettias, for example, are likely to be poisonous, while cacti are obviously dangerous as well.

Houseplants may be poisonous or prickly

Stairs should be made inaccessible with a stairguard

Doors should be kept closed

Sofas may cause injury if the rabbit falls off

▲ *If you intend to persuade your rabbit to use a litter box regularly, make sure it always has easy access to it. Tipping some droppings into the box in the first instance may encourage your pet to use it as a latrine.*

◄ *The illustration left shows many of the potential dangers that could confront a rabbit left to roam freely without supervision. The best place to locate a rabbit's pen is alongside a wall, away from direct sunlight.*

The Rabbit's Digestive System

THE RABBIT'S DIGESTIVE SYSTEM IS QUITE UNLIKE our own, and is designed for their specialized feeding habits. They have a system that allows them to obtain maximum benefit from their food, which is comprised entirely of plant matter. Since the nutritional value of such foods is relatively low, rabbits must eat large quantities to meet their needs. However, in common with other herbivores such as sheep and cattle, they do not possess the necessary enzymes to break down the cellulose in plant cell walls, which is a crucial first step in the digestive process.

Instead, rabbits rely on beneficial bacteria and protozoa to undertake this task for them, and they have developed a unique digestive process as a result. When food is eaten, it passes via the stomach and small intestine into the cecum. This is a blind-ending tube located at the junction of the large and small intestines which terminates in the appendix. In the cecum, food—especially plant cell walls—is partly broken down by microbial action before passing to the large intestine and being voided from the body in the form of soft, brownish droppings usually produced at night. The rabbit then consumes these predigested droppings again—a process called refection. Here, on this second passage through the digestive system, the nutrients are fully absorbed, and the waste material continues on through the large intestine where water is reabsorbed into the body. After this, the typical rounded, dry fecal pellets are expelled from the rabbit's body for the last time.

Therefore the rabbit eats its predigested food again to obtain maximum nutritional benefit from it. The microbes in the digestive tract are also important in the manufacture of certain key vitamins in the body, such as vitamin B12. The rabbit's digestive system is finely balanced, with

▼ *The digestive system of a rabbit is designed to cope with the problems associated with eating plant matter with tough, indigestible, cellulose cell walls.*

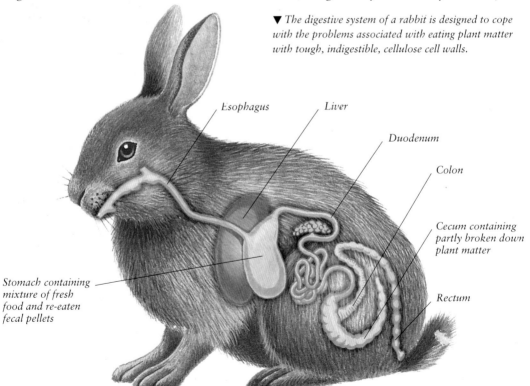

Esophagus

Liver

Duodenum

Colon

Cecum containing partly broken down plant matter

Rectum

Stomach containing mixture of fresh food and re-eaten fecal pellets

the microbes being very sensitive to any sudden change in diet.

Diet and Health

Whenever acquiring a new rabbit, therefore, it is vital to obtain a diet sheet at the same time, so you can match the food it has been receiving. Otherwise, the stress of the move to new surroundings, coupled with a change in diet, might have a fatal outcome. Most breeders are aware of this problem, and will give you some food if necessary, although you can buy your own supply if you obtain this information first.

Changes to the rabbit's diet must be made slowly, preferably over a period of a week or more, so that the microbial population can adjust accordingly. This applies not just to dry food but also to fresh food. Under no circumstances should a rabbit which has spent the winter in its hutch be allowed outside into a run to gorge itself on fresh spring grass, because this will inevitably trigger a digestive disturbance.

Treatment of ailments can be equally hazardous as far as the digestive tract is concerned, because antibiotics, in addition to killing harmful microbes, will also upset the delicate bacterial flora. This in turn can open the way for other infections to gain access to the body via the digestive tract.

▲ *Rabbits benefit from a balanced diet. Here two rabbits are eating a dried food mix comprising cereals and vegetables, with the addition of some fresh leaves.*

● *I've heard that a probiotic may help a rabbit's digestive system. What is this?*

It is a preparation containing beneficial bacteria that can effectively reinforce those already in the digestive tract. Specially formulated small animal products of this type can be obtained from pet stores and should be used as directed—often being mixed with the drinking water.

● *Are rabbits more vulnerable to changes in their diet at any particular age?*

It seems that young rabbits, from the time they start eating solid food at around four weeks of age until they are about 12 weeks old, are particularly susceptible to sudden changes in their diet. This is because the microbial component of their digestive system is not fully established at this stage.

● *How should I change my rabbit's dry food mix?*

Start by mixing a small amount of the new food to the food your pet is already eating. Then, over successive days, gradually increase the amount of the new food, while reducing the percentage of the previous ration, until all the old food has been replaced with the new mix.

Feeding Rabbits

ALL WILD RABBITS ARE BROWSERS, NIBBLING AT vegetation with their sharp incisor teeth, and their natural diet is low in energy. In the past, this diet was traditionally reflected in the food offered to pet rabbits. They used to be fed mainly on seasonal greenfood, along with root vegetables such as carrots, and hay which also serves to increase the fiber level of their diet. Cereal seeds did not predominate in their diet.

The demand for faster-growing meat rabbits and advances in nutritional science saw a rapid development in formulated foods. Most notable of these were rabbit pellets, which gave a much quicker growth rate and provided all the nutritional needs to keep a rabbit in good health. Such foods could also be used to combat illness, since it also became possible to manufacture rabbit pellets with drugs to prevent the disease known as coccidiosis.

● *How should I store a bale of hay?*

It must be kept dry, and you may prefer to break it down into sections which can then be stored in paper sacks. Ensure these are kept out of reach of unwanted rodent visitors that may contaminate the bedding so that it has to be discarded.

● *Will rabbits eat straw instead of hay?*

This is far less palatable, and not as soft for bedding purposes—which may lead to eye injuries, for example. However, it is possible to obtain straw that has been softened and treated with a non-toxic disinfectant, to create a hypoallergenic bedding.

● *What is the best way to keep dry rabbit food?*

Store it in a suitable container with a lid. Sacks can be kept in metal trashcans, where they will be out of reach of rodents. A feeding scoop will allow you to top up the food bowls easily. Never pour new food on top of old, because your pet may eat food which is out of date.

▲ *A low-sided bowl is often recommended for lop rabbits, to avoid their ears trailing in their food. Do not place food bowls directly under water bottle spouts.*

▶ *A selection of the prepared foods which you can buy for rabbits. Pellets contain all the necessary ingredients to keep rabbits in good health. Pellet diets are available for both maintenance and breeding conditions. Treats (near right) should only be given occasionally.*

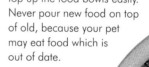

Dry Food

Pet rabbits today tend to be fed on a cereal-based mix, rather than one which is comprised solely of pellets. These contain a range of ingredients, including items such as flaked corn (or corn-flakes), alfalfa, crushed oats, and wheat, along with smaller quantities of other ingredients like crushed dry peas and even dried herbs. Although locust bean pieces have been used in mixes in the past, they have now been dropped by some manufacturers because of concerns that they could be harmful to rabbits. There is a possibility that they may lodge in the throat or possibly lower in the digestive tract.

The precise ingredients and percentages vary from one mix to another, as is evident from the packaging. It is better to buy a branded mix, rather than one which is sold loose, simply because you can be certain of the level of vitamin supplementation in a packet. The "use by" date will be clearly visible, and it is false economy to buy a large bag which will not be used up before this date is passed.

Dry food should be offered in a heavyweight ceramic bowl. This will prevent the rabbit tipping it over and scattering the contents. (Rabbits may sometimes engage in this behavior if they become bored.) Aim to provide just sufficient food to meet your rabbit's daily requirements, based on the recommended amount stated on the packaging. Avoid uneaten dry food accumulating in the bottom of the container, where it is likely to deteriorate.

When feeding a rabbit housed outdoors, always make sure that the bowl containing dry food is positioned away from the mesh door. This should ensure there is no risk of the rain blowing in and wetting the contents of the bowl.

A Balanced Diet

As we have become more reliant on complete foods for pets such as dogs and cats, so this also applies in the case of rabbits. This is actually proving to be to their detriment, certainly in the case of those being kept as pets. It is very easy to simply tip food from a packet into a food bowl, especially when the pack suggests that it contains a complete diet. This may be true in a strictly nutritional sense, but it does not apply in terms of the rabbit's regular feeding habits, because dried food offers a much higher calorific ration than would be the case in the wild. Most rabbits with free access to nothing other than dry food are likely to become obese before long, and this will not only spoil their appearance but is also likely to shorten their lifespan.

Although dry food provides a vital component of a rabbit's diet, it should be supplemented each day with greenfood as well as with vegetables. Hay is also important, to increase the bulk of the rabbit's food. This will have the effect of reducing its appetite by filling the digestive tract. Studies have shown that good-quality hay is helpful in lowering the incidence of enteric disorders, as well as the behavioral problem of hair-chewing, which is generally regarded as being due to a shortage of dietary fiber. The quality of hay offered to a rabbit is very important. It needs to be free from dust, and it must not be musty or moldy. Special hay, such as timothy, can be purchased in bags from pet stores, but if you have the space, a bale is likely to be more economical.

Greenfood

Rabbits can be fed many different types of plants, as can guinea pigs. It may be possible for you to grow such items in your yard. This will not only reduce the cost of feeding your rabbit but also ensures that your pet will receive maximum nutritional benefit from fresh-picked food, which will be free from pesticides. Even some plants that are considered weeds are traditional rabbit fodder.

A number of crops can be grown throughout the year. Most seed catalogues provide advice on which crop is most suitable for sowing at a specific time of year. Root vegetables such as turnips can also be provided, usually during the winter

Safe and Unsafe Greenfood

Some wild plants are beneficial to rabbits but others are poisonous. The main ones are listed below.

Safe greenfood

Plantain, clover, dandelion, shepherd's purse, groundsel, thistle, dock, chickweed, mallow, coltsfoot, yarrow. Also marigold, aster.

Unsafe greenfood

All bulbs, ragwort, privet, yew, foxglove, laburnum, lilac, lupin, bracken, buttercup.

months when greens are in short supply. As with carrots, they should be washed off and peeled, before being cut into small pieces for the rabbit. Fresh food of this type is perishable, and it is wise to use a feeding tray for your rabbit, to help it find its food easily. You can then remove any fresh food which is uneaten, without having to search through the bedding. Provide fresh food on a daily basis, removing it within 24 hours before it can turn moldy.

Hay for Angora rabbits should be provided in a special hay rack that allows them to pull out pieces for eating. If the hay is left on the floor of the hutch—as it is for most other rabbits that also use the hay for bedding—it will become entangled in their fur.

Other Dietary Items

A mineral block is often provided for rabbits and is extremely beneficial. Another popular

▼ *Greenfood should form part of your rabbit's regular diet, although you may not be able to grow such foods at home. It is, of course, possible to buy suitable supplies at vegetable stores.*

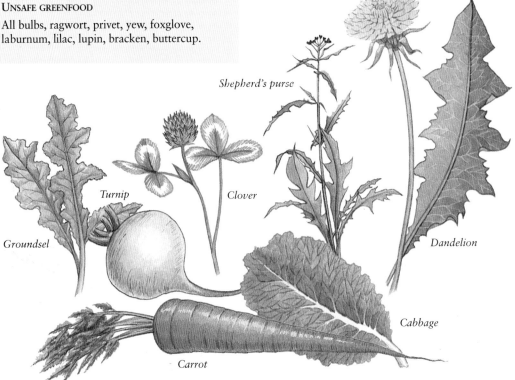

Shepherd's purse

Turnip

Clover

Groundsel

Dandelion

Cabbage

Carrot

means of helping to keep their teeth in good condition, and deflecting them away from the wood of the hutch, is to offer hard-baked crusts. These are very easily prepared from wholemeal bread, by baking the crusts in the oven on a low heat. Allow the crusts to cool before giving them to your rabbit. Unlike a mineral block, however, these should be replaced every few days—especially if they become wet, when they will rapidly turn moldy.

It is especially important to provide fresh drinking water in such a way that it cannot be spilt or tipped over the floor of the rabbit's quarters. Using an open container for this purpose is not satisfactory because hay and bedding will inevitably contaminate the water. A special drinking bottle, which attaches to the mesh on the outside of the hutch, is recommended. Fix this at a convenient height so that your rabbit can drink from the spout without difficulty.

Q&A... ● *Are there any areas where I should not collect greenfood for my rabbit?*

Avoid collecting greenfood from roadside fields and other areas where herbicides or pesticides may have been used. It is also not recommended to pick greenfood where dogs may have fouled it, and all greenfood collected from the wild should be washed as a precaution.

● *What precautions should I take in freezing weather?*

Avoid filling the water bottle to the top. You need to allow space here because the water will expand when it turns to ice, and if there is insufficient space the bottle is likely to crack and will then leak. After a mild frost, always squeeze the bottle to check the water flow. Sometimes, a hidden plug of ice may form in the stainless steel spout, causing a blockage.

● *My rabbit keeps dislodging its water bottle, and it ends up on the floor. How can I prevent this?*

Replace the piece of wire holding the bottle in position with another piece that wraps around the bottle completely, and twist the ends together before replacing it on the cage. Your rabbit will soon stop this behavior once it realizes that it can no longer dislodge the bottle.

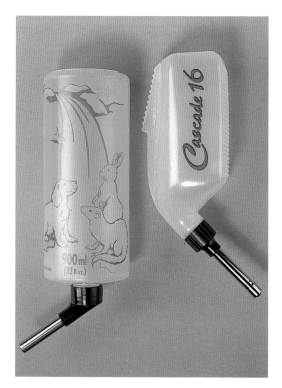

▲ *A drinking bottle provides clean water for your rabbit. Two of the many kinds of bottle available are shown here. Most rabbits instinctively seem able to obtain water without difficulty, but check a new rabbit is not having problems.*

▲ *Mineral blocks not only supplement a rabbit's natural intake, but nibbling on the hard surface also helps to keep teeth healthy. Blocks of this type are generally available from pet stores and simply need to be placed in the rabbit's quarters.*

Handling and Carrying a Rabbit

RABBITS ACCUSTOMED TO BEING PICKED UP AND handled from an early age are obviously much better companions than those that are not tame. It is especially important if you are seeking a rabbit as a child's pet, therefore, to start out with a young individual which can become accustomed to this procedure.

Beware of taking on an older rabbit in need of a good home, because if it has been neglected the likelihood is that it will resent being handled. Although generally placid by nature, rabbits can prove surprisingly strong and agile in terms of struggling to avoid being picked up. They also have claws that can inflict painful scratches. They may even bite occasionally. Should a rabbit be dropped because of this, even if only a short distance to the ground, the fall could be fatal.

There are three basic steps to follow when handling a rabbit. The first step is to restrain the animal in its quarters. This is usually much easier within the confines of a hutch rather than a run. Place your left hand on the rabbit's shoulder and your right hand over the rump (assuming you are right-handed) to restrain it. Lift the rabbit up by sliding your right hand underneath its body and gently sliding the left hand round to give support to the chest area. Now you can lift the rabbit out of its hutch toward you, ensuring that it is adequately supported with your hands beneath its body. When holding the rabbit

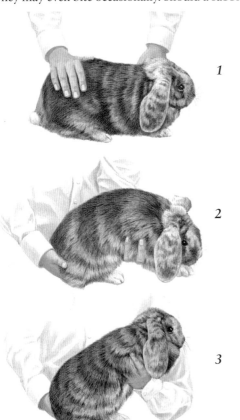

1

2

3

▲ *Rabbits do not usually struggle when their body is adequately supported. Wearing a long-sleeved top will, however, guard against painful scratches on bare arms.*

◄ *The stages in picking up a rabbit, as described in the text. Always train a rabbit to become accustomed to being picked up from weaning time onward, especially in the case of one of the larger breeds.*

cradle it with your arm providing support, so that it feels secure.

It is when the rabbit is being lifted up initially that it is most likely to start struggling. Do not allow its hindquarters to hang down, because this will also provoke a similar response. It is important that young children especially are supervised when they are picking up a rabbit, both to give them confidence and to avoid any injuries. It is also important that they do not try to pick up a rabbit without their forearms being covered, because even a minor scratch will be painful and may be enough to cause them to drop their pet.

Always take care not to hurt your pet when carrying it. One of the myths about handling rabbits is that they should be picked up by their ears. This is actually very painful for your pet. If your rabbit is reluctant to be picked up or becomes very excitable, then placing your hands gently on its ears may help to calm it down, but never use the ears to support its body weight.

Pet Carriers

If you need to carry your rabbit any distance—from hutch to run, for example—after picking it up, then transfer your pet in a secure carrier. The types sold for cats are also ideal for rabbits, but avoid cardboard carriers if possible, especially for large rabbits. It is not just their weight which can cause the bottom of the box to collapse, for rabbits may also urinate as the result of being moved, and this can weaken the cardboard as well. Line the carrier with hay, so that the rabbit will not slip about on the base. Avoid placing newspaper in the base, because if this becomes wet, the ink could stain your pet's fur. Always travel with the box in a cool part of a vehicle, such as behind the front seats, where it will fit firmly without sliding around. It is also more likely to be out of the sun here. Never be tempted to place a rabbit in its carrier in the trunk of a car. The temperature may rise to a fatal level, while any exhaust fumes seeping into this compartment are likely to prove deadly, too.

Q & A...

● **Do I really need a carrier to take my rabbit back and forth to its run?**

There is always the risk that you could trip over, or that your rabbit will be badly frightened and escape from your grasp if, for example, your dog slips out of the house while you are carrying it. Accidents do happen, even in the most organized households! A carrier really is the safest option.

● **When might a rabbit bite?**

This can happen if you put your hand close to your rabbit's mouth or pick up a frightened rabbit incorrectly. If you leave your finger in the way when feeding your rabbit, this is also likely to result in you being bitten.

● **Are show rabbits more friendly than non-show stock?**

Certainly, one of the most important attributes which show rabbits need is a docile nature, allowing themselves to be handled readily by complete strangers during judging, but this is really just a reflection of regular handling.

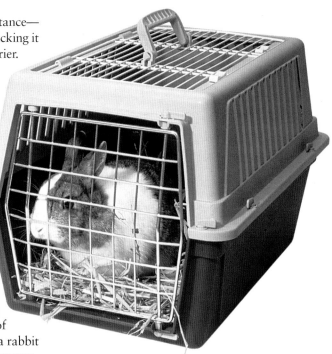

▲ A secure, ventilated carrier enables you to move your rabbit safely from hutch to run, or for traveling further afield, such as to the veterinarian or to a show.

Cleanliness and Grooming

RABBITS ARE ACTUALLY VERY CLEAN CREATURES, which is why they can be trained to use a litter tray in the house. In the confines of a hutch, they are likely to use only one corner as a latrine. It is therefore possible to spot clean this area on a daily basis, using a small trowel, while cleaning out the entire floor area once a week. Being able to shut your rabbit in one part of the hutch while you carry out this task will make it much simpler, or alternatively, you can transfer your pet to a carrier. Trays on the floor of the hutch can be emptied into a rubbish bag. Use a brush to clean off any material still sticking to the tray.

▲ *Cleaning out a rabbit hutch. With the animal safely removed, a small shovel or trowel can be used to scoop or scrape out the old bedding (top). Spray the hutch thoroughly with a safe disinfectant (above). Allow the hutch to dry before replacing bedding, water, and food.*

A regular cleaning routine is very important, especially during warmer months, because flies are otherwise likely to be attracted here, and this can lead to fly strike. In addition, soiled bedding predisposes rabbits to the condition known as hutch burn, when the hocks become sore and inflamed, with a corresponding loss of hair.

The water bottle and feed bowls must also be washed regularly. It is quite likely that traces of greenish algae will soon start to appear in the water bottle. These deposits should be removed with a bottle brush, which will also be useful for cleaning the interior of the bottle, as well as the nozzle of the spout. Adding a dish detergent to the water will make this task easier, but rinse the bottle out well with clean water afterward.

Be sure to use only disinfectants which are safe for use in your rabbit's quarters. Disinfectants work most effectively when the surfaces have been cleaned beforehand, and they need to be left in contact with the surface for a few minutes rather than being rinsed off at once.

The ideal hutch lining consists of good-quality wood shavings (not sawdust, which can irritate the rabbit's eyes) on top of which is placed a layer of good-quality hay. Make sure there is enough hay to make a bed for the rabbit. The hay will also be eaten by your pet, adding to the fiber content of its diet.

Grooming

Most rabbits need relatively little grooming, but if you opt for one of the long-coated breeds—such as the Cashmere Lop or the Angora—you must be prepared to spend time nearly every day caring for your pet's coat. If the coat becomes matted, it will be almost impossible to break down the knots, and they will have to be cut out of the coat, spoiling the rabbit's appearance. Matted fur, especially on the hindquarters, also predisposes the rabbit to fly strike.

Special grooming tools are available, and one of the most useful is a comb that has revolving,

● *How do I clean my rabbit's ears?*

... It is important to inspect the ears regularly, particularly in the case of lop breeds, since these can become dirty. They can be wiped clean with a piece of damp cloth, but never be tempted to probe down into the ear itself, because this could cause a serious injury.

● *Are any foods recommended to help a rabbit through its molt?*

Groundsel is traditionally recommended for this purpose, but overall, a well-balanced diet containing all the necessary vitamins and minerals will speed your pet through this debilitating period.

● *Is it worth using a supplement?*

Provided that your rabbit is receiving a balanced diet, with a dry food mix supplemented with vital vitamins and minerals, then there is little to be gained by using a supplement. In fact, an excess of these dietary components can be harmful.

▶ *Long-haired rabbit breeds need daily grooming. Use a comb or brush to work steadily but gently through the fur, ensuring all tangles are removed. Don't forget to brush the fur on the underside of the body.*

▼ *Occasionally brushing the coat of smooth-coated rabbits for a few minutes, especially during the molt, will keep it clean and in good condition.*

rather than rigid, teeth. These help to break down any knots in the coat without pulling at the fur and causing your rabbit pain. Natural bristle brushes can also be effective, since they will not impart a static charge to the fur.

The fur will be shed in greater amounts during the molt, and grooming at this stage is particularly useful in removing the old coat, which will spoil the rabbit's appearance. The molt will be most obvious in the spring when the rabbit sheds its dense winter coat, but hair is also likely to be shed in increased amounts at the end of the summer. Rabbits that are molting cannot be shown, since their usually immaculate appearance is spoiled at this stage.

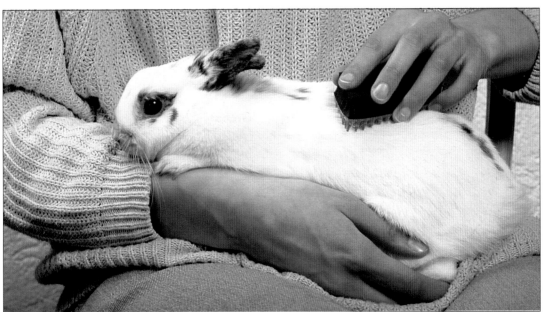

Breeding Rabbits

RABBITS WILL BREED VERY READILY, ALTHOUGH before allowing a pair to mate, it is important to ensure that the young will have good homes in due course, bearing in mind that a doe (female) may easily produce ten or more offspring (known as kittens). Sometimes, inadvertent breeding occurs when two supposed females turn out to be a pair when they mature. It is possible to keep does together successfully, especially if they have grown up sharing a hutch, although this does increase the risk of pseudo-pregnancies (see page 44). Bucks (males) are likely to fight fiercely as they become mature, however, and they must be housed individually.

The age of onset of sexual maturity depends mainly on the size of the breed, with smaller breeds such as the Dutch being able to breed at just 18 weeks, whereas the giant breeds may not attain maturity until they are about 28 weeks of age. Does will attain maturity earlier than bucks, so if a first mating fails, it is likely that the buck's low sperm count is the cause. When breeding for the first time, most rabbits can be paired successfully at about five or six months old.

Sexing mature rabbits is much easier than with youngsters, because the external genitalia are fully developed by this stage. The scrotum of the buck, containing the testes, lies in front of the penile opening, which in turn is in close contact with the anus. The inguinal pouches, which are small, hairless scent glands, can also be seen lying to the sides of, and just above, the penis. In does, the genital opening is slitlike rather than rounded, and they lack the obvious swellings formed by the testes and inguinal pouches. There may be other signs that help to distinguish the sexes after maturity, such as the swelling under the chin of mature bucks—known as a dewlap—that creates the appearance of a double chin.

The Breeding Cycle

Various factors influence the breeding cycle of rabbits, with light exposure being a significant trigger. This is why rabbits start to become reproductively active at the onset of spring, with their breeding success then falling off again in late summer, as daylength declines. It means that the young are likely to be born at the time when they are most likely to survive.

Rabbits have an unusual breeding cycle compared with most mammals. Does do not ovulate on a regular cycle, but only in response to mating, with the eggs being released from the ovary between nine and 13 hours later. This ensures the greatest likelihood of reproductive success, as both ova and sperm are then certain to be in

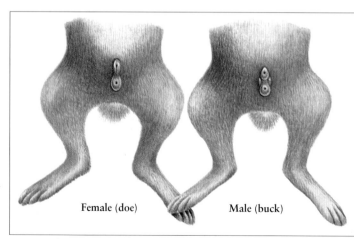

Female (doe)   Male (buck)

◀ It is relatively easy to sex rabbits once they are mature, thanks to the slightly swollen area of the buck's scrotum, although it can be more difficult in youngsters. At the time of weaning, however, the buck has a circular-shaped orifice, whereas the doe's is in the shape of a V. If in doubt, gentle pressure can be applied to evert the buck's penis.

the reproductive tract at the same time. If mating does not occur, then new follicles will develop on the ovaries over the course of a couple of days, at which time the doe will not be willing to mate. At other times, however, her readiness to mate is likely to be revealed by the reddish, swollen appearance of her vulva. She should be transferred to the buck's quarters and left here for up to 30 minutes or so, during which time mating should take place. It is sometimes recommended to reintroduce the doe to the buck again for a second mating.

Exhibition breeders usually have a much higher number of does in their studs than bucks, simply because a buck can mate successfully with up to five different does each week. The buck is therefore very important in ensuring the overall quality of a stud, because he is likely to play a much greater role in the breeding program than a doe. Most studs are based on at least two separate bloodlines, which can be mated together as well. Accurate record keeping, allowing you to trace the parentage of different rabbits, is crucial in terms of planning breeding programs.

▼ *Mating in rabbits is a brief encounter. It should take place soon after the pair are introduced, assuming that the doe is receptive.*

▼ *The breeding cycle of the rabbit, showing the development of the young.*

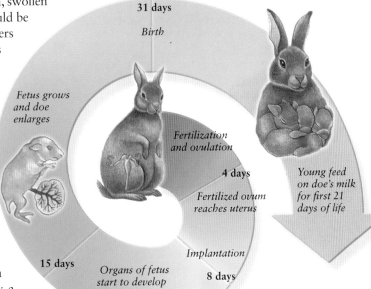

31 days
Birth

Fetus grows and doe enlarges

Fertilization and ovulation

4 days
Fertilized ovum reaches uterus

Young feed on doe's milk for first 21 days of life

15 days
Organs of fetus start to develop

Implantation
8 days

Q&A...

● Can I transfer the buck to the doe's cage, instead of the other way round?

This is not recommended, because she will prove to be much more territorial, and this is likely to result in the buck being attacked.

● What is the likelihood of my doe becoming pregnant after mating?

As a result of the coordinated breeding cycle between buck and doe, it is very high—with more than eight out of ten matings producing offspring.

● My buck appeared to fall off the doe. Does this means mating was unsuccessful?

No, quite the reverse. It is quite usual for the buck to lose his balance at this stage, when mating has been achieved. Equally, either buck or doe may call out during mating, but this also is not a cause for concern.

Confirming a Pregnancy

● First, stand the doe on a firm surface, where she cannot slip. If she does not feel relaxed, it will be harder to examine her.

● Feel very carefully and gently under the body just in front of the pelvis, with your fingers and thumb on either side of the abdomen.

● If the doe is pregnant, you should be able to detect a number of marble-sized swellings in the uterus here. These are the developing embryos. They will be larger than fecal pellets, with which they could be confused.

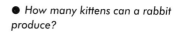

● *How many kittens can a rabbit produce?*

... There may be any number from a single individual up to as many as 22, but these extremes are rare. Typically expect between six to eight offspring. Young does breeding for the first time often have smaller litters, as do smaller breeds such as the Netherland Dwarf.

● *Is it possible to breed rabbits by means of artificial insemination?*

Yes, with rabbits helping to pioneer this technique for use in other mammals. Fertility is almost guaranteed under these circumstances, but it is only generally used on commercial rabbit farms, although the method can be helpful with particularly rare breeds.

● *I thought my rabbit was pregnant because her mammary glands enlarged and she started to build a nest, but no young were born. Why was this?*

Almost certainly it was because she suffered a false or pseudopregnancy. This results on occasions because the hormonal output from the structures known as the corpora lutea (which form after ovulation) can then produce signs of pregnancy. A pseudopregnancy can occur even if mating did not take place.

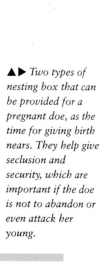

▲▶ *Two types of nesting box that can be provided for a pregnant doe, as the time for giving birth nears. They help give seclusion and security, which are important if the doe is not to abandon or even attack her young.*

◀ *The doe will make a nest for her young, which is usually comprised of soft fur pulled from her own body. She will do this whether she has a nesting box or not. This is natural behavior, and the fur soon regrows.*

▼ *Newborn rabbits. Note how small their ears are at this stage. Rabbits are blind and helpless at birth. The black areas of skin indicate where, in due course, the coat will be dark.*

The Period of Pregnancy

Even if the doe has previously been sharing accommodation, she should be transferred to a hutch on her own for the duration of her pregnancy. After 10–14 days it will be possible to determine whether the mating was successful, by carrying out the procedure on page 44. It will not be possible to detect the number of offspring with any certainty, and once you have determined that the doe is pregnant, she should be returned to her quarters. If the doe is not pregnant, early remating will be desirable.

External signs of pregnancy will be apparent by the 24th day following mating, when the mammary glands will appear swollen, compared with a doe that is not carrying young. Handling should again be kept to a minimum now, because of the risk of spontaneous abortion. Provide the doe with a kindling or nesting box, where she can make a nest for the young. As the time for birth approaches, she will start to pull fur from the underside of her body to create a soft lining among the hay of the nesting box.

At this stage, the doe will be eating more food than before, since the last third of the pregnancy is the period of maximum growth of her offspring. Some breeders like to add raspberry leaves to the diet right at the end of the pregnancy period, in the belief that this will ensure an easy birth. Pregnancy typically lasts for about 31 days, but the young may be born any time between 29 and 34 days, although after a longer interval, kittens are likely to be stillborn.

The Birth

Young rabbits are normally born in the early morning, with the entire litter often being produced within a hour or so. Difficulties during birth are rare, usually being linked with abnormally large fetuses. If you suspect a problem, with a doe appearing to be in obvious discomfort and persistently straining, then contact your veterinarian for advice without delay. A simple injection of oxytocin is likely to be sufficient to resolve this problem, although there is no guarantee that the young will be born alive. On rare occasions, a Caesarean section may be required.

Keep a close watch on a doe when the births are imminent, but do not interfere if all appears to be proceeding normally. In particular, do not start checking the nest to see how many young have been born. This is likely to cause a doe to abandon or even attack her young if she detects your scent here. If you do have to investigate, distract the doe with food and then probe the nest apart carefully, using a pencil which has been wiped in the nest litter and rubbed on the doe's coat beforehand. Hopefully, this will then not disturb the doe.

Rearing

Although totally helpless at birth, young rabbits grow very quickly. Between four and seven days after birth, their fur will start to become clearly evident. In another two or three days, their eyes will have opened, followed by their ear openings. Their outer ears, too, which are relatively small at birth, will start to grow rapidly. The kittens will continue to suckle their mother until about seven weeks old, first emerging from the nest at about three weeks of age.

There are rarely any problems when the doe is rearing a litter. If there is a crisis that prevents her feeding her young, you will normally be alerted to it by the distress calls of the hungry kittens. The most common cause for this is an infection of the mammary glands, called mastitis. Infected mammary glands are red and sore at first and then, as the infection develops, the teat area is likely to turn blue. The disease is often described as "blue breast" for this reason. Mastitis requires

urgent treatment and you should take the doe to a veterinarian without delay, not only for her own health but also to save yourself the task of hand-rearing the kittens. Always have supplies of cow's milk and calcium caseinate available during this period in case you need to hand-feed.

If your doe has produced a very large litter, it may be advisable to foster some of the kittens to another doe that gave birth at roughly the same time. Ideally, this should be within ten days of the litter being born, but it can be carried out successfully up to three weeks after birth if necessary. It is not wise to foster a litter if their mother falls ill, however, because of the risk of spreading the infection. Always aim to move the younger, smaller individuals, since they are more likely to be accepted. Place the kittens alongside their new litter mates, giving them time to settle. This will help to disguise their scent. Remove the doe from the nest for an hour or so. This will cause no harm, since rabbits

Q&A

● *Is it true that rabbits sometimes cannibalize their young?*

... This does happen on rare occasions soon after birth, usually when there is a very small litter. It has been suggested that the doe kills her young under these circumstances with the aim of mating again and producing a larger litter. Excessive disturbance can also trigger such behavior.

● *Why are orphaned rabbits hard to rear?*

They may not have received the immunity present in the doe's first milk, or colostrum, which normally protects them against infections until their own immune systems are working. During the hand-rearing process, there is also significant risk of aspiration pneumonia, with fluid entering the lungs—especially if the young are weak.

● *What milk should I use for bottle-feeding?*

Cow's milk alone is too low in protein, so add calcium caseinate at 0.5oz (14g) to 10fl oz (296ml), increasing this figure to 0.7oz (20g). Warm to blood heat and feed the kittens drop by drop, using an eyedropper.

▲ *This rabbit has a ring, or band, on one of its hind legs. Rings are produced in various sizes to fit different breeds of rabbit.*

only feed their litters once a day, with suckling lasting for as little as three minutes.

For the first three weeks or so, the kittens will feed only on the doe's milk. She will drink much more water during this period, because of her milk output, and another drinking bottle may be required. Most rabbits require 0.3fl oz (10ml) of water per 3.5oz (100g) body weight daily, but this rises to 3fl oz (90ml) during lactation.

Weaning and Ringing

As the young rabbits start to eat solid foods, they should be encouraged to eat a prepared ration with a high level of protein, to meet their growth requirements. It can be beneficial to offer some greenfood at this stage, but it must not form a major part of their diet.

If you intend to ring your rabbits for exhibition purposes, this can be undertaken when they are between six and eight weeks old. Do not delay in banding, because the lower leg will soon grow too large for the band to slide over.

Although a doe can mate again while she is suckling young, it is usual practice in exhibition rabbits not to mate does again until after their young are weaned. Allowing a doe to mate during this period can cause a more rapid decline in her milk production, which may adversely affect the growth of the young.

◄ *Young rabbits develop very rapidly, as shown by this litter of lops that will soon be ready to be weaned. Be sure to provide extra food and water as they grow.*

Health Care in Rabbits

RABBITS ARE NORMALLY HEALTHY ANIMALS, especially once settled in their surroundings. They need relatively little in terms of routine health care, although vaccinations may be advisable. But always take time each day to check your pet over, noting anything out of the ordinary that could be an indicator of impending illness. It might be that your pet is not eating as much as usual, or may be less active. Perhaps its droppings have altered in consistency, or its breathing might have become audible. If you can detect a problem early, the likelihood of successful treatment will be greater.

There are a number of ways in which infections can be spread, some of which may be more obvious than others. It is important to remain alert to the possibilities, to safeguard the welfare of your pet. The bedding can be a particular concern, because rabbits are susceptible to respiratory ailments. The hay must be clean and free from dust as far as possible. Beware of cheap hay—not only may this be old, but it may also contain potentially deadly plants such as ragwort that can poison a rabbit.

Keep the floor of the rabbit's quarters clean, because soiled bedding in the confines of a hutch can give off ammonia, which in turn will attack the lining of the rabbit's respiratory tract, leaving it more vulnerable to infection. Food should be fresh and must not be allowed to deteriorate and turn moldy. Wild rabbits can also introduce disease, so keep them away from your pet. Insects, especially flies, are likely to be attracted by dirty surroundings.

Some breeds, such as Rexes, are especially susceptible to health problems if kept under

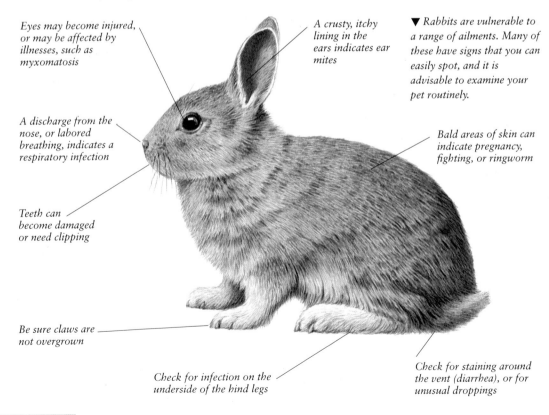

Eyes may become injured, or may be affected by illnesses, such as myxomatosis

A crusty, itchy lining in the ears indicates ear mites

▼ Rabbits are vulnerable to a range of ailments. Many of these have signs that you can easily spot, and it is advisable to examine your pet routinely.

A discharge from the nose, or labored breathing, indicates a respiratory infection

Bald areas of skin can indicate pregnancy, fighting, or ringworm

Teeth can become damaged or need clipping

Be sure claws are not overgrown

Check for infection on the underside of the hind legs

Check for staining around the vent (diarrhea), or for unusual droppings

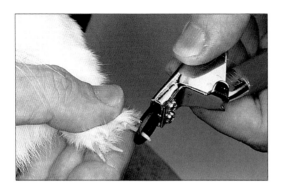

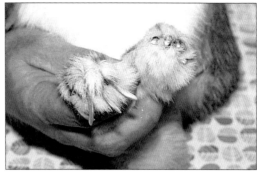

▲ *Use guillotine-type clippers for cutting nails, not scissors. Cut at the point where the pinkish vein disappears. If you cut the vein, it will cause bleeding.*

▲ *The claws of the foot on the right have been cut correctly with guillotine-type nail clippers. Compare these with the uncut claws on the left.*

these conditions, because of the relatively thin covering of fur on the undersides of their hind legs. Small blisters may start to form here, and these invariably become infected by staphylococcal bacteria. Hutch burn, caused by soiling of the fur that then infects the skin, can become more of a problem in older animals, which tend to be heavier. Soon, these inflamed spots develop into extensive areas of infection, and the bacteria invade the body. Rapid veterinary treatment will therefore be necessary to safeguard the rabbit's life under these circumstances. However, this problem can often be avoided, simply by ensuring that the rabbit always has clean bedding in its hutch.

Cutting Claws

Claw clipping is often required, however, because if the nails become too long they can be a serious handicap to the rabbit. If you are in any doubt about whether the nails need cutting, or how to do it, seek veterinary advice. The procedure itself is relatively straightforward, particularly in the case of a rabbit with pale nails, because the blood supply to the nail—which you should avoid cutting—will be clearly visible.

Place the rabbit on a table in good light and, preferably with someone else restraining your pet, work around each foot in turn with nail clippers. Should you nip a nail too short, however, then pressing gently on the tip for a minute or so with a damp piece of cotton should stem the blood flow quite rapidly.

● **I think my Netherland Dwarf is suffering from maloccluded teeth. How easy is it to trim these back?**

Unfortunately, this particular problem is quite widespread in the Netherland Dwarf breed. Trimming the teeth is something that is best left to your veterinarian, because they have to be trimmed at the correct angle to ensure that the rabbit will be able to continue eating without difficulty.

● **I heard a breeder at a show talking about Pasturella. What is this?**

It is a bacterium which is a common cause of respiratory illness. In some cases, the signs are relatively minor—such as a runny nose and eyes—whereas in others, it can cause pneumonia and rapid death. Much depends on the actual strain of the bacterium and the susceptibility of the rabbit. Mild cases, described as "snuffles," sometimes appear to clear up without treatment. They often recur during stressful periods such as the molt, for example.

● **Can "snuffles" be cured successfully?**

It can be very difficult, because although specific antibiotics may appear to overcome the infection, they usually only suppress it, with the *Pasturella* bacteria still remaining localized in the rabbit's nasal cavities. The risk of infection is greatest when rabbits are housed indoors in sheds, rather than outside in hutches, because the bacteria responsible are spread in confined spaces by sneezing.

▶ *The mucus staining around the nose indicates that this rabbit has snuffles. Sneezing may accompany the illness.*

Parasitic and Intestinal Problems in Rabbits

NOT SURPRISINGLY, BECAUSE OF THE SENSITIVE nature of their digestive tract, rabbits are vulnerable to intestinal disorders. These can be caused by bacteria such as *Escherichia coli*, viruses, and parasites. The most obvious sign of this type of illness is likely to be diarrhea, which can be blood-stained in more severe cases where the intestinal lining is seriously damaged. Diarrhea can strike at any age, with young rabbits being particularly vulnerable.

You will need to seek veterinary advice immediately. Fluid therapy is usually the first line of treatment. This helps to protect the vital body organs from the effects of dehydration, and this is usually combined with a drug such as loperamide, which will stop the diarrhea. Antibiotics are only prescribed in the most serious cases, since they may be ineffective against

▼ *A veterinarian examining the abdomen of a Silver French Lop, by gentle palpation. This can be a helpful method of determining various intestinal problems.*

● My rabbit has brown deposits forming in its ears, and keeps scratching them. What could be the cause?

Almost certainly, ear mites are the problem. These microscopic pests may be introduced on bedding, and will then cause inflammation and severe irritation in the ear. Treatment by dusting with flowers of sulfur is recommended. Do this as soon as possible, because if the parasites reach the inner ear they will affect the rabbit's sense of balance. The hutch must also be disinfected.

● *What should I do about fly strike?*

The best course of action is to try to prevent it. Ensure the rabbit's coat is not soiled, because this will attract blowflies which are likely to lay their eggs here. Maggots hatch rapidly and will then burrow into the skin where they will produce deadly toxins. Veterinary treatment is advisable in cases of fly strike, to ensure that not only are all the maggots removed from the wound, but also so that the wound can be dressed properly to prevent any recurrence.

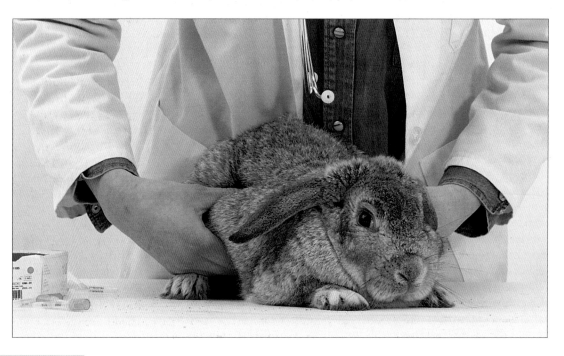

some causes of diarrhea, and also because they can worsen a case of diarrhea. You can try to rekindle your pet's appetite when it is suffering from diarrhea by offering human breakfast cereal that has been soaked in water to soften it and reintroducing its own food as it recovers.

Coccidiosis

One of the most significant causes of diarrhea and death in rabbits is the parasitic illness known as coccidiosis. This occurs in two forms, affecting either the intestines or the liver—the latter being described as hepatic coccidiosis. At least eight different types of the *Eimeria* parasite responsible for coccidiosis affecting the intestinal tract of rabbits have been identified, with some strains having much more serious effects than others. Some result in very serious diarrhea and are almost invariably fatal, whereas others have a mild effect, usually just slowing the rabbit's growth. A fecal examination arranged by your veterinarian is necessary to identify these parasites with certainty.

Since coccidia can be spread very easily, some rabbit foods may contain drugs known as coccidiostats which help prevent the illness. Even so, this gives no guarantee that rabbits may not fall ill. If this happens, treatment with sulfonamide drugs and fluid therapy may be required.

The cause of hepatic coccidiosis is a species of *Eimeria* called *E. steidae*. Unfortunately, this cannot reliably be controlled by coccidiostats but rarely proves fatal. It causes swelling of the liver and often affects the rabbit's growth rate.

Coccidiosis is spread via droppings which have contaminated the rabbit's environment, and the infection can be very difficult to eliminate. The risk is much greater in commercial rabbitries, however, where a large number of rabbits are kept together.

Cysticercosis

One parasitic illness which is more common in backyard rabbits, however, is the illness known as cysticercosis, linked with tapeworms. These parasites mature in the intestinal tract of dogs, with their microscopic eggs passing out in the dog's feces. These in turn can contaminate grass, and if your rabbit then eats this grass the

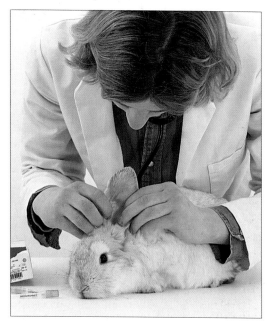

▲ *Here the veterinarian is examining a rabbit's ears. The ears of rabbits such as this Platinum French Lop can become infested with ear mites, which can lead to crusty swellings in the ear canal.*

tapeworm begins its development, usually forming a cyst in the abdomen or liver. A build-up of these can prove fatal, although there will be few symptoms beforehand. Therefore do not let your rabbit graze grass soiled by dogs' feces.

Dietary Disorders

A problem affecting the lower part of the rabbit's digestive tract, which appears to be increasingly common, is mucoid enteropathy. It is also known as cecal impaction, and is most often seen in young rabbits soon after weaning. The actual cause is unknown, but it has been suggested that a high protein diet may at least worsen the illness, if it is not the actual cause. Affected rabbits lose their appetites and drink considerably more than usual. Once again, rapid veterinary attention will be needed to treat this condition, with the cecum being discernible as a hard mass in the right-hand side of the abdomen. A change of diet, with more fiber added, will be beneficial, although mortality is often high, especially if there is an associated pneumonia.

Viruses and Miscellaneous Problems in Rabbits

THERE ARE TWO MAJOR VIRAL DISEASES OF rabbits, neither of which can be treated successfully once contracted. Therefore, susceptible rabbits should be protected by vaccination. Ask your veterinarian for details.

Myxomatosis
This is caused by a pox virus that originated from South America and results in only a very mild illness in the native species of rabbit there. But when the virus was introduced to Europe and Australia during the 1950s as a means of controlling wild rabbit populations, it caused massive mortality. Since then, wild rabbit populations have built up some immunity to the illness, but domestic rabbits are still vulnerable.

Contact between wild and domestic rabbits is one way in which the virus can be spread. It can also be transmitted by rabbit fleas, which are localized on the rabbit's ears, and also via mosquitoes, especially in warmer areas. Symptoms include swelling of the head and eyelids, leading to blindness.

Viral Hemorrhagic Disease
In 1984, a previously unrecognized disease was first recorded in China, causing widespread mortality in rabbitries there, and has since spread to most parts of the world. It attacks the liver and is rapidly fatal. Now known as viral hemorrhagic disease (VHD), the cause of the illness has been identified as a calcivirus. It is highly infectious and can be easily spread by direct contact between rabbits. Like myxomatosis, it can also be transmitted by flies and fleas.

VHD has an exceedingly short incubation period, with affected rabbits dying within a day or two of being exposed to the virus. The only symptom is often a very slight bloody discharge from the nose and sometimes around the vent. In rabbits over two months of age, nervous signs are often more apparent, with the outcome again usually proving fatal. Vaccination is now possible, however, and it affords good protection. Boosters are usually required every six months for rabbits at risk.

Broken Bones
Rabbits may sustain bone injuries, such as a fracture resulting from a fall. The tibia in the lower leg is often broken in this way, and unfortunately, it can be very difficult to treat injuries of this type successfully. Internal fixation (by the insertion of a surgical pin, for example) has the best chance of success, but it is an expensive procedure. The other usual method—applying an external cast to the affected leg—is often not successful, partly since the rabbit's skin is very flexible and also because the rabbit will try to remove the cast itself. Even more serious is a fracture of the

▼ A 10-week-old rabbit suffering from the incurable viral disease myxomatosis. The incubation period typically lasts from seven to 14 days.

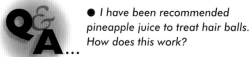

● *I have been recommended pineapple juice to treat hair balls. How does this work?*

Encouraging an affected rabbit to consume approximately 0.3fl oz (10ml) of fresh pineapple juice, using it to mix a bran mash twice daily, for example, can be beneficial because of the presence of an enzyme called bromelin, which helps to break down the hair ball directly.

● *Why are pregnant does most likely to die from hair balls?*

This is partly because they will be pulling their fur to create a nest, and so are likely to swallow it in large amounts, while the presence of a hair ball in the stomach means that they will have difficulty in obtaining sufficient nutrients to meet the demands of the young developing in their body, which results in the condition known as pregnancy toxemia.

● *Why does my veterinarian suggest neutering my doe, which lives in the home?*

Because does that do not breed are at much greater risk of developing malignant tumors of the uterus than those kept for breeding purposes. In contrast, bucks are neutered for behavioral reasons.

▼ *The only protection against myxomatosis is by vaccination. There is no treatment, and an infected individual will have to be painlessly destroyed.*

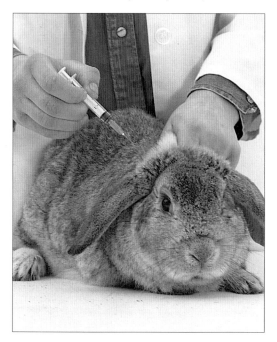

▲ *This Rex rabbit is shedding. This change in coat is quite normal, but rabbits are likely to be more vulnerable to illness during this period.*

lumbar vertebrae in the lower back. The rabbit will become unconscious for a period afterward and then, when it recovers, its hind limbs are likely to be paralyzed, with incontinence also being evident. There is little that can be done under these circumstances, with euthanasia often being the kindest option.

Fur Chewing

In the case of Angora rabbits especially, fur-chewing can become a life-threatening problem, not because of the amount of hair being removed from the body but because of the resulting blockage that can occur in the stomach and lower down in the intestinal tract. This can be fatal if the hairs clump together. The traditional treatment is to give 0.7fl oz (20ml) of liquid paraffin oil orally with a syringe (obtainable from your veterinarian) twice daily for a week. The rabbit's stomach area should also be massaged by gently rubbing the belly region for a few minutes after each dosage, in the hope of clearing the obstruction.

Pet Insurance

As rabbits have become more popular, a number of the pet insurance companies are offering specific policies for them. These can be very valuable in cases where the rabbit has sustained a major injury, such as a fracture resulting from a fall. Insurance can also be valuable for covering the cost of diagnostics such as radiography, to determine other problems in the body.

Rabbit Breed Development

THE NUMBER OF RABBIT BREEDS HAS INCREASED greatly over the past 150 years, and new breeds are still being developed. However, there is often confusion between breeds and varieties. A **breed** is a type of rabbit defined by certain recognizable characteristics, such as coat type, ears, and size. These features combine to create a distinctive appearance. There can often be a number of different **varieties** of the same breed, each based on differences in coloration. For example, the Dutch breed is instantly identifiable by its distinctive coat patterning, but there are currently eight color varieties recognized, as well as a tricolored form.

The Breed Standard

The characteristics of a breed are laid down in the official breed standard, which is used for judging purposes. At a show, the rabbits in a particular class are not judged against each other, but are assessed on the basis of how closely they correspond in all respects to the ideal, as described in the breed standard. Revisions to the judging standards are made from time to time, after extensive consultation with breeders and judges, and judging standards can be drawn up for new breeds which attain a level of popularity. The awarding of points for particular features is influenced by the particular characteristics of the breed in question. Patterning, for example, is more relevant in some instances than the quality or texture of the coat.

Although there have been moves to create international judging standards for particular breeds, especially in mainland Europe, there is no universally agreed standard. This also applies in the case of the breeds themselves, with the American Rabbit Breeders' Association recognizing breeds for show purposes—such as the Jersey Wooly, which is presently unknown in Europe. Conversely, some European breeds are not kept in North America.

Classification

Rabbit breeds are classified in various ways, being divided traditionally into fur and fancy groups in Britain, based on their origins. Breeds that have been of commercial importance for their pelts feature in the fur category, whereas those which have been developed essentially for exhibition purposes, such as the Dwarf Lop, are considered to be members of the fancy group. In the case of fur breeds, the judging emphasis is always placed far more upon the quality of the coat rather than the overall type or appearance.

The fur category is further subdivided to embrace both the Rex and Satin breeds. Within these groupings, however—which exist as the result of changes in the structure of the coat—there are a wide range of colors and patterns, not all of which may even have been fully developed as yet, in the various forms.

◄ *Domestication has led to a greater variance in size developing between the different breeds of rabbit than in any of the other popular small animals kept as pets.*

If you are interested in showing your rabbits, then it is important to begin with quality stock obtained from an established breeder. Start by joining the national rabbit organization in your country, which will be able to give you local contacts and direct you to a specialist club for the particular breed concerned. Searching the Internet can also provide useful contacts, especially with overseas fanciers.

Most breeders are eager to assist newcomers and will often give advice on recommended pairings of rabbits which you purchase from them. Bear in mind that most does are generally considered to be coming to the end of their reproductive lives at about three to four years of age, with litter sizes decreasing, but bucks can sire offspring for significantly longer. It may therefore be better to start out with young does and an older, quality buck.

▼ *Rabbit shows have helped to encourage the development of today's breeds, with competition inevitably being fierce at larger events. This is a prize-winning Black Silver, with its many awards.*

● *How can I find out about the dates of shows in my area?*

Newsletters produced by rabbit societies usually contain such information, and magazines devoted to rabbits also contain details of such events. If you want to enter, you will need to obtain an entry form from the show secretary, which must be returned before the closing date, along with the appropriate entry fee.

● *Which rabbit breeds make the best pets, especially for children?*

Generally, smaller rabbits such as the Dutch and Mini Lop are to be recommended, not just in terms of their size but also because of their friendly natures. Dutch rabbits are a traditional favorite and are widely available in a range of colors. However, they are not the best choice for exhibition purposes because of the difficulty of breeding well-marked individuals. Mini Rexes are also growing in popularity as pets—thanks in part to their soft fur. Polish and Netherland Dwarf rabbits are also often recommended as pets, but they can prove to be less friendly than the lop breeds. Rabbits with particular grooming requirements—especially the Angora but also the Cashmere Lops and Lionheads—are not good choices for most children.

Rabbit Breeds and Varieties

APART FROM THE DIVISION INTO FUR AND FANCY categories which applies in the case of British breeds, there is no universal system of classification for rabbit breeds. Some still remain quite localized and uncommon outside their area of origin, whereas others, such as the Dutch, have built up a strong international following.

ALASKA

This particular breed provides a good example of the difficulties in classifying rabbit breeds. It is thought to have originated in Germany, being first exhibited there in 1907. Other distinct strains may have existed for a period in France and in England, being evolved from crosses between melanistic (black-coated) Himalayans,

Q & A...

● *How did the Alaska obtain its name, since it has completely black fur?*

The original aim of those who created the breed was to produce a rabbit which had a black coat but with white tips to the hairs, creating an appearance resembling that of the Arctic Fox in its winter coat. Although this attempt clearly failed, the chosen name remained in use!

● *Breeders were talking at a show about the American Checkered Giant's butterfly markings. What are these?*

These are the dark areas of fur that extend from the sides of the mouth to above the nose. They should be symmetrical, so they resemble the outline of a butterfly. There should also be a small cheek spot below the dark circle of fur encircling each eye in this breed, plus dark markings along the back extending along the top of the tail. Finally, there should also be two prominent dark areas of fur on each flank.

● *Is it true that the American Checkered Giant is descended from a Flemish Giant crossed with a wild white hare?*

This is a story that is actually more legend than truth, particularly as hares and rabbits do not hybridize together in the wild. A white hare is exceptionally rare anyway, so the likelihood of any breed of rabbit being developed in this way is very remote.

● *The Alaska looks similar to the Havana. Are they related?*

It is likely that Havanas may have been involved in the development of the Alaska. This is borne out by the fact that both breeds display a similar stocky, rounded body shape and a short neck.

◀ *The shiny black fur of the Alaska is a particular feature of this breed. The Alaska played an important part in the development of the Rex breed.*

which were probably crossed with Argentes. The British strain, originally recognized under the name of Nubian, then died out during the 1930s. These rabbits typically weighed about 5lb (2.3kg), being slightly heavier than the French strain. Today, the Alaska has evolved into a bigger breed, typically averaging 7–9lb (3.2–4kg).

The rich, black, glossy color of their coats helps distinguish these rabbits, which are quite compact in terms of type. They have no obvious neck, and a relatively broad, yet short, head.

AMERICAN

One of a number of breeds created in the United States, the American first came to prominence when it was exhibited in 1917. The breed was developed in California. At first, all Americans were blue, but before long, occasional whites were appearing in litters as well, and today both varieties are now recognized for show purposes. The blue coloration should be of a dark slaty shade, and of an even depth over the entire body, with the undercoat being very dense. The white variety has pink eyes, whereas they match the coat color in the blue variety. Bucks should weigh approximately 10lb (4.5kg), with does typically being 1lb (0.45kg) heavier.

AMERICAN CHECKERED GIANT

The origins of this breed can be traced to Germany, with stock being taken from there to the United States around 1910. Its origins are unclear, but these rabbits were probably bred from Flemish Giants crossed with Checkered Lops, with the Flemish input being used as a means of reducing the size of the Lop's ears.

Sometimes simply referred to as the American Giant, this breed has now become much larger, with some individuals weighing 11lb (5kg) or more, although bucks are generally slightly lighter than does. The appearance of these rabbits also suggests that Belgian Hares, which were very numerous in the United States in the early 1900s, also played a part in the development of the breed. It has a long, well-arched body carried off the ground.

The American Checkered Giant is also quite a challenging breed to exhibit, because of its distinctive markings. They resemble those seen in the English Spot, but there is no line of clearly defined spots in this case. Two color varieties—black and blue—are recognized in this breed. The coat is short and dense, which helps to emphasize these colored markings set against predominantly white fur. One of the most appealing features of this rabbit is the distinctive area of dark fur encircling each eye.

▼ *The dark markings around the eyes of the American Checkered Giant must be symmetrical in shape and must not merge with other dark areas on the face.*

ANGORA

While most rabbits are considered to have fur, the Angora breed has a woollen coat. The structure of the coat is very different from that of other rabbits because the downy, insulating undercoat, which is short in other breeds, grows much longer in Angoras, merging with the outer guard hairs that normally lie sleekly above it.

The Angora is one of the oldest of all rabbit breeds and has probably been kept in Britain since the 1600s. Ultimately, some of these rabbits were smuggled to France in about 1723, before reaching Germany in 1776, where slightly different variants have been developed. The name "Angora" was given to the breed because of the long-coated forms of

▲ *A Smoke English Angora displaying the difference in depth of body color which typifies this form, due to the varying amount of dark pigmentation in its wool.*

▼ *The fur around the nose shows the true color of a particular Angora variety more accurately than the paler body fur. Young Angoras are relatively darker in color.*

other livestock originating from Turkey which bear this name, notably breeds of cat and goat.

The traditional English form of the Angora weighs approximately 6lb (2.7kg), and although it produces less wool each year than other forms, this is of a finer quality. French Angoras are about 8lb (3.6kg) in weight, with German stock weighing 9lb (4kg) or so. The French Angora can also be distinguished by the lack of hair, called furnishings, in its ears. The fur of these rabbits is traditionally plucked, not clipped, as in the case of the English Angora.

The unique coat of these rabbits needs particular care. They are not kept in ordinary hutches but in cages with wire floors. Otherwise, bedding will become stuck to the long coat and will be very difficult to extract. It is also not possible to bathe them if their coats become soiled. The dense nature of the fur means that if it becomes wet, it will dry very slowly, leaving the rabbit at risk of hypothermia. It is also quite likely to become matted as it dries out.

The density of the coat can also cause other problems, particularly during the summer months when Angora rabbits are especially prone to heatstroke. Therefore, even if you do not intend to use the wool of these rabbits, clipping the fur approximately every three months is essential, by which time it will have grown to more than 3in (7.5cm) long. Use round-ended scissors to carefully cut away the excess thick coat.

It is possible for a single Angora to produce over 2lb (0.9kg) of wool during the course of a year, although that of the smaller English Angora is unlikely to exceed 12oz (340g). The traditional color associated with all forms of the Angora is the Pink-eyed White, but there are around a dozen other different varieties. These include solid colors such as blue and black, as well as Chinchilla and smoke varieties, which have dark tipping on the hairs. The dark tipping alters the appearance of these rabbits as they move or when groomed.

Acceptance of colors for show purposes varies, as usual, from country to country. The breed is popular in exhibition circles, in spite of its rather time-consuming requirements, and shows well—often taking top honors.

Q&A...

● **At what age can a young Angora be clipped for the first time?**

Young Angoras are born with coats which are less profuse than those of adults, but their hair grows quickly and they can be clipped for the first time around seven weeks of age.

● **My Angoras appear to mate, but their fertility is low. Why is this?**

This is often the result of the physical barrier created by the rabbits' fur. Most breeders therefore mate their Angoras after clipping them. Toward the end of a doe's pregnancy, it is also a good idea to trim back the fur carefully around both her genitals and teats, using blunt-ended scissors, to ensure that she will have no difficulty in giving birth, and that her offspring will be able to suckle without difficulty.

● **Does coat length matter in exhibition circles?**

Yes, this is an important feature. The coat should be a minimum of 2.3in (6cm) in length, and preferably longer. However, these rabbits are assessed primarily on features such as the quality of their wool, as well as its density and texture.

▼ *Grooming an Angora rabbit's fur must be carried out gently, otherwise it is likely to result in the undercoat being pulled out.*

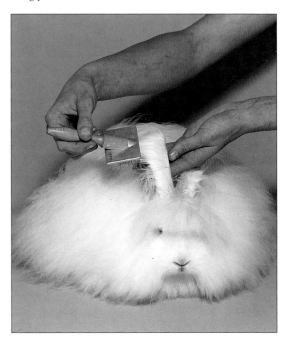

ARGENTE GROUP

The Argente group consists of four different varieties, whose origins can be traced to the Champagne region of France. The name Argente means "silver" and describes the characteristic tipping apparent in the coats of these rabbits. The Argente Champagne was first described in 1631, although its ancestry is unknown. The original standard for this breed was drawn up in 1912. Its distinctive appearance results from a change in the coloration of the tips of the under-coat, which becomes apparent at the first molt. The Argente Champagne has a dark, slate-blue undercoat, which is then transformed to silvery-white at its tips. The contrast in the coat results from the color of the undercoat set against the long, black guard hairs. For show purposes, the coat must be evenly colored. Any particular con-centration of black hairs spoils the overall effect. The Argente Champagne is the largest of the four varieties, weighing around 8lb (3.6kg).

Other varieties now include the Argente Bleu, with lavender-blue rather than black hairs, and a smoother textured coat. There are differences in

▼ *The long, elegant shape of the Belgian Hare is highly suggestive of a true hare, but it is a rabbit. Its ancestry is believed to include the now-extinct Patagonian, as well as Flemish Giant stock. This is a black and tan form.*

Q & A...

● *At what age will the Argente's distinctive coloration begin to appear?*

This usually starts at about five weeks of age, with the molted hairs then being replaced by the typical tipped hairs which are characteristic of this breed. It usually takes up to six months for these rabbits to acquire their adult coats.

● *How easy is it to exhibit a Belgian Hare successfully?*

In terms of show preparation, they are quite straightforward, but you will need to train young Belgian Hares to adopt the characteristic "sitting up" show stance, that emphasizes the long, slim, straight front legs of the breed. This is not difficult and, not surprisingly, this highly distinctive breed often features among the winners at major shows.

▲ *Beverens have a dense coat that feels very soft, with the individual hairs being over 1in (2.5cm) long. They typically weigh about 9lb (4kg). This is a blue variety.*

terms of type as well, with the Argente Bleu having a far more compact shape. The Argente Brun is very similar in terms of size and appearance to the Argente Bleu, weighing about 6lb (2.7kg). It is probably the scarcest member of the group and has a silvered brown appearance. In fact, today's stock is a recreation of the original bloodline, which had died out by the 1940s.

Corresponding more closely in type to the original Champagne form, the Argente Creme is the smallest variant, weighing little more than 5lb (2.3kg). In this variant, the orange undercoat has creamy-white tips, with the guard hairs being orange. This creates a stunning silvery-yellow effect, especially since the coat lies quite flat.

BEIGE

Rabbits displaying this unusual coloring were bred first in Britain during the 1920s and then developed in the Netherlands in the following decade. What makes this unusual breed so attractive is the fact that there are very delicate light pastel blue tips to a number of the hairs, which are often most apparent on the head. The original strain died out in Britain and was then reintroduced in the 1980s. It is also known as the Isabella. These are medium-sized rabbits—they typically weigh up to 7lb (3.2kg)—with a rather square body profile. Their origins are unknown,

but in overall shape they bear some resemblance to the Havana.

BELGIAN HARE

These rabbits were first seen in Britain in 1874, and they were soon in great demand in the United States, triggering what became known as the Belgian Hare Boom (see pages 16–17). The traditional variety associated with this breed is the agouti form, described as "hare colored." The agouti has been subjected to selective breeding, however. Cross-breeding with Beverens has produced the rich chestnut coloration combined with black banding on the individual hairs.

In the black and tan form, the tan markings are restricted to the undersides of the body. There is also a pink-eyed albino form, which is most commonly seen in Britain. The coat is sleek and glossy, emphasizing the athletic poise of these rabbits. They weigh about 9lb (4kg).

BEVEREN

This breed takes its name from the town close to Antwerp, Belgium, where it was developed. The traditional color of the breed is blue. It was first exported to Britain in about 1915, and then to the United States, where they were first called Sitkas. Other colors now include blue and pink-eyed white variants, black, and a chocolate form. More recent developments include a lilac form, bred in Britain in the 1980s, and pointed varieties with darker extremities—which are often regarded as a separate breed.

BLANC BREEDS

The three existing Blanc breeds are of European origin. The Blanc de Hotot is the oldest member of this group of white-coated rabbits, being first bred in 1902. Pairings involving patterned rabbits, including the Dutch, contributed to its ancestry. The Blanc de Hotot can be distinguished by the black areas of fur which encircle its eyes, in combination with black eyelashes. They typically weigh around 9lb (4kg) or so, with rather a square body shape, although a smaller dwarf form also exists.

The Blanc de Bouscat was bred during the early 1900s in the Gironde area of France, being derived from Angora and Pink-eyed White Flemish Giant crosses, with an input also from the Argente Champagne. It is a bigger breed than the Blanc de Hotot, with does as usual being slightly heavier than bucks, weighing up to 15lb (7kg). The Blanc de Bouscat is pure white in color, with the dense fur having a slightly frosty appearance. This is due to the coarser guard hairs distributed through the coat, which is at least 1.2in (3cm) long. The head of these rabbits is a feature of the breed, being both broad and well rounded.

Belgium is the home of the Blanc de Termonde, derived from Beveren and Flemish Giant stock. These rabbits correspond in size to the Blanc de Hotot. They have a relatively long body and ruby-colored eyes, with short, silky fur.

BRITISH GIANT

Developed during the 1940s, the British Giant is descended from the same stock as the Flemish Giant. Breeders were seeking to increase the size of the Flemish form and create new varieties, since only the Steel-gray Flemish was recognized in Britain for show purposes. This resulted in the importation of Flemish Giants from the United States, where a great range of colors had been created. Interest in the new breed continued for nearly a decade but then declined, and it was not until 1981 that fresh attempts were made to promote the British Giant again. The breed today is slightly smaller than its Flemish relative; bucks weigh a minimum of 12.4lb (5.6kg) and does weigh at least 13.5lb (6.1kg).

These are friendly rabbits, which have grown in popularity as house-rabbits, but they must have a spacious hutch if being housed outdoors (see page 19). A number of varieties has since been created. These include solid colors such as black and blue, as well as both blue and pink-eyed whites. Other varieties include rabbit-gray, which is light brown with black ticking, as well as the Steel-gray where the brown coloration is replaced by gray. At present, however, the

▼ *The dewlap—the fold of skin beneath the chin—is visible in this buck Blanc de Bouscat. The ears measure up to 7in (18cm) and form a V-shape when held erect.*

British Giant has not established a strong inter-national following compared with the Flemish.

BRUN MARRON DE LORRAINE
This is one of the rarer small breeds of French origin. Its weight ranges between 3.3lb and 5.5lb (1.5–2.5kg). Its coloration is very similar to that of the Deilenaar, being chestnut-brown with black tipping and with yellower underparts. It has a more slender, rounded appearance, how-ever, with its fur being both short and very dense.

BURGUNDY YELLOW
Another ancient French breed, these rabbits started to become known elsewhere in Europe during the early 1900s, but are still not widely seen today. The Burgundy Yellow is a relatively large breed, which can weigh up to 11lb (5kg). Its natural color is a yellowish shade, being much paler on the underparts. The fur is rela-tively long and soft, thanks to a profuse under-coat. The eyes are encircled with fur which appears almost whitish in color.

▶ *The brown-gray form of the British Giant can be distinguished by the brownish tone to its fur, with this color being especially evident in the vicinity of the neck.*

▼ *Two Black British Giant youngsters, aged 14 and five weeks respectively. They start to grow rapidly after weaning, as is the case of other large breeds.*

● *Will a large breed such as the British Giant have a shorter lifespan than a smaller breed, as is the case with pedigree dogs?*

There appears to be no significant difference in this respect in the case of rabbits. Some bloodlines do, however, appear to be longer-lived than others.

● *I saw two examples of Burgundy Yellows that looked rather red to me. Does this breed vary much in color?*

The yellowish color that distinguishes the breed is quite distinctive, but what has happened is that breeders have carried out crossings with red-colored rabbits of other breeds. This in turn has affected the Burgundy Yellow's color, causing it to become more reddish.

CALIFORNIAN

The Californian was created in the early 1920s by a breeder in the United States. Although intended as a commercial breed for farming purposes, it is now widely kept by exhibition breeders as well. It was bred originally from crossings between New Zealand Whites and Himalayans, with Chinchilla rabbits also contributing to its development. The new breed was not actually recognized by the American Rabbit Breeders' Association until 1939 and did not become well known in Europe until the 1960s.

It is a pointed breed, which means that the points, or extremities, of the body—the feet, tail, ears, and nose—are dark, offset against a white body color. The eyes are pink. There are now four different varieties of the Californian, differing in the coloration of their points. The normal form is distinguished by its black points, while there are also chocolate, blue, and lilac varieties—although the acceptance of these newer varieties in exhibition circles is not universal. They are most common in Britain, where they were first bred.

A slight variance in type has also arisen, with a more elongated body shape being preferred in the United States. The weight is somewhat variable, but it is typically between 8.8lb and 10lb (4–4.5kg). The Californian is a powerful rabbit, with broad hindquarters, but it also has a gentle disposition. This has helped encourage its acceptance in show circles.

▲ *A Normal Californian doe and her litter. In common with other pointed varieties such as the Himalayan, the young are pale at birth; the dark fur develops with age.*

CHINCHILLA

This breed gets its name because the coloration of its fur is similar to that of the rodent known as the chinchilla. Its origins are mysterious, since the French breeder who developed the strain suggested it had resulted from crosses between Himalayans and Blue Beverens, which appears to be unlikely on genetic grounds. Certainly, early pairings of the Chinchilla revealed that there were a number of other breeds in the genetic makeup, with Sables and Squirrels appearing in their litters. The breed became very popular among commercial breeders, because the pelts of these rabbits could be marketed when they were just five months of age—significantly earlier than in the case of other breeds.

The characteristic feature of the Chinchilla is the loss of red and yellow pigment from the hair. The coat is dense, with a blue undercoat over the entire body. In contrast, the longer guard hairs are white with obvious black ticking, which helps to create the distinctive appearance of this breed. The underparts are entirely white. The Chinchilla is quite a small breed, typically averaging between 4.4lb and 6.6lb (2–3kg).

Other colors have been created, but they are rare. The brown form used to be bred on quite a large scale in France. Another form, with blue ticking, was bred in Britain. Meanwhile a separate American form of the breed, called the American Chinchilla, has been created, although it remains unknown in Europe.

A large form of the Chinchilla, the Chinchilla Giganta, was developed during the 1920s, with the maximum permitted weight of these rabbits being 11lb (5kg). Their coat coloration is very similar to that of the Chinchilla but tends to be slightly darker overall. Subsequent crossings of such rabbits (better known as Giant Chinchillas in the United States) with Flemish Giants has led to the creation of another breed here, called the American Giant Chinchilla. This weighs about 15lb (7kg), making it the heaviest of the group.

Such was the impact of the Chinchilla that even discarded rabbits produced in the early days of the Chinchilla breeding program helped to spawn other breeds, notably the distinctive Chifox, which had a coat that was 2.5in (6.5cm) long. The Chifox was a combination between the Chinchilla and Angora, with a fox-like body shape. Although it now appears to be extinct, it could be recreated in the future, especially since Chinchilla kittens with longer coats still appear occasionally in litters, reflecting the past input of the Angora breed.

▼▶ *The Chinchilla was bred as a fur rabbit and has a fine, dense coat, with the individual hairs varying in color along their length. The quality of the fur can be checked by seeing if the bands line up (inset).*

● *I've seen the term Apoldro mentioned in regard to Chinchillas. What is this?*

This is the name given to a modern recreation of the Brown Chinchilla, which was originally developed in the Netherlands. It was then bred again in Britain in 1981, using Chinchilla and Havana stock.

● *Do Chinchillas make good pets?*

Yes, and they are probably underestimated in this respect. Their relatively small size, compact shape, and friendly nature mean they deserve to be more popular in this regard. They have a strong following among exhibitors, so obtaining one of these rabbits should not be too difficult.

● *Are there any other localized forms of the Chinchilla?*

There is a larger version of the Chinchilla in Germany, sometimes described as the German Grosse Chinchilla. It is still lighter than the American Giant form, weighing about 12lb (5.4kg). In Switzerland, there is no division between normal and giant breeds of the Chinchilla; instead, there is one breed of intermediate size.

DEILENAAR

The attractive Deilenaar breed is of Dutch origin. Chinchilla, New Zealand Red, and Belgian Hare stock were used in its development. The Deilenaar was recognized in its homeland in 1940, but progress was slow because of the outbreak of the Second World War. The breed finally attained recognition in Britain in the 1980s, but remains scarce elsewhere. The coats of these rabbits are very attractive, being reddish-brown with a variable degree of black ticking in them. Deilenaars can weigh up to 7.7lb (3.5kg). They have a solid appearance, with ears that should not exceed 5in (13cm) in length.

DUTCH

In spite of its name, the widely kept Dutch rabbit originated in Belgium, being descended from an old breed called the Brabancon. The standard for the Dutch is very precise, calling for a symmetrical white blaze extending down between

● Can I mate my Blue and Black Dutch together?

This pairing will be fine in the short term, but avoid repeating it over several generations, because it tends ultimately to result in Blues with excessively dark coats.

● My Black Dutch rabbit's coat has acquired a rusty hue. What has caused this, and will her coat return to its usual color?

It sounds as if your rabbit's coat has become bleached by exposure to bright sunlight. If this is the case, the coat is unlikely to revert back to its usual black color until she molts this fur. For this reason, exhibition rabbits should be kept out of bright sunlight at all times. Sometimes, however, this bleaching effect can occur naturally just prior to a molt.

▼ *Coat color is very important in the exhibition Deilenaar. A yellowish or gray hue is a serious flaw, with paler fur on the hind legs also being considered a fault in show stock.*

▲ ▶ *Dutch have proved to be very popular, not just because of their size and appearance, but also because of their friendly nature, being a good choice as pets. Here are a Black Dutch and (inset) a Yellow Dutch.*

the eyes and over the throat area, which may taper to a point at the front of the ears. The neck should be free of colored fur, with the remainder of the front half of the rabbit, including the forefeet, also being white. The rear of the body is the same color as the sides of the face and ears.

Today's Dutch rabbits have a cobby shape and weigh 4.5–5lb (2–2.3kg). The coat is now short and dense with a good sheen, whereas in the past it was actually longer, with a silky texture. The markings will be consistent throughout the rabbit's life, so a well-marked individual is likely to have a long, successful show career.

A range of color varieties has been successfully developed, adding to the breed's appeal. The traditional black and white variety is a firm favorite. The black areas must display no hint of browning or odd white hairs scattered through them. Evenness of coloration is vital, and this can be a particular flaw which mars the Blue Dutch, since its extremities are often paler than the body itself. Overall, a medium shade of blue is preferred. Chocolate Dutch can also suffer from this particular fault; they need to be an even shade of deep, dark brown.

Three different shades of the Gray Dutch are

recognized, of which the steel-gray color is most commonly seen. It is dark gray, with clearly defined steel ticking. The brown-gray form is similar but has a brown undercoat. These rabbits can be quite variable in terms of their depth of coloration. In this case, it is often the cheeks that are too pale, spoiling the desirable even effect. There is also a recognized pale gray form.

The Yellow is the lightest of the eight different varieties in this breed. It can be confused with the Tortoiseshell Dutch, sometimes showing slight traces of darker shading. These are a well-defined feature of the Tortoiseshell Dutch, which has a yellow ground color and black shading over the ears and cheeks as well as the haunches. These dark areas must not be smudged.

The Tricolored Dutch bears some resemblance to the Tortoiseshell Dutch, but it is usually regarded as a separate breed. It was created by matings between Harlequin and Dutch rabbits, with the Harlequin itself being descended from Tortoiseshell Dutch. Tricolors are rare, partly as the result of the difficulty of breeding well-marked specimens.

ENGLISH

The English was one of the original fancy breeds, first recorded in 1849. It appears to have become very popular at that stage, before fading into obscurity later in the century. The patterning of these rabbits is highly distinctive. It is predominantly white, offset against dark areas of fur. Black is the traditional color for the dark areas. The ears should be jet-black, displaying no trace of white fur, with the eyes being encircled by black fur. The area including both the nose and the mouth is also black, with the pattern here being described as the butterfly smut, because of its shape. A black spot below each eye completes the head markings.

A black line, called the saddle, extends from the top of the back to the tip of the tail, while there is a series of black spots evident on the sides of the body. The spots forming the so-called chain markings extend from the base of the ears and increase in size toward the loins. There should also be a spot on each of the legs, with six teat spots present on the belly as well.

One of the particular challenges of this breed is the fact that it does not breed true. Pairing English together will, on average, result in only half of the youngsters being similarly marked. The others will be either black, or what are described as "charlies." These are rabbits which possess only part of the pattern of markings associated with the breed —normally just a very small, dark area on the face and dark ears.

These are very attractive rabbits, with their dense, short fur helping to emphasize their markings, while the well-proportioned body shows off this unique patterning to good effect. The English weighs about 7lb (3.2kg).

FLEMISH GIANT

This is the largest breed of rabbit in the world today, although smaller than the now-extinct Angevin which contributed to its ancestry. Bucks should weigh at least 11lb (5kg), with does weighing a minimum of 12lb (5.4kg). Exhibition

Q & A...

● *Should I offer as pets the charlies produced by my pair of English?*

No, keep them as part of your breeding program. Pairing a charlie with a well-marked English increases the likelihood of producing English with improved markings, compared with English to English matings. (This name "charlie" is probably derived from the moustache worn by the comedian Charlie Chaplin—a similar dark area of fur being a feature of such rabbits.) If you mate the Selfs produced in their litters, however, these will breed true, and no English-marked offspring will result.

● *What are the common faults associated with the English, in terms of their markings?*

White hairs breaking up the saddle running down the back are common faults, but the chain is the hardest part of the pattern to replicate to show standard.

▲ *The Black is the color form most often associated with the English. The short, close-lying fur of these rabbits helps to highlight their black markings.*

◀ *A Tortoiseshell English. This variety of the breed was created after the Black, and this has now been followed by blue, gray, and chocolate variants of the breed.*

▼ *Flemish Giants are powerfully built. When compared together, there is a distinct variance in head shape between mature bucks—which have larger heads—and does. The ears form a distinct V-shape when held erect.*

Flemish Giants today may weigh 14lb (6.3kg), with individuals as heavy as 21lb (9.5kg) having been recorded on occasions—although it is the size of these rabbits, rather than their weight, which impresses judges. The weight must correspond with the rabbit's body frame, rather than indicating obesity. (Any tendency toward obesity will be penalized for show purposes.)

Known in their Belgian homeland under the name of Vlaamse Reus, these rabbits first came to prominence in the 1850s, in the area around the town of Ghent, where Flemish language predominates. The earliest examples of this breed were a sandy color, with steel-gray individuals also becoming common. A much wider range of colors now exists, although not all are recognized internationally for show purposes. White Flemish Giants with pink eyes have become popular over recent years, but tend to be slightly smaller than the traditional colors. Other self variants now available include blue and black. Gray forms should be relatively dark in color.

FOX

The Fox breeds are descended from Chinchilla stock, with the popular Silver Fox having been created from crossings between Chinchillas and Black and Tans. Breeders hoped to improve the pattern of ticking as a result, with the markings of these rabbits now broadly corresponding to those of their tan ancestor. The Chinchilla gene causes the loss of tan pigmentation, resulting in the longer guard hairs having silvery tips, offset against black. The breed was originally called the Black Fox as a result, but the advent of other colors, beginning with blue, and then lilac and chocolate variants, meant that this name was inappropriate.

The quality of the fur is very important. It must be soft, silky, and dense, averaging about 1in (2.5cm) in length. The characteristic ticking should be present on the chest and flanks and also extends over the feet. It is also present on the back, where it tends to be darker. There are pale circles of fur around the eyes, with other white areas including the fur inside the ears. The belly and underside of the tail are white. These rabbits average 5.5–7lb (2.5–3.2kg) in weight.

The American Silver Fox does not share a common ancestry with European strains of the Silver Fox; in fact, it is a separate breed, created from the crossings of Silvers with Self-colored American Checkered Giants. It was first recognized in 1925, and resembles a larger version of the Silver, weighing between 9 and 12lb (4–5.4kg). Both black and blue varieties of the American Silver Fox have been developed, with silver tipping being present throughout the coat. The Swiss Fox (see page 87) is also of separate origins.

GIANT PAPILLON

This French breed is similar to the English, although significantly larger in size, weighing about 12 or 13lb (5.4–6kg). Instead of a chain of spots on the sides of the body, there are more solid dark patches.

● *What are the Silver Fox's pea spots and triangle?*

... The pea spot describes the shape of the whitish area of fur just in front of the base of each ear. There is also a small triangle of similarly colored fur to be found at the base of the neck. The eye circles of pale fur, which need to be even in shape, are also important in exhibition stock, with points being awarded for all these features.

● *Do the various Papillon rabbits breed true, unlike the English?*

No. Such pairings are again likely to produce the same three possible variants that exist with the English (see page 68), with poorly marked specimens being called charlies (see page 68).

● *Why are breeders so concerned that their Papillon rabbits have a relatively long body shape?*

This feature helps to emphasize the characteristic markings, both down the back and on the sides of the body in particular. The spots on the flanks must be well spaced in a good exhibition rabbit of this breed.

● *How did the name "Fox" become associated with these rabbits?*

It originated because the appearance of their fur resembled that of the North American gray fox.

▼ *The Black Fox is now described as the Silver Fox in Britain, where it was created during the 1920s, and as the Silver Marten in North America.*

However, other characteristics, such as the black spot beneath each eye and the butterfly marking on the nose—responsible for the breed's name—are identical to those of the English.

The Giant Papillon was bred in the district of Lorraine when it was under German control during the late 1800s. It arose from a combination of Flemish Giant and French Lop stock, crossed with spotted rabbits. This rabbit is also known as the Giant Lorrainese for this reason.

While development of the breed occurred in France, stock also became widely kept in Germany, with these rabbits becoming known as the Deutsche Riesenschecke there. They were taken to the United States in the early 1900s, laying the foundations for the creation of the American Checkered Giant.

A recent addition to the Papillon group of breeds is the small Dutch form, known as the Klein Lotharinger. These rabbits, which typically weigh 7lb (3.2kg), were bred by crossing Giant Papillons with Netherland Dwarfs. A wide range of color varieties has been developed, including a tricolored form. The breed has grown rapidly in popularity, particularly in its homeland, since first attaining recognition there in 1975.

▼ *The Glavcot is one of the breeds of rabbit which occurs in only one color—described in this instance as golden. The Glavcot is not especially common.*

GLAVCOT

The Glavcot breed used to exist in both silver and golden forms, coming to prominence in the 1920s in Britain where the breed was created. Neither attained great popularity, and only the golden variety was standardized in 1934. Both became extinct soon afterward, but during the 1970s the golden form was recreated using a combination of Beveren, Siberian, and Havana stock. It was first shown again in 1976. This is a relatively small, fine-boned breed weighing about 5.5lb (2.5kg).

▼ *Although the black variety is the most commonly seen form of the Giant Papillon, other colors have also been created. These include blue, brown, and amber, as well as combinations like steel and rabbit-gray.*

HARLEQUIN

The Harlequin is descended from the Brabancon and so shares a common ancestry with the Tri-colored Dutch. It was first exhibited in France during 1887, becoming known as the Japanese.

Everything about the Harlequin's coat pattern should contrast; if one ear is black, for example, then the other should be orange, with the coloration of the head being split and reversed in this instance. This type of patterning continues right down to the feet. The coat is silky, fine, and dense. Apart from black, there are three other colors—blue, brown, or lilac—that can be combined with orange. Rabbits in which white fur replaces orange are called Magpies.

HAVANA

The Havana was first bred in 1898 in the Netherlands. Subsequently, a separate lineage

▼ *In terms of type, the Havana is quite short and cobby, with rounded hindquarters. The coat of these rabbits should be dense and glossy.*

was developed in France as a result of a mating between a Himalayan and a wild rabbit. They were originally known as Fiery Eyes in Britain, thanks to the ruby-red glow of their eyes, which was offset by the rich, dark, chocolate-colored coat of this variety.

Another variety of the Havana, lacking the purplish sheen to its coat, was subsequently introduced from the Netherlands to the United States in 1916. There once existed a distinctly larger form of the breed, which now averages about 6lb (2.7kg), but this is now extinct.

Havana rabbits have played a significant role in the development of a number of other breeds, including the Marburger in Germany, which has been bred from crosses with Vienna Blues, and the English breed called the Lilac. In the Netherlands, the similar breed is called the Gouwenaar, with rabbits of this color appearing unexpectedly in litters alongside Havanas. They closely resemble the Havana in terms of type, being short and powerfully built, with a broad head and rounded hindquarters. Both the Lilac, which was originally known as the Essex Lavender, and the Marburger are a soft, pastel blue color, with the latter becoming significantly

▼ *The Harlequin is one of the most distinctive breeds. The colors should be clearly defined, but a relatively common fault of this breed is brindling, or the colors merging together. Harlequins weigh 6–8lb (2.7–3.6kg).*

▲ *An Agouti Lop Lionhead. Lionheads get their name because of the distinctive ruff of longer fur around the face, which looks rather like the mane of a lion.*

● **Why is the Himalayan also called the Egyptian Smut?**

... This is because these rabbits were widely bred in Egypt, with the description of "smut" referring to the dark area of fur on their faces.

● **Do both sexes of the Lionhead have a mane?**

Many does do display traces of manes, although some lose their mane as they mature. Generally, it is better to choose does with manes, in the hope that they will pass this trait onto their offspring. The remainder of the coat should be relatively short, with no furnishings of long hair in the ears.

● **My litter of Himalayans are much whiter on their extremities than the doe. Is this normal?**

Yes, this is normal. Their patterning is unusual, being temperature-sensitive. This means that the young are pure-white at birth. The darker markings normally present on the face, legs, and tail will usually take several weeks to develop to their fullest extent.

● **Does a giant form of the Himalayan exist?**

In continental Europe a strain weighing about 9lb (4kg) is often kept. This form also has a very placid nature and makes a good pet.

darker in color since it was first recognized in Germany during the 1920s.

HIMALAYAN

The origins of this breed lie in the east, where it probably originated in China before being introduced to Britain during the 1800s. Wild rabbits displaying similar markings have also been documented in Russia, which is why they are called Russian rabbits in some countries. Although Himalayans with black markings are common, there are also blue, lilac, and chocolate color varieties. Himalayans are very placid rabbits.

LIONHEAD AND JERSEY WOOLY

Created in Belgium during the 1990s, the Lionhead is one of the latest breeds to be developed, and it has since become very popular in many countries around the world. Weighing about 3.5lb (1.6kg), these rabbits were bred from crosses between the Dwarf Swiss Fox and a Netherland Dwarf, with the original aim being to create a long-coated dwarf breed.

In North America, the Jersey Wooly, developed in New Jersey and recognized as a breed in 1988, also played a part in the subsequent development of the Lionhead there. It has a much more wooly texture to its coat, however, compared with the Lionhead, and so requires more grooming. Both breeds are of similar size and bred in a wide range of colors.

Lop

The Lop family of breeds are characterized by ears that hang down over the sides of their heads. Such rabbits first appeared in the early 1800s. They had enormous ears and were to be the forerunners of the breed now known as the English Lop. They weighed over 20lb (9kg) and had ears more than 25in (63.5cm) long and over 4.5in (11.5cm) in width. Today's English Lops are smaller overall and kept mainly for exhibition purposes.

In France, crossings with Flemish Giants in the mid-1800s created a shorter-eared breed of Lop. French Lops typically weigh in excess of 12lb (5.4kg). Their ears form a distinctive horseshoe shape, with the crown of the head being arched. Agouti coloring is most common in this breed, although other colors also exist. These Lops

▼ *The French Lop has a stocky shape, often described as having an almost cuboid body. Various shades of gray are common in the breed, such as this Blue-gray Lop.*

Q&A…

● *How should I measure my Lop's ears?*

To measure the length, gently line up the tip of one ear against the start of the scale on a ruler. The ruler should extend over the top of the rabbit's head. Now measure the distance from the tip right across the head and down to the tip of the other ear. The width of the ears is measured at the broadest point.

● *Are there any particular precautions I need to take with the ears of my English Lop?*

Be sure to keep the front claws trimmed short, otherwise these may injure the trailing ears. Clean surroundings, as always, are essential.

● *The six-week-old Mini Lop rabbits I saw recently had erect ears. Is this normal?*

It depends. The ears will not start to droop until four weeks of age and it can take as long as three months. The earlier they droop, however, the better, because in some individuals they may remain erect throughout the rabbit's life.

were paired by German breeders with spotted rabbits, resulting in what is now known as the German Lop. It is significantly smaller than the French Lop—weighing about 7lb (3.2kg)—but has a similarly stocky body shape, with a short neck and broad head.

The Meissner Lop breed is also of Germanic origin, being first bred in the town of Meissen from crosses between German Lops and Silvers plus Argente Champagne stock later in the century. Young are born with plain coats, and the characteristic silvering only starts to become apparent from the age of about five weeks onward. Black is their traditional color, but other forms including blue and brown have also been recognized. The ears must hang down in a straight line, without any signs of folding. Meissners display distinctive raised crowns where the ears attach to the skull, with the ears being rounded at their tips. The weight of this breed is quite variable, generally being between 9 and 11lb (4–5kg). It remains one of the rarer members of the group.

The appealing appearance of Lops, with their floppy ears, has meant that more recently breeders have sought to create further breeds of smaller size, both for exhibition purposes and as pets. The Dwarf or Holland Lop was developed in the Netherlands in the early 1950s, initially by mating a French Lop with a Netherland Dwarf. This was unsuccessful, however, since all the resulting offspring had erect ears. The use of English Lops helped to correct this situation, but a high percentage of the young again displayed either normal ear carriage, or had one ear up and one ear down. It took more than 12 years to stabilize the lop-eared characteristic in this case. The breed was then taken to Britain in 1968, and to the United States in the following year. These rabbits are now available in a wide range of colors and have become very popular.

During the early 1980s, a long-coated form of the Dwarf Lop emerged in Britain, probably reflecting an Angora genetic influence. These rabbits have now been developed into a breed called the Cashmere Lop. Since then a bigger variety, known as the Giant Cashmere Lop, has also been bred. This has yet to win widespread recognition for show purposes, however.

▲ *The Dwarf Lop now ranks among the most popular of all rabbit breeds for the pet-seeker, thanks to its attractive appearance, small size, and friendly nature. This is a sooty-fawn variety.*

Cashmere Lops require more grooming than ordinary Lops, thanks to their long, dense coats. The Rex characteristic (see pages 80–81) has also been introduced to Lop bloodlines, giving rise to what is described in North America as the Velveteen Lop, thanks to its sleek, soft coat.

Miniaturization of the Dwarf Lop has also continued in the Netherlands, creating the Mini Lop, which was recognized in 1994. The weight of these rabbits must not exceed 3.5lb (1.6kg). They are quite sturdy and make ideal pets.

▼ *Fawn is the most common color variety seen in the English Lop, which is recognizable by its long, trailing ears. Shades of gray, solid blacks, and rare albinos are also seen on occasions.*

● *Are there any problems associated with the Netherland Dwarf because of its small size?*

Scaling down in size has produced a few unwanted effects, but these are now less common. Maloccluded teeth were a particular problem, thanks to the smaller head size, while does sometimes encountered difficulties when giving birth because of the size of their kittens. If you suspect any such problem, contact your veterinarian without delay.

● *How did the description "New Zealand" arise in these rabbit breeds?*

It seems that some wild rabbits were imported to California at about the time that the New Zealand Red developed. It therefore was assumed that they played a part in its development, and that of the White as well, but there is no evidence to support this view.

● *Why do New Zealand Reds bred on mainland Europe differ from those seen in Britain and North America?*

The European version of this breed has a significantly longer body and head, which is a reflection of the greater part played by the Belgian Hare in its development. There is also a difference in the coat, which tends to be slightly shorter. The original examples of the breed brought to Europe from the United States in 1919 were much paler, being more yellowish in appearance compared with those bred today.

▼ *The Netherland Dwarf is one of the smallest rabbit breeds. Its weight must not exceed 2.5lb (1.1kg) and its ears should be a maximum of 2in (5cm) in length.*

LUX

Some rabbit breeds can be distinguished primarily by their shape, whereas others can be recognized easily by their coloration. The color of the Lux is highly unusual. Resembling the Havana in type, the Lux has a white undercoat, with orangish guard hairs tipped with silvery-blue, which creates its unique coloration. The coat is sleek, soft, and springy, while the eyes often appear reddish, depending on the light.

This breed was developed in Dusseldorf, Germany, with Marburgers, Sables, and Tans all contributing to its ancestry, along with the Perlfee. Although first exhibited in 1919, and represented in many European countries, it has yet to establish any significant following in Britain or North America. Its weight ranges between 4.4 and 7.7lb (2–3.5kg).

NETHERLAND DWARF

This breed was evolved in the late 1800s from Polish stock taken from England and bred with Dutch rabbits. At first, white examples predominated, occurring both as pink-eyed and blue-eyed variants, with colored Netherland Dwarfs being bred in the 1930s.

Today, a very wide range of colors and patterns is recognized in this breed, which was first seen in North America in 1969. Self-colored examples of the breed, such as lilac or blue, must be evenly colored, with no white hair evident in their coats. Agouti variants are also well established in this breed of rabbit, as is the tortoiseshell form.

Many of the features associated with other, larger breeds have now been incorporated into the Netherland Dwarf, too. These include Himalayan patterning (with such rabbits having white bodies offset against dark points) and Silver Foxes. Others show Dutch and Harlequin markings, with a Netherland Dwarf form of the Blanc de Hotot—a Swiss creation—having become very popular. These rabbits

should display characteristic black rings measuring 0.1–0.2in (3-5mm) around the eyes, with the rest of the coat being pure white. More recently, Netherland Dwarfs with English-type patterning have also been created.

The scope offered by such a wide range of varieties has helped to ensure their popularity among exhibitors, with their small size also appealing to pet-seekers as well. Regular handling of young stock is important, however, otherwise they may not turn out to be the most friendly of rabbits.

▼ *A New Zealand Red doe and young. In terms of temperament the Red has proved to be more lively than other New Zealand rabbits. This variety is also somewhat smaller, not exceeding 10lb (4.5kg).*

NEW ZEALAND BREEDS

There are four different varieties of New Zealand rabbit. Confusingly, none of them was bred there initially; their development began in the United States. To add to the confusion, the New Zealand Red is quite different from the other varieties, forming a separate breed. The New Zealand White was originally created as a commercial breed, although its ancestry is unknown. Since being brought to Britain in the 1940s, both black and blue varieties have also been developed. As might be expected, these rabbits grow fast, attaining weights of about 9–11lb (4–5kg).

The New Zealand White remains the most common variety and has been used to create the smaller Florida White breed. The New Zealand Red is believed to have evolved from crosses between Flemish Giants and Belgian Hares—which are responsible for the breed's distinctive reddish-buff coloration.

▲ *A medium shade of blue-gray is preferable in the Perlfee. The underparts are white, with white areas of fur encircling the eyes and nose, as well as extending inside the ears and along the jaw line.*

PALOMINO

This American breed of rabbit acquired its name because of its golden coloration, which resembles that of a Palomino horse. It was originally exhibited in 1952 under the name of Washingtonian, being bred from tawny and yellowish-brown rabbits. The coat is a striking golden color, with a cream-colored undercoat, while the area around the eyes and the underparts are of a paler shade.

A second color variety of the Palomino, known as the Lynx, has also been developed. This form is a bright orange color, with even, lilac tipping and a white undercoat, creating a silvery effect overall. The fur is thick and even in length. These rabbits typically weigh between 9 and 10lb (4–4.5kg) and have a broad head that is carried on a short neck. They remain almost completely unknown outside North America at present, however.

PERLE DE HALLE

These rabbits are also closely related to the Havana, arising from a mutation which appeared in a litter of this breed in the Belgian town of Halle. The breed is also sometimes described as the Halle Pearl-gray. Its coloration is a soft shade of bluish-gray, with the glossy fur enhancing its appearance. The eyes are a distinctive bluish-gray color. The Perle de Halle is a small breed, weighing 4.5–5.5lb (2–2.5kg). It is still not well known internationally, although it is regularly exhibited in its homeland.

PERLFEE

This attractively colored breed is not especially common, even in its German homeland. Two different strains were originally developed. The first was created by the Dusseldorf breeder responsible for the Lux breed (see page 76) and was called the Dusseldorfer Perlfee, while the other strain was evolved from Havanas crossed with agouti rabbits in the town of Augsburg, and so was called the Augsburger Perlfee. These two bloodlines were ultimately merged together, with their disparate geographical origins being dropped, and the breed is now known simply as the Perlfee.

It corresponds closely to the Havana in terms of its type, but is uniquely colored, being blue-gray with a pearl-like tipping on the ends of the individual hairs. The coat has a decidedly glossy appearance overall. Perlfee rabbits weigh between 4.5 and 8lb (2–3.6kg).

PICARD

This old French breed was created by crossing Flemish Giants with wild rabbits, as reflected in its coloration today. It is most likely to be encountered in Picardy and the northwest and central regions of the country. The Picard weighs about 8–9lb (3.6–4kg) and is also sometimes described as the Giant Normand.

POLISH OR BRITANNIA PETIT

The Polish is better known in North America as the Britannia Petit. The earliest examples were pure white, being bred in both pink-eyed and blue-eyed forms. At that stage, during the 1860s, Polish rabbits had a reputation for being rather weak. This was probably partly due to the fact that cows' milk figured prominently in their diet, because at this time the rabbits were regarded as a gastronomic speciality.

Subsequently, the breed has flourished in the show arena. A much wider range of color varieties has been created, similar to those seen in the related Netherland Dwarf (see pages 76–77). The coat of the Polish is a very distinctive feature, having been used as a substitute for ermine in the past. It must be short and with a fine texture, being described as "fly back." (This means that when ruffled, it flies back to lay flat again.)

Q&A...

● **Is the Britannia Petit actually an American variety of the Polish?**

No, these are separate breeds. The American Polish is larger, with a rounder, heavier body and with a more rounded face than that of the Britannia Petit.

● **Do Polish rabbits make good pets?**

Compared with some breeds, these small rabbits are surprisingly lively and active. If you want a rabbit that enjoys being stroked for long periods, however, then a breed such as the New Zealand White may be a better choice. Provide a Polish rabbit with plenty of attention to help tame it.

▼ *Descended from Belgian stock, the Polish was developed in Britain and is one of the smallest breeds in the world—weighing between 3.3lb and 4.5lb (1.5–2kg). This is a Pink-eyed White Polish.*

REX

The Rex characteristic is a very distinctive mutation, which affects the length of the guard hairs in the coat. These should be reduced to, or just below, the level of the undercoat, giving these rabbits a very distinctive, soft, short coat with a texture not unlike that of velvet. The hairs themselves measure about 0.5in (12mm). When this mutation first occurred, such rabbits became very popular in the fur trade, although they had a reputation for being rather delicate. The full beauty of the Rex's coat can only be appreciated in the case of mature individuals, typically from about eight months of age onward.

It has proved possible to introduce the Rex characteristic into many breeds, as well as creating specific Rexes. The original form was the

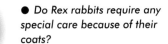

● *Do Rex rabbits require any special care because of their coats?*

They can be slightly more susceptible to cold, so provide them with plenty of bedding. This is also essential to stop the fur on the underside of their hocks being rubbed off on the floor of their quarters. The grooming requirements of the breed are very minimal, since there is no risk of the fur of true Rexes becoming matted. During the molt, however, they will look unsightly as their new coat starts to emerge. This is quite normal.

● *What other colors exist in the Rhinelander?*

The black form is most common, but a blue variety has also been created. It was recognized for show purposes in the 1980s.

● *Do Rhinelanders make good pets?*

If you can find a breeder, a young Rhinelander is an excellent choice as a pet, although you will probably have to settle for a somewhat poorly marked individual, since the breeder will probably want to keep the best-marked ones.

◀ *The Orange Rex is a very highly valued variant of this breed, thanks to its attractive coloration.*

▼ *A Blue Rex. This was one of the first color varieties to be created, and the color in this case should be a distinctive medium shade of blue, reflecting the Blue Beveren influence in its ancestry.*

▲ *Five-week-old Rhinelanders. The Rhinelander is tricolored in appearance, typically displaying both black and yellow markings on a white background.*

Castor Rex. This has an agouti pattern, being a combination of dark slate-blue and orange. Among the solid colors, the Black Rex is very impressive, as is the Havana, with its rich brown chocolate coat. The Ermine Rex, a pink-eyed white form, is also highly valued.

Color variants include the Chinchilla Rex which, because of the shortened guard hairs, is an exceedingly difficult variety to breed with the required degree of contrast. Harlequin Rexes are also seen, again being bred from the ordinary Harlequin variety. Pointed varieties exist, too, with the Himalayan Rex being especially attractive. The Spotted Rex, called the Dalmatian, is also popular.

There are two very distinctive forms of Rex, although neither is commonly seen today. The Opossum Rex was created in Britain in 1924, and has a significantly longer coat which measures about 1.5in (3.75cm) in length. Its coat has a consistent appearance from every viewpoint, since the hair lies at right angles to the skin. The color of the rabbit can be seen from the face and ears, as well as from the feet, which are not silvered. Black is the most popular color. These rabbits were bred from Chifox Rexes, with Wooly Argentes also contributing to the silvery color.

The Astrex was evolved slightly later, during the early 1930s. It is now very rare. The fur is very tightly curled over the entire body, apart from the face, ears, and feet. Any artificial curling of the fur is strictly outlawed for show purposes. These rabbits can be bred in a very wide range of colors.

The latest addition to the Rex group, which has become increasingly popular since been officially recognized for the first time in 1990, is the Mini Rex. These rabbits are distinguished by their size, which should be between 3 and 4lb (1.4–1.8kg). They are now being bred in an increasing range of colors.

RHINELANDER

This marked breed was developed in the area of Rhine-Westphalia during the early years of the 20th century, first being recognized in 1905 in its German homeland. Its markings reflect both Harlequin and English patterning.

Although well-marked examples are especially striking, the breed has not gained great popularity among exhibitors, only becoming known in Britain and the United States in the 1950s. This is probably due to the difficulty in meeting the show standard. Both colors must be clearly apparent in the saddle, which runs down the center of the back from the nape to the tip of the tail. This also applies to all other markings, such as the butterfly smut on the face, the fur encircling the eyes, and on the ears. Only the cheek spots should be of a single color. Rhinelander are docile rabbits, weighing 6.5–9lb (3–4kg).

▲ *The overall color of the Marten Sable is sepia. The fur is paler on the sides, with the underparts being white. Silvery-white ticking is present on the flanks and rump, creating an attractive contrast.*

SABLE

The Marten is one of the popular varieties of Sable, first exhibited in Paris during 1914. These rabbits were developed from brown offspring that appeared in litters of Chinchilla rabbits. As with the related Siamese form, the Marten Sable is bred in light, medium, and dark shades, although the medium variety is the one most commonly seen. The sable coloration has also been combined with coat variants such as Rex and Satin-coated forms.

The Siamese form is identical in type to the Sable, but here the points, comprising the ears, face, feet, and tail are darker compared with the light body, creating an appearance like that of a Siamese cat. The eyes are dark red. The weight of both varieties is also similar, being in the range of 5–7lb (2.3–3.2kg).

The Sable des Vosges, or Sable Rex, is a French breed of more recent origins, first recognized in 1964. The body color of these rabbits is a light shade of sandy brown, with the points again being significantly darker, while the belly is paler. What distinguishes this breed is the texture of its coat, which is dense and shiny, with both Angora and Rex bloodlines also having contributed to its ancestry.

ST. NICHOLAS BLUE (BLAUWE VAN ST. NIKLAAS / BLEU DE ST. NICHOLAS)

This Belgian breed is now very rare. It originated from St. Niklaas, in the area of Waas, during the late 1800s. Its origins are unknown, but Blue Flemish Giants and Blue Beverens were probably involved in its ancestry. This is a large breed, weighing between 11 and 13lb (5–6kg). It is a beautiful light bluish-gray shade, traditionally broken by white markings on the face and sometimes the feet.

SALLANDER

This rabbit originated in the Salland region of the Netherlands. It has resulted from a combination of Chinchilla and Thuringer stock, being recognized for show purposes in 1975. Sallanders resemble a pale form of the Thuringer, with a unique off-white coat which has black or

● I recently saw several St. Nicholas rabbits with no white markings. Is this acceptable?

This change in appearance dates back to 1928, when it was decided that the breed in the future should be entirely blue, and so breeders sought to eliminate the unique white markings, notably the blaze between the eyes. Unfortunately, this in turn contributed to the declining popularity of the breed.

● Pairing Medium-colored Sables together has resulted in only a few such offspring. The others have been dark, or even white. Any suggestions?

What you need to do is pair one of the resulting Pink-eyed whites back to a Dark Sable. All the offspring will then be of a medium shade. By way of contrast, mating Dark Sables together will result in all the young matching their parents in terms of depth of color.

● What other Satin colors exist?

Other solid colors that have been combined with the Satin characteristic include red, blue, chocolate, and black. Patterned varieties include the Californian. Not all correspond exactly to the equivalent normal-coated variety, however, with the Satin form of the Siamese Sable, for example, being paler than normal.

▼ A Bronze Satin. This breed typically weighs between 6 and 8lb (2.7–3.6kg), and its fur is about 1.25in (3cm) long. These rabbits have very glossy coats.

brown tips. The points and underparts are of a corresponding darker shade, which is especially prominent on the face and ears. They are medium-sized rabbits, weighing 7–9lb (3.2–4kg) on average. The breed is still quite scarce outside the Netherlands, but it became increasingly popular in Britain during the 1990s after being recognized there in 1994.

SATIN

The Satin mutation reflects a distinctive change to the rabbit's coat and, like the Rex forms, this distinctive characteristic has now been introduced to many breeds. It has even been combined with the Rex itself. Satin rabbits have a very glossy coat, resembling satin, thanks to changes in the microscopic structure of the individual hairs. These are smoother than normal, and this helps to create the distinctive appearance of the breed.

This recessive mutation was first established in the state of Indiana during the 1930s, from a Havana buck, before being brought to Britain in 1947, from where it has been taken to other European countries. Although bred in a wide range of colors today, the Ivory Satin, which has an off-white coat combined with pink eyes, is one of the most popular varieties.

SIBERIAN

The earliest form of the Siberian rabbit, which was bred from crosses between Angoras and Himalayans, is now extinct. It resembled the Angora in terms of its coat type but was marked like a Himalayan, with dark points. The breed now known as the Siberian is very different from its predecessor, being developed in the 1930s from a combination of self-colored English and Dutch crosses. The original color of these rabbits was brown, but since then, other colors have been created, including blue, black, and lilac.

The fur is a very important feature of the breed. It must have a very dense and soft texture, combined with a glossy sheen. When folded back with the hand, there should be very few guard hairs visible, because they are covered by the undercoat. The coloration of individual hairs is even along their length, right down to the skin.

SILVER

Rabbits with silver fur may have first evolved in the Orient, possibly in present-day Thailand. This mutation also appeared in wild rabbits in Britain, however, and it is from these individuals that present-day strains probably evolved. Records of rabbits in mainland Europe with silver tipping on their coats go back to the 1600s, but these appear to have died out.

Silver rabbits were first recognized officially for show purposes in 1880, with stock being taken to the United States soon afterward. The original color variant of these rabbits was black, with the undercoat being bluish-black and evenly broken by longer, silvery guard hairs. Loss of pigment from the guard hairs results in the silvery coloration. Subsequently a silver-fawn was created, using Argente Creme rabbits initially.

There is also a silver-brown variety, bred from Belgian Hare crosses, which is relatively popular in continental Europe but scarce in the United States and Britain. A silver-blue form also exists but is rare at present, having been created using Vienna Blue stock. It is the latest addition to the group, originating during the 1980s.

Young Silvers resemble Selfs at birth, gradually developing their silvered appearance from about five weeks of age. It is likely to take up to six months for the coats of these rabbits to develop to their full extent, with individuals differing to some extent in terms of their depth of silvering. The hairs themselves must be a definite shade of bright silver, and never white. The coat should be quite short, and must fly back to its original position when brushed forward, against the lie of the fur. Adult Silvers weigh about 5–7lb (2.3–3.2kg). Although quite small, they are very lively and not the most placid of rabbits for those seeking a breed as a child's pet.

SMOKE PEARL

These rabbits are closely related to Sables, being bred from them in the 1920s. They are in effect a dilute version of this breed, originally known as the Smoke Beige until their name was changed in 1932. Both Marten and Siamese patterning occur in the Smoke Pearl as well. In the Marten variety, long white guard hairs will be evident over the area of the chest and back, extending down from the rump onto the flanks and feet, with the underparts being white. The color distribution on the coat again matches the black and tan pattern (see page 88), with the tan pigment being replaced by white, although the distribution of black areas of fur is unchanged. Although not especially common in the United States, these rabbits are quite often exhibited at European shows.

● *I've bred a litter of Silvers, but the offspring vary quite widely in color. Why is this?*

The color of these rabbits is directly influenced by the extent of the silvering, which starts to appear on the head, ears, and feet. This color is subject to natural variance as the rabbits mature, so they can be any hue from a light shade, through medium (which is preferred), to dark. Light coloration is caused by extensive silvering, which obscures the dark undercoat, whereas the reverse situation applies in the dark form of the Silver.

● *One of my Silvers has several white toe nails. Does this matter?*

Unfortunately, this is a serious flaw if you want to exhibit your rabbit, but in other respects it is of no significance. You should be able to locate the blood supply easily if you need to cut the nails.

▲ *In the Silver, the distribution of color must be even throughout the coat, as in this fawn variety, so there are no light and dark patches discernible on the individual.*

▼ *In the Smoke Pearl, the smoke-colored saddle extends right along the back, from the neck to the tail, with the fur becoming a pearl-gray shade on the flanks.*

● Is there only one color form in the Steenkonijn?

... No, there are three different agouti varieties, all of which have black ticking on their fur and brown eyes. The two which are most commonly seen today are the rabbit-gray, which corresponds most closely to the wild rabbit, thanks to its light gray fur. There is also the hare-colored form, which is easily distinguished by its more reddish-orange coat. The rarest form is the steel-gray, where the coat consists entirely of gray hairs, apart from the black ticking.

● I would like a Swiss Fox as a pet, but do these rabbits require much grooming?

The amount of grooming required for this breed is far less than is required for its Angora ancestor, but daily brushing and combing is still recommended. Grooming is simplified by the fact that the hairs of the coat are usually straight, and that the coat is less susceptible to becoming matted because it does not have a wooly texture. The Dwarf Swiss Fox has a medium-length coat and also needs regular grooming.

SQUIRREL

This breed stemmed from Chinchilla stock, with the first examples appearing occasionally in litters of these rabbits. They were so called because of the similarity between their coat color and that of Siberian squirrels. Originating during the 1920s, the breed received a provisional show standard but then became extinct. It has been recreated successfully, however, by crossings carried out during the 1980s between Chinchillas and Argente Bleu stock, with these rabbits weighing 5.5–6.5lb (2.5–3kg).

The Squirrel has also been bred successfully as a satin variety and in a dwarf form. The color is very distinctive, being light slate-gray with longer hairs of deeper slate evenly distributed

▲ The Squirrel was once known as the Blue Chinchilla, thanks to the patterning of its fur and its coloration. These rabbits have a compact body shape.

◄ The Sussex is one of the newer breeds of rabbit to be developed and has yet to establish a strong international following, in spite of its attractive coloration. This is an example of the cream form.

throughout the coat. The undercoat is slate, even beneath the white fur on the belly. The fur encircling the eyes is gray, with the nape triangle being small and a light shade of slate. The coat itself is dense and shiny, measuring about 1in (2.5cm) in length. These rabbits display a cobby body shape overall.

Steenkonijn

The Flemish name for this rabbit breed literally means "stone rabbit," although this refers not to their wild agouti coloration but rather to an old Belgian measure of weight, which corresponds roughly to 8lb (3.6kg). This was the required table weight for this breed, with natural agouti coloration being preferred in such breeds, since it was thought that their meat quality was better. The ancestry of the Steenkonijn is unknown, but possibly Flemish Giants and even wild rabbits played a part in its development. The breed declined dramatically in the late 1800s, but it was revived in the 1900s, and the rabbits were exhibited again in 1932. Their weight today is slightly less than it was formerly, averaging about 5.5lb (2.5kg).

Unfortunately, however, the Steenkonijn has not yet established an international following, although it is still popular in Belgium. It is probably its similarity to the wild rabbit which is responsible for this situation, because these rabbits can certainly become friendly companions.

Sussex

This breed is a relative newcomer, whose origins can be traced back to 1986 as the result of cross-breeding between a Lilac and a Californian, which was being carried out to improve the point color of a Californian bloodline of this color. The breed, named after the county in southern England, was accepted for show purposes in 1991, having an ideal weight of about 7.5lb (3.4kg).

▲ *Swiss Foxes have a medium-length coat that needs regular grooming. These rabbits have a reputation for being placid, which has helped popularize them.*

The original form, described as the Sussex Gold, is a rich, reddish-tortoiseshell shade with brown or lilac shading. The more recent paler cream variety is pinkish-cream in color, with lilac ticking. Although still quite localized, the popularity of this breed seems set to increase, thanks mainly to its attractive appearance and friendly nature.

Swiss Fox

These rabbits were developed in both Germany and Switzerland during the 1920s, but it was in the latter country that the breed remained popular. Havana and Angora stock were used to create the Swiss Fox. The coat of the breed today is therefore quite long, with the hairs measuring 2–2.5in (5–6.5cm) over the body, creating a fine, dense body covering. Pink or blue-eyed white examples of this breed are common, as well as other self colors, notably blue and black, with other forms such as the Chinchilla variant being scarce. These rabbits weigh between 5.5 and 9lb (2.5–4kg) and have a very short neck.

A dwarf form of the breed has recently been created from crossings between Swiss Fox and Polish rabbits, gaining recognition in the Netherlands during 1994.

TAN

These rabbits trace their origins back to a warren in England where a number of domestic and wild rabbits were being kept. The first example of this breed appeared in about 1880 and is believed to have resulted from a pairing between wild and Dutch rabbits. Since then, the breed has been considerably refined, becoming smaller and more docile as a result. Crosses with Belgian Hares subsequently helped to lengthen the body shape and darkened the tan coloration on the underparts.

There must be clear delineation between the tan and colored areas of fur in the case of these rabbits, with the tan areas being clearly defined. Tan fur encircles the eyes and extends from the nose around the jawline, forming a triangular-shaped patch behind the neck. It is also present in the ears and extends over the entire underparts, from beneath the chin. There are also tan patches on the feet and on the hind legs.

The blue and tan variety was created after the black. Brown, and then lilac, forms followed, with lilac coloration being introduced as the result of crossing with the Marburger. The type of these rabbits today is quite cobby, and they have a decidedly rounded profile. They weigh between 5 and 7lb (2.3–3.2kg), with their attractive markings making them a popular choice with exhibitors and pet-seekers alike.

THRIANTA

These beautiful orange rabbits were originally created in the Netherlands, being recognized there in 1940, but subsequently they declined in popularity. In Germany, however, there was a separate breed called the Sachsengold, which partly shared the Thrianta's Tan and Havana ancestry, although it was a paler color. Breeders in Germany sought out the last remaining Thriantas, in a bid to improve the color of their breed. They succeeded, with these rabbits being taken back to the Netherlands in the 1960s.

The breed was introduced to Britain during the early 1980s and seems likely to continue to grow in popularity. These are small rabbits, weighing the same as Tans, with soft fur (thanks to their dense undercoat). Meanwhile, the Sachsengold breed is still kept mainly in Germany, being slightly stockier and paler in color.

▼ *The Tan is one of the most striking of the smaller rabbit breeds, and its smooth, glossy coat displays its coloration to excellent effect. This is a black and tan form.*

THURINGER

This is another German breed, developed in the east of the country, in Thuringer Wald. It is believed to have been created in the late 1800s from crossings between Himalayans and Silvers, mated with the plain form of the Giant Papillon. This resulted in the creation of offspring with amber-colored fur, which were originally called Chamois rabbits. Subsequent crosses with Flemish Giants then created the breed of today, which may weigh 9lb (4kg) or more.

VIENNA BLUE

The creation of this attractively colored breed relied on the mating between a Self yellow rabbit obtained in France, a blue doe, and a Flemish Giant buck. It was once larger than now, and its

color less vivid, but the color has been refined over the years and is now a particular characteristic of the breed. Other colors have been bred, but are not universally recognized. The chocolate variety now seems to be extinct.

VIENNA WHITE

In spite of the similarity in name, this breed is not simply a color variant of the Vienna Blue, but has evolved from this breed being crossed with Blue-eyed white Dutch stock. It has since become very popular in mainland Europe, after having been first exhibited in Vienna in 1907. These rabbits tend to be slightly lighter than the Vienna Blue, weighing 7–11lb (3.2–5kg). The coat is white, offset against blue eyes.

Q&A

● **What are the common faults in Thriantas?**

... Paleness of color is a serious flaw, as is any ticking in the coat, which spoils the overall color effect. It is normal for the hair on the underparts to be paler than usual, but there must be no areas of white fur evident here.

● **Is there a dwarf form of the Vienna White that my daughter could have as a pet?**

The nearest equivalent is the Hulstlander, which was developed during the early 1980s in the Netherlands. It was named after the district in Overijssel province where it was created. This dwarf breed has been developed by crossings between the Vienna White and the Blue-eyed Polish, which maintained its characteristic eye coloration.

◀ *A breed that remains surprisingly quite scarce, the Thrianta is a friendly and very colorful rabbit with a soft coat. Its size makes it an ideal choice as a pet, especially since these rabbits are easily handled.*

▼ *Only one color form of the Thuringer exists, with dark tips on the amber-colored hairs. This shading is most pronounced on the face, ears, and underparts, with the coat having a dense, silky texture.*

Guinea Pigs

THESE ATTRACTIVE AND LIVELY RODENTS HAVE A LONG HISTORY
of domestication in their South American homeland. Ancient artifacts
suggest they may have been first kept in the Andean region of modern
Peru and Bolivia over 3,000 years ago, and even today it is not unusual
for them to be seen around villages and in people's homes. Five different
species make up the genus *Cavia*, and it is because of this name that these
rodents are known as cavies, as well as guinea pigs. No one is sure which
species was the ancestor of today's domestic varieties. In all probability,
more than one has contributed to the development of the domesticated
guinea pig in South America and thus to the ancestry of these pets. The
main ancestor, however, is thought to be the Brazilian cavy (*C. aperea*).

Guinea pigs were probably introduced to Europe in the late 1500s by the
Spanish. Why they became known as guinea pigs is less clear. It has been
suggested that the name could be linked with the way sailing ships crossed
the Atlantic, using the fast trade winds. Vessels heading for Europe from
South America would cross on these winds to the Gulf of Guinea before
sailing north. This meant that these rodents became linked with Guinea,
although it has also been suggested that "guinea pig" is derived from a
corruption of the name of the countries of South America formerly called
the Guianas. Certainly, there were regular passages between Dutch Guiana
(now Suriname) and the Netherlands—one of the first European countries
in which guinea pigs became popular as pets. Initially, these rodents were
rarities, cherished by wealthy owners, thus a third explanation of the name
might come from the fact that they may have sold for a guinea.

The second part of the guinea pig's name is much easier to explain, thanks
to their rather porcine appearance, coupled with the distinctive "oinking"
and squealing sounds of their calls, which are often uttered when they are
excited. In spite of these vocalizations, however, guinea pigs are not noisy
companions. Today, they are popular both as pets and as exhibition
subjects, with an ever-increasing range of color varieties and coat
types having been developed over recent years.

▶ *There is an ever-increasing range of colors,
patterns, and coat types now being bred by
enthusiasts of guinea pigs. A crested variety
is shown here.*

Guinea Pig Lifestyles

THE NATURAL FORM OF THE GUINEA PIG IS described as agouti, with the typical mottled coloration resulting from dark and light banding running down individual hairs. This type of coloration is very common among wild rodents as well as rabbits, helping to provide these creatures with camouflage. As domestication has proceeded, however, a wide range of colors has been created, and differences in coat types have also arisen. Color changes first arose in the guinea pig's South American homeland, but they have since been developed to a much greater extent in North America and Europe where these rodents are now widely kept for showing.

Biologically speaking, guinea pigs belong to the caviomorph group of rodents. The most significant feature of this group, whose members are found in the wild mainly in the New World,

▲ *Only small breeds of rabbits can be housed safely with guinea pigs. Large breeds may cause injury or even death if they accidentally squash a guinea pig.*

Fact File

Name:	Guinea Pig or Domestic Cavy
Scientific name:	*Cavia porcellus*
Weight:	1.5–4lb (0.7–1.8kg); boars generally heavier than sows.
Compatibility:	Generally quite compatible if housed in single sex groups from early age. Boars may sometimes be aggressive, but sows more tolerant together. Sometimes kept with rabbits.
Appeal:	Ideal children's pets, becoming very tame if handled regularly from early age. Can be kept in indoor or outdoor hutch.
Diet:	Commercially produced guinea pig food, greenfood, root vegetables, and hay. Also eat bran mash readily.
Health problems:	Especially vulnerable to skin ailments—often due to vitamin C deficiency—and skin mites.
Breeding tips:	Sows must be mated when relatively young to minimize likelihood of subsequent birthing problems.
Pregnancy	69 days
Typical litter size:	4 young
Weaning:	30 days
Lifespan:	5–8 years

is their reproductive habits. These differ markedly from the other two rodent groups. Female guinea pigs, called sows, produce relatively small litters—typically comprised of four offspring—and have a long gestation period averaging 69 days. Their young are born as fully developed miniature adults, rather than being totally helpless at birth. In fact, young guinea pigs will start to feed by themselves at barely a day old.

Guinea Pigs as Pets

Part of the popularity of guinea pigs as pets stems from their attractive appearance. In noticeable contrast to rats and mice, they lack a tail. Guinea pigs are also essentially terrestrial in their habits and are not inclined to climb. If threatened, they will simply retreat into their bedding. In the wild, guinea pigs do not display any great tendency to burrow, instead seeking refuge among rocks from possible predators.

Although guinea pigs are relatively hardy, and can live in an outdoor hutch throughout the year in temperate areas, they will adapt just as well to being housed permanently in the home. In contrast to rats and mice, guinea pigs do not have any unpleasant odor associated with them. Handling them is also quite straightforward, since they display no instinctive tendency to bite when picked up, nor are their claws as powerful as a rabbit's, so being scratched is less likely.

It is even possible to house guinea pigs and rabbits together, providing their accommodation is suitably spacious. In a relatively small hutch, however, a large rabbit especially could inadvertently injure a guinea pig by trampling on it, or could even smother it. Again, it helps to obtain both pets at an early age, allowing them to grow up together. Their needs are similar, although the specific dietary requirement of guinea pigs for vitamin C must be reflected in the food offered to them, because rabbit food is not normally supplemented with this vitamin.

Guinea pigs have a life expectancy of six years or so, making them longer-lived companions than many pet rodents. Unfortunately, however, it is impossible to tell their age accurately once they are adult, and since they are not rung for exhibition purposes—unlike rabbits—the aim should be to start with a youngster as a pet. Older individuals that are not handled regularly will not be as friendly as youngsters that grow up with plenty of human contact.

● *How suitable are guinea pigs as children's pets?*

They are ideal, being easy to pick up and handle, as well as feeding readily from the hand. Their grooming requirements are minimal in most cases, and the fact that they can be kept easily both indoors or outside means that even if you do not have a backyard, they can be kept quite satisfactorily in the home.

● *What would be the best type of rabbit to choose as a companion for a guinea pig?*

One of the smaller breeds such as a Mini Lop or a Mini Rex would be most suitable. Choose a doe if possible, because they are more tolerant than bucks, although this is not necessarily critical—particularly if you are intending to have your rabbit neutered.

● *Are certain types of guinea pigs less suitable as pets than others?*

It is usually best to avoid long-coated varieties such as the Peruvian, because they will require a lot of grooming. But there is little difference between the various types of guinea pigs in terms of their temperament.

▼ *Guinea pigs make ideal pets for children because of their small size, friendly natures, and the ease with which they can be tamed and handled.*

Keeping Guinea Pigs Outdoors

ALTHOUGH GUINEA PIGS ORIGINATE FROM A warm part of the world, they live at high altitudes in the Andes, where the winters can be bitterly cold. Therefore it is quite possible to house them outdoors in hutches throughout the year in temperate areas, although they must obviously be protected from the worst of the winter weather. Prolonged periods of damp, foggy weather are far more likely to be harmful to their health, and their hutches must be kept dry at all times.

The basic design of a guinea pig hutch does not differ from that used for rabbits, although they are usually less tall. This is partly because guinea pigs are smaller animals, and also because they do not climb, or stand up on their haunches like rabbits. Guinea pigs require a fairly large floor area, however.

▲ *Guinea pigs can be allowed to forage for food outdoors when the weather is fine. They should always be housed in a secure run, however, to avoid being attacked by cats or other animals.*

Tiered Cages

Groups of guinea pigs are often kept in tiered cages. The design of these cages is such that they are built in a single block. Again, however, it is important that the bottom unit is kept off the floor, to prevent the guinea pigs here from being exposed to damp conditions. The floor sections will be the weakest part of the hutch under these circumstances, and these sections should be made of marine plywood. Floor trays (see pages 22–23) should also be included, to minimize the risk of urine penetrating here, which is unhygienic and could also cause rotting over time.

The design of the doors is especially important in tiered cages, to minimize the risk of guinea pigs falling to the ground with fatal consequences. It is obviously quite easy to open the wire mesh door

▼ *A solidly constructed run and house. Easy access to the run is vital, to enable the guinea pigs to be caught when necessary. Here the roof is hinged for this purpose. Bedding should be supplied in the hutch area.*

with little risk of the guinea pigs tumbling down, because they will be visible inside, but it is more difficult with a solid door. As a safety precaution, hinge all doors from the bottom, so that a guinea pig is less likely to fall out if it is sitting close to the door.

Morant Hutch

Guinea pigs will benefit from being able to roam on a lawn. The Morant hutch is very popular for this purpose. It is comprised of two sides that join at the top and, with a base, create a triangular-shaped structure. Within one of these sides, there is a large, hinged door that allows easy access to the interior of the run.

The floor of the run is covered with mesh about 2in (5cm) square. This mesh is more open than the mesh on the sides, so it will not flatten the vegetation but will still provide a barrier to prevent the guinea pig slipping out and escaping, as could otherwise occur if the run was placed on uneven ground. It is also more comfortable for the guinea pig to walk on and will provide security against a cat gaining access to the run from beneath. Attached to one end of the run is a covered wooden area in which the guinea pig can shelter. This also has a door, and in this part of the run the floor is made from solid wood.

When it comes to siting the run, choose an area where there will be shade during the hottest part of the day. Guinea pigs prefer to browse on grass which is relatively short, rather than coarse dry clumps that will be flattened by the base of the run, so an area of lawn which has been regularly cut will suit them well. Beware of using grass that has been treated with chemicals or recently reseeded, since this could be harmful to their health. There will usually be little need to check the grass for plants which may be harmful, because guinea pigs seem to ignore these instinctively. You must avoid positioning the run on a lawn where bulbs may be dying down, because their leaves are likely to be harmful.

● **Are there any steps I can take to prevent guinea pigs falling out of tiered cages?**

The best precaution is to add a strip of plywood as a barrier on the front edge of the tray. Always tap the door before opening it in any case, to ensure that your guinea pig isn't sleeping against it.

● **Can I introduce guinea pigs from both of my hutches into the same run?**

This is possible, but you should check their sexes first to ensure that you are not presented with unwanted offspring in due course. Fighting is unlikely to break out, but keep an eye on them at first to ensure they settle down together.

▶ *Tiered cages are ideal for housing a larger collection of guinea pigs. The unit can be designed to fit into a shed (like this one) or be kept outdoors, depending on the amount of weather-proofing.*

◀ *This type of run is known as a Morant hutch. Access is through the sides of the unit. Keep the hinges well oiled. Bedding should again be supplied in the dry sleeping quarters.*

Keeping Guinea Pigs Indoors

IF YOU DON'T HAVE A YARD YOU CAN STILL KEEP a guinea pig as a pet. If you decide to keep a guinea pig in the home, you can dispense with the conventional hutch design—which will look rather out of place in domestic surroundings in any case. Instead, there are various cages or runs available specifically for use in the home. Cages usually consist of a plastic base or tray with a detachable top. The base unit helps to retain the bedding so that it cannot spill into the room, as well as providing an area where the guinea pig can feel secure. You may want to include a small wooden shelter within the base area, too, that will allow your pet to retreat out of sight on occasions. The rest of the cage floor can be covered with absorbent shavings.

An alternative system of indoor housing for guinea pigs entails building a simple run, with a plywood base, one end of which can be lifted out. This is preferable to fitting a hinged door, because it will take up less space when it is open. The guinea pig can then come and go at will, and be able to return here when it feels hungry or needs a drink. This arrangement will also help to discourage it from chewing at carpeting or trying to nibble any plants within reach.

◀ *Guinea pigs housed indoors, especially long-coated individuals, are usually kept on a bed of wood shavings, with hay supplied separately in a hay rack, as seen in the cage below.*

▼ *A modern unit designed for keeping guinea pigs indoors. The mesh lid can be opened to gain access to the animal or for replenishing food and bedding, and the whole top section can also be removed for cleaning.*

Siting a Cage or Run

The best place for the guinea pig's cage or run is often in the living room area. Here, you can let your pet out when you are at home relaxing and enjoy its company. It is not a good idea to allow a guinea pig to roam freely around the home, however, because of the dangers that may be present. A barrier roughly 1ft (30cm) in height will prevent a guinea pig from slipping out of a room if the door is open. This can be slotted into channels and put in place when required.

Hazards in the Home

Open doors may allow your guinea pig to escape outdoors, be accidentally stepped on, cause someone to trip, or stray into potentially dangerous places like kitchens.

Cats and dogs should be removed from the room before you let the guinea pig out.

Cat flaps can enable guinea pigs to escape or allow a cat to enter and catch the guinea pig.

Fireplaces should be adequately protected by guards.

Chemicals such as carpet sprays and some insecticides can be hazardous to your pet.

Items that may be gnawed such as carpet fibers, painted or treated wood, electrical cables, or houseplants should be kept out of reach.

● *I have just purchased a young guinea pig from our local pet store. Can I transfer him to an outdoor hutch, even though it is winter?*

It is not to be recommended at this stage. Instead, you will need to keep him indoors in the relative warmth of the home, and then transfer him outdoors once spring arrives. Then he will be able to stay outside permanently.

● *Do guinea pigs like being petted?*

They will soon become used to sitting contentedly for quite long periods on their owner's lap, especially if accustomed to this routine from an early age. It is advisable for them to sit on an old towel, however, even though guinea pigs are not messy creatures.

● *Will guinea pigs disturb the neighbors?*

This is most unlikely. They are generally quiet, and their calls are usually only uttered if they become excited or they cannot reach their food. (This latter problem can be overcome by providing food and water for your pet on a tray in the room when it is out of its quarters.)

▼ *A young guinea pig explores the home environment accompanied by its mother. It is especially important to block off all possible escape routes through which baby guinea pigs can easily disappear when loose.*

Feeding Guinea Pigs

GUINEA PIGS ARE HERBIVOROUS IN THEIR FEEDING habits, with a correspondingly adapted digestive system. They have a large cecum in which beneficial bacteria and microscopic protozoa are present to enable the digestion of cellulose to occur. The large intestine (or colon), where vitamins and water are absorbed into the body, is also much longer than in other rodents.

Like rabbits (see pages 32–33), guinea pigs first produce what are described as cecal feces. These contain partly digested food. Once these have passed out of the body, the guinea pig consumes them. On the food's second passage through the tract, the nutrients are then absorbed through the wall of the small intestine.

Guinea pigs require a high-fiber diet, and they also require an adequate level of vitamin C to be present in their food. All other rodents—and indeed every other mammal apart from ourselves and some monkeys—can manufacture

▼ *A variety of dry and pelleted foods is available for guinea pigs. Never give food formulated for other rodents to guinea pigs because, although the food may look the same, it will contain too little vitamin C. Store food carefully and ensure it remains dry.*

this particular vitamin in their bodies. Greens, which will help provide some vitamin C, should therefore be offered on a daily basis. Most breeders give fresh supplies of greenfood in the morning and the late afternoon.

A wide range of greens is suitable guinea pig fodder, and they can be given garden weeds such as dandelion, yarrow, chickweed, and plantain, but avoid those which are likely to be poisonous. These include convolvulus (bindweed) and buttercup, plus some cultivated plants such as lupins. During the winter it is harder to provide a range of greenfood, but crops such as broccoli are very valuable because of their vitamin C content, especially if freshly picked. This can be augmented with root crops such as carrots and turnip tops, although these are not such valuable sources of vitamin C. Good-quality hay should also be regularly available, adding to the fiber content of the guinea pig's diet.

Dry Foods and Supplements

It is also possible to ensure that guinea pigs do not suffer from a vitamin C deficiency by providing them with specially formulated dry foods. These are now widely available and offer a more balanced alternative than items such as crushed oats. Alternatively, pelleted foods produced for guinea pigs are also available, but it is important not to change their diet suddenly, because this will upset the vital microbes present in their digestive tract. A fatal diarrhea may then result.

to purchase guinea pig food elatively long shelflife indicated 1e packaging. Otherwise, the imin content will be adversely fected—especially if exposed) the air for any length of time. 1 any event it must not be used fter the recommended date, nce the vitamin C content will variably have declined.

One useful supplement which

can be given throughout the year is a bran mash. This is easily prepared using oat bran, mixed with sufficient water to moisten it thoroughly. This can then be poured into a suitable container. Remove this on the following day and wash the bowl out thoroughly before refilling it.

Although guinea pigs may receive quite a high fluid intake through their food, they still need to be provided with fresh drinking water every day. A drinking bottle should be provided for this purpose, because an open, heavyweight ceramic bowl will almost inevitably become soiled with bedding. If your guinea pigs have been used to this type of water container, keep a close watch to ensure they have adapted to drinking from the bottle. You may need to encourage them to begin with by putting the spout to their mouths and gently squeezing some water out.

▼ *Guinea pigs will benefit from a daily supply of greenfood as part of their diet, with both cultivated and wild greens being suitable for this purpose. Such foods should be washed first and must always be fresh.*

Q&A...

● *Can I use lawn clippings as food for my guinea pigs?*

These can be used safely, provided that the grass has not been treated with any chemicals, and that there is no risk of the grass being contaminated by oil from the mower blades. Beware of grass that has been recently fertilized or treated for weeds—some of the chemicals used may be poisonous.

● *Is it possible to maintain a supply of dandelion leaves through the winter?*

If you dig up these plants complete with their deep roots and set them in pots, with the leaves just protruding above the surface of the soil, this should be possible. You will need to place the pots in a light, warm area and keep them well watered, to ensure good growth.

● *What value is rosehip syrup for guinea pigs?*

Some breeders favor this product, which is a traditional source of vitamin C. It can be mixed into a bran mash, or added regularly to the drinking water at the rate of 12mg of vitamin C per 3.4fl oz (100ml) of water.

Routine Care of Guinea Pigs

GUINEA PIGS ARE EASY CREATURES TO HANDLE because they do not bite readily, in spite of having sharp incisor teeth. However, a guinea pig can use its short legs to burrow into its hay very quickly to escape being caught, so you need to try to place a hand across the animal's back at the earliest opportunity. This will stop the guinea pig from running off and, if you are right-handed, you can then use your left hand to lift the rodent from beneath while keeping the right hand in place on the top of the body. Once you have lifted the guinea pig out of its quarters, be sure to provide support to the underparts, otherwise your pet will feel insecure and will start struggling to escape.

Always discourage a child with bare arms from picking up a guinea pig, in case its claws inflict a painful scratch and cause the animal to

▼ *Guinea pigs can be picked up and handled quite easily. Always ensure that the guinea pig is being supported firmly from beneath to prevent it struggling.*

be dropped. The method recommended for picking up a rabbit (see page 38) can also be used for guinea pigs.

When carrying a guinea pig to and from its run it is preferable to place it in a suitable pet carrier, or even a clean cat basket. This means that even if you trip, or perhaps your pet dog slips out into the yard and jumps up at you, your guinea pig will remain relatively safe. Always take particular care when placing the guinea pig in its run, to ensure that it cannot slip past you. If it escapes, it may run into dense vegetation or even out of your backyard completely. If this happens, you should make every effort to catch your pet again without delay before it disappears.

Cleaning Out

A guinea pig's quarters will need to be cleaned out thoroughly at least once a week, with any uneaten fresh food being taken out on a daily basis. A dustpan and brush are recommended for this task, although it will be easier if the

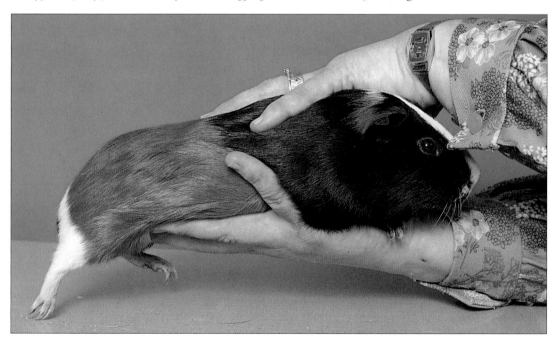

▲ *Grooming a long-haired guinea pig on a special non-slip burlap-covered stand. Only choose a long-haired breed if you are prepared for daily grooming sessions.*

hutch incorporates sliding trays like the ones provided for rabbits (see page 22). With breeds such as the Peruvian that have long, trailing coats, it may be preferable to restrict them to hay supplied in a special hay rack (see page 96), rather than providing this for general bedding purposes, since this will almost inevitably become entangled in their coats.

If the hutch is outdoors, it will be easier if you keep all the necessary items such as hay, wood shavings, and dry food within easy reach, possibly in a nearby shed. It is obviously important that the bedding and the food remain dry, but it must also be kept out of reach of wild rodents. A clean trash can provides an easy means of storing these items safely. While the bedding can be kept in sacks in the can, it is important to store the dry food in an airtight container, to prolong the life of its vitamin content.

Food bowls for dry food must be washed out each week, using a detergent and a small brush. They should then be allowed to dry thoroughly before being refilled. The water bottle should also be washed out on a regular basis, partly to prevent the growth of green algae within the container. A bottle brush, as sold for household use, provides the simplest way of cleaning the bottle, but take particular care not to scratch the sides of plastic bottles with the brush, because algae will become established in these scratches, where it will be hard to remove. Glass bottles are less likely to scratch, but they are not as satisfactory overall because they will smash very easily if they are dropped.

● *I find wood shavings tend to stick to the tray when they become damp. Any suggestions for removing them?*

The simplest way of ensuring the tray is thoroughly clean is to use a small shovel or trowel to scrape the soiled bedding into a plastic bag, or alternatively, you can use a paint scraper for this purpose. Stick to shavings rather than sawdust, since sawdust will be too fine and could irritate your guinea pig's eyes.

● *Do I need to provide my guinea pig with anything to keep his incisor teeth in trim?*

A range of chews (right) are available for this purpose, while short lengths of branches cut from apple trees can also be provided, as long as they have not recently been sprayed. Mineral blocks are also beneficial, since gnawing these will help to keep the teeth in trim.

● *Why does the guinea pig's water bottle keep dripping?*

Probably because it is only partially full. Filling it to the top will drive out all of the air, and then you should have no further problem.

Taming Tips

● Start with a young guinea pig—about five weeks old if possible.

● Accustom your pet to being handled regularly—on a daily basis if possible.

● Offer the guinea pig food from your hand while it is still in its quarters.

● Encourage your pet to sit quietly on your lap (below), even if it is reluctant to begin with. Offering a piece of fresh greenfood may help.

Breeding Guinea Pigs

IT IS IMPORTANT NOT TO WAIT TOO LONG BEFORE mating sows for the first time. This is because their pelvic bones become fused at about ten months of age. Under normal circumstances they slacken off, allowing the young to pass through the birth canal easily. If mating occurs too late, however, the bones will have permanently fused together, greatly increasing the risk of birthing difficulties. This may even necessitate a Caesarean birth, in order to save the sow's life.

The ideal time to allow guinea pigs to breed for the first time is when they are about five months old. No special precautions need to be taken. The boar can simply be left together with the sow for approximately six weeks, by which time mating should have occurred successfully, since females come into heat approximately once every 18 days. The sow should be kept on her own for the duration of her pregnancy, which lasts typically for 69 days, with the young often being born at night.

The sow will require a similar diet to that which she has been receiving previously, possibly augmented with a special supplement, which can be sprinkled as instructed over moist greenfood. As the time for giving birth approaches, the sow's abdomen is likely to have increased dramatically in size. Try to avoid handling her more than strictly necessary at this late stage, and be very careful not to drop her.

It is also very important to provide the sow with the correct diet, because her vitamin C requirement will have doubled during this period. Young can be born with paralysis of their hind limbs if a pregnant sow did not receive sufficient vitamin C. You also need to a watch for signs of pregnancy toxemia, which causes a sow to appear depressed and her condition to deteriorate rapidly, with muscular twitching soon becoming apparent. This requires emergency veterinary treatment.

The Newborn Guinea Pig

A sow usually gives birth to about four young, although this figure may range from just one to six. It is very important not to allow the boar into the hutch during the period following the birth. Although he will not harm the young, the sow comes into heat again about 48 hours after giving birth, and she will be likely to conceive again immediately.

The young are normally reared without any problems, although complications can sometimes arise, especially following a difficult birth. Although guinea pigs can start nibbling at solid food within a couple of days of birth, they still need to suckle from their mother. Look for any signs of resentment on the part of the sow—such as driving her young away. This could suggest inflammation of the mammary glands (a condition known as mastitis) or could reflect a shortage of milk (a condition known as agalactia).

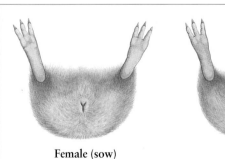

Female (sow)

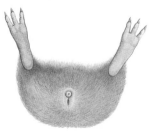

Male (boar)

◀ *Sexing guinea pigs at an early age is not as straightforward as later in life, but applying gentle pressure just above the anogenital opening should result in the penis appearing in the case of a young boar. Later, the testes will be evident as swellings below this part of the body.*

Q&A

● **What is the best substitute for the sow's milk?**

... In an emergency, evaporated milk diluted with twice the volume of cool boiled water can be used, augmented with a baby cereal. Although guinea pigs require a higher level of protein than is present in this type of milk, they can make up this deficiency by eating pelleted food. Alternatively, you can use a milk replacer of the type sold for puppies, diluted with water. Encourage them to eat fresh foods as well, since excessive milk has been linked with the subsequent development of cataracts in young guinea pigs.

● **Is it better to foster young guinea pigs rather than hand-rear them?**

Fostering is certainly preferable if you have another sow which gave birth at the same time and has just two or three offspring. To overcome the possibility of rejection by the foster mother, allow all the youngsters to mix together in a small box, to mask the smell of the newcomers, before placing them with her.

▲ *Guinea pigs are born in a fully developed state, with their markings remaining consistent throughout their lives. They grow rapidly and can soon feed themselves.*

Mastitis requires urgent veterinary treatment, but agalactia soon resolves itself once the sow has become more relaxed—therefore keep disturbances to a minimum in the first few days after she has given birth. Be prepared to hand-feed as soon as any such problems arise.

While she is suckling her offspring, especially if it is a large litter, it is important to provide a good source of calcium, such as leafy vegetables, corn, or cornmeal. This will help prevent the condition known as eclampsia, in which the sow suddenly loses coordination and has fits. Treatment at this stage is then very difficult.

Young guinea pigs grow fast, and they should be separated from their mother once they are a month old, with boars and sows being transferred to separate accommodation at this stage.

Illnesses in Guinea Pigs

ALTHOUGH GUINEA PIGS RARELY FALL ILL, THEY are susceptible to skin ailments. This may be related to a lack of vitamin C in their diet, which results in hair loss and can lead to bleeding and general weakness. Treatment by means of a suitable supplement will be needed, and the diet should be improved as well.

Mange and Other Skin Problems

Mange, caused by microscopic mites, can also cause signs of hair loss. It usually occurs first in the vicinity of the head and shoulders, before spreading if left untreated over the rest of the body. The guinea pig will appear distressed, because this condition causes intense itching, with the mites actually multiplying in the skin. In severe cases, nervous twitching may be seen.

Early treatment is very important, and can now be achieved quite successfully by means of the drug known as ivermectin, given by injection. Your veterinarian will be able to confirm the cause first by taking skin scrapings which are viewed under a microscope. Repeated doses of

● **Can guinea pigs suffer from sunburn if kept in a run?**

This can be a problem during hot weather, notably for guinea pigs with pink ears. The run should always be sited in a shaded part of the garden if possible—certainly when the sun is at its hottest—to protect against sunstroke. As a further precaution, it is possible to purchase sun blocks for pets, which may be used on vulnerable guinea pigs. Avoid using a human preparation, since this might be harmful if ingested.

● *Is ringworm a parasitic illness?*

No, this is a fungal disease. Although it is very rare in guinea pigs it is significant, because it is a zoonosis—a disease that can be spread to people. Skin signs in people take the form of reddish circular patches, usually on the forearms, with similar scabs being evident in the guinea pig's coat. Seek veterinary advice if you suspect this condition.

▼ *Treatment for mange mites in guinea pigs used to involve giving regular medicated baths, but now medication by injection from a veterinarian offers an easier way to kill these parasites.*

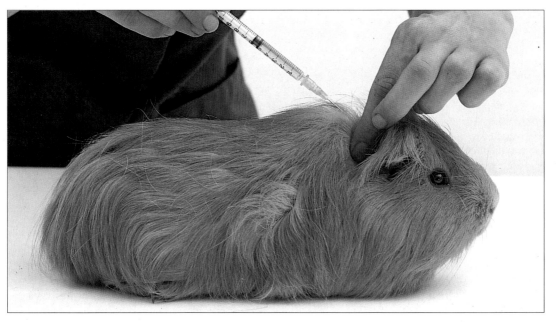

Dangers in the Hutch

Insects Flies can enter the hutch and cause fly strike—a serious condition in which the fly's eggs are laid in the coat.

Food Poisonous or sprayed plants may be fed to the guinea pig. Rodent-contaminated, or out-of-date, dry food can also be a hazard.

Other animals Dogs or cats may reach a guinea pig if the door is not securely locked.

Contamination Hay which has toxic weeds present, or is moldy, may harm your pet. A hutch which has not been properly cleaned can also harbor diseases.

this drug may need to be given at roughly three week intervals, to kill off all the mites. Thorough disinfection of the guinea pig's quarters will be needed as well, to destroy any mites which survive here. Mites can be introduced in bedding, while secondhand hutches may also pose a danger and should be scrubbed out with a suitable disinfectant before being used again.

Skin problems often strike sows during, or soon after, pregnancy. Typical among these is the condition described as "broken back," which is most common in pale-coated individuals and usually seen in the warmer months of the year. It takes the form of hair loss along the back. This may be linked with the guinea pig's diet, with flaked corn often being identified as the cause of this condition. Once other causes such as mites have been eliminated, dietary changes and topical treatment can resolve this problem. Hair loss may also arise during pregnancy but, unlike the situation with mites, it is not accompanied by itching. The hair should grow back in due course, although it is quite common for the situation to worsen over subsequent pregnancies. A vitamin B supplement, which should be sprinkled over greens, is often recommended to assist this condition.

Nutritional and Other Problems

A serious nutritional problem seen in boars is metastatic calcification. This causes stiffness, and often weight loss, in its early stages. It is the result of calcium nodules forming in various parts of the body, ranging from the lungs and stomach to major blood vessels such as the aorta. The condition results from an imbalance in the body's calcium and phosphorus metabolism, which is regulated by vitamin D. Prevention is the best course of action and is achieved by offering a balanced diet. Should you notice that your guinea pig starts to display difficulties in moving, seek veterinary advice without delay to minimize the problem.

A relatively common and unpleasant ailment which can strike guinea pigs as they grow older is impaction of the rectum. This causes distortion of the anus, with an accumulation of droppings being apparent here. The only solution is to lubricate the affected area and gently squeeze out the offending mass of droppings, wearing disposable gloves. Since this condition is caused by loss of muscle tone, there is little that can be done to resolve the problem, although a high-fiber diet should help to minimize it.

Damage to the ears sometimes occurs, often as the result of overlong claws when guinea pigs are being housed together in groups. A mother may inadvertently injure her young as they start using the food bowl under her feet. If the ears are bleeding, pressing on the wound with some damp cotton for a few moments should stem the blood flow, allowing a scab to form. If this area becomes extensively damaged, it may spoil the youngster's exhibition chances in the future. Always pay attention to the guinea pig's nails, therefore, cutting them back as demonstrated previously for rabbits (see page 49).

▲ *If the outer part of a guinea pig's ear becomes soiled, it can be wiped clean with a damp cotton bud. Never probe inside the ear canal, however.*

Guinea Pig Breeds and Varieties

GUINEA PIGS ARE CATEGORIZED PARTLY ON THE basis of their coloration and also on the appearance of their coat, with the number of varieties having increased rapidly over recent years.

SOLID COLORS

Members of the Self group are very popular, consisting of smooth-coated guinea pigs whose short hair consists of one color. The Self Black is the darkest member of the group; it has a jet-black coat. Any reddish hairs in the coat are deemed to be a serious fault in this variety. Self Chocolates are another dark variant, and their color should be a deep, rich shade. They have ruby-colored eyes. The color of the underparts of exhibition guinea pigs of this variety must be as dark as the hair elsewhere on the body.

These two Self varieties are also bred in red-eyed dilute forms, creating the Self Lilac, which corresponds to the Self Black, and the Self Beige, which corresponds to the Self Chocolate.

Reds and Creams

The rich, mahogany-red shade of the Self Red lightens with age, to the extent that it is best to pick the darkest-colored offspring. White hairs are a relatively common problem with this variety, spoiling the appearance of some individuals for show purposes. The Self Golden is a paler color form, which should be of a ginger shade, rather than yellow. The pink-eyed form of the Self Golden is most common, being better known in North America as the Red-eyed Orange, but there is a dark-eyed variant as well. Check that the undercoat of these guinea pigs matches their top coat. Paleness here will cause an uneven, streaked appearance.

Self Creams are a well-established variety, but

◀ *A Self Lilac. The lilac coloration should be a pale dove-gray, with a pinkish hue, but it can be hard to achieve a consistency of color over the entire coat. Some areas often appear darker than others.*

● *Is it possible to breed crested Self colors?*

... This is quite feasible, since the crested characteristic occurs independently of color. Two distinctive forms of the crested mutation have been developed. In the English Crested form, the rosette of hair forming the crest should match the coat color, whereas the American Crested form has a white crest. The crest should be of even shape and well positioned on the head. The crest can be groomed gently with a toothbrush if necessary.

● *What features are judges likely to look for when assessing Self guinea pigs at shows?*

In general terms, the head should be broad and the face short, while the body is cobby in shape. The ears must be perfect, with no signs of nicks around the edges. The ears should droop down, resembling petals in appearance. The eyes should be bold and bright, while the nails should not be overgrown or distorted.

● *Do young guinea pigs alter in appearance?*

They often appear to have rather elongated bodies at first, but tend to gain a more cobby profile as they mature. Depending on the variety, their coloration may also alter slightly—with odd reddish hairs often being lost in the case of the Self Black, for example.

▼ *This group of three Self varieties—from left, Cream, Buff, and Golden—reflects the differences in the depth of coloration between them, with the Buff, for example, being darker than the Cream.*

▲ *An example of an American Crested Self. Note the contrasting white fur here, which should serve to highlight the entire crest and must not be broken by the main body color.*

again, it is not easy to achieve the desired level of coloration. A lighter shade is preferred, but this often means that the color of the undercoat is too white. Even coloration, as in the other Self varieties, is vital. The deep ruby eyes of the Self Cream, which can appear blackish, help separate this variety from the rarer, pink-eyed dilute form called the Saffron, with its pale lemon fur.

Whites and Other Selfs

The Self White exists in two forms, which can be distinguished by their eye coloration. The Dark-eyed White has black eyes, as its name suggests, with dark pigment also sometimes being present on the ears and feet, in contrast to the pink-eyed form, which is a true albino, displaying no pigmentation whatsoever. The fur in both cases should be pure white, but it can be difficult to retain this color, because the fur of these guinea pigs may become stained by their bedding.

Other Self varieties are being developed, including a Self Blue form, bred in the United States. As with other members of this group, these guinea pigs need to display an even depth of coloration on their coats.

The development of the Satin mutation has helped to reinforce the attractive glossy coat coloration of members of the Self group in particular, although this characteristic can be combined very effectively with other short-coated varieties as well. Satins should not be paired together, but always outcrossed to other varieties in order to maintain the quality of the coat.

PATTERNED VARIETIES

There are a number of other smooth-coated forms of the guinea pig which are of mixed coloration, and they are included in the Non-self category. These include the agouti forms, so called because of the light and dark ticking running down their individual hairs and corresponding to that seen in the guinea pig's wild ancestor. The Golden Agouti has brighter coloration than the Silver Agouti, and its underparts have a more reddish tinge compared with those of the Silver, which are of a bluish-black shade. Other newer agouti variants include Argentes, which have red eyes.

Tortoiseshells and Other Color Combinations

There are a growing number of breeds displaying colored and white areas of fur. They include the Tortoiseshell and White, whose coat consists of a patchwork of red, black, and white areas. This should ideally be arranged in the shape of even squares, with clear delineation between them. It is also important that the red areas of the coat are of a deep, even shade. The same applies in the case of Tricolors, in which other

▼ *A Black Himalayan. The name of these attractive guinea pigs reflects the influence of the Himalayan gene, which is responsible for the distinctive patterning of dark pigmentation on their bodies.*

colors are offset against white markings. Tortoiseshells and Bicolors have a similar patchwork of markings, with neither a solid band of color encircling their bodies nor any white areas in their coats.

The Dutch guinea pig should have markings similar to those of the corresponding rabbit breed (see pages 66–67). Again, this is a difficult variety to breed for exhibition purposes. There must be a central white area of fur around the body, with a white blaze present on the face. Darker colors including agouti are often favored in the Dutch, since paler shades such as cream do not stand out well against the white areas.

In some varieties, clear delineation between the colors is not required. This is true of the Brindle, which displays streaks of red and black hair in its coat. There must be no white hairs in the coats of these guinea pigs, however, nor should the colors cluster together.

Even mixing of white and colored hairs characterizes Roan guinea pigs. A combination of black and white fur underlies the appearance of the Blue Roan. Both the head and feet should be solidly colored in roans. The Strawberry Roan is another popular member of this group, displaying a combination of red and white hair, with the white again evenly distributed over the body.

White areas of hair are far more evident in the Dalmatian breed, which has been named after

the popular breed of spotted dog. The face is a solid color, separated by a white blaze running down the nose. The spots, which are roughly the size of peas, extend over the body. While black and white examples of the Dalmatian are most common, a chocolate and white variety has also been developed, along with other colors, but the distinctive contrast is most pronounced in the dark-coated varieties.

Himalayans

The Himalayan is another variety that occurs in both a black and a lighter chocolate form, with the coloration in this instance being confined to the extremities of the body, comprising the nose, ears, legs, and feet. Young are white at birth and then start to develop their characteristic coloration in a few days. Their coloration is sensitive to external temperature, becoming paler when these guinea pigs are housed in relatively warm conditions—in the home, for example.

▼ *A Harlequin (left) and a Tortoiseshell and White (right). The term Harlequin has been applied to guinea pigs in which there is a brindled overlap between the two colors in their coat. The white area between the eyes of the Tortoiseshell and White is called a blaze.*

Q&A...

● *Why is the coloration of Argentes less obvious than in normal agoutis?*

This difference in color is a result of the dilution factor, which affects the black pigment. This means that the dark bands of ticking in the coat are also paler, and so the contrast here between the light and dark areas is less marked.

● *I'm trying to breed well-marked Tortoiseshell and White guinea pigs, but without great success. Any advice?*

These rank among the hardest of all colors to breed for exhibition purposes, because of the unpredictability of the patterning in the offspring. If you have a guinea pig in which one of the colors is very restricted, then try to pair this individual to another in which that particular color is dominant. Hopefully, the markings will then be balanced better in some of their offspring.

● *Why is it not recommended to pair either Roans or Dalmatians together?*

This is because of a genetic problem which causes white offspring in their litters to be born blind. Therefore always mate these varieties to their self-colored counterparts.

OTHER COAT TYPES

There have also been a number of changes to the appearance of the guinea pig's coat as a result of domestication.

Abyssinians

The Abyssinian breed is characterized by the series of rosettes which cover its body, creating ridges where they meet. The wiry hair must not lie flat, although it is short, measuring a maximum of 1.5in (3.75cm) in length.

Great emphasis is placed on the quality and positioning of these rosettes for show purposes. Four rosettes must be present on the rump area, with another four clearly defined rosettes encircling the saddle area in the center of the body. A further two are present on each shoulder. It is therefore quite difficult to breed Abyssinians with a perfect pattern of rosettes, and having a pair of Abyssinians which excel in this respect gives no guarantee that the offspring will inherit this patterning as well.

In terms of coloration, Self Abyssinians are not favored, simply because their fur tends to be softer than that of some other varieties. Both Tortoiseshells, and Tortoiseshell and Whites, have coarser coats which stand up better. These are therefore more commonly seen in

● *My Abyssinian boar mated accidentally with a smooth-coated sow. What will their offspring look like?*

Since the Abyssinian coat pattern is genetically dominant, all the young will have an Abyssinian-type coat, but the rosettes themselves are likely to be less clearly defined, because the coat texture will be softer.

● *Why are long-haired guinea pigs often not shown after two years of age?*

This is because their long coats become stiffer and display less of a sheen, placing them at a disadvantage compared with young individuals.

● *Do long-haired guinea pigs have any special needs?*

Provide hay for them in a special hay rack, because pieces of hay become caught up in their long coats—which may measure 20in (50cm) in some cases.

▲ *A Roan Abyssinian. The ridges that are formed by the meeting of adjacent rosettes of fur are clearly apparent on this individual. The centers of the rosettes must be aligned, as shown here.*

◄ *The Rex characteristic can be combined with any color or length of coat. This is a Silver Agouti Rex. Rex guinea pigs require only minimal amounts of grooming to keep their coats in top condition.*

▶ *The Sheltie variety can be distinguished from the similar Peruvian by the fact that its face is not covered by long fur. There should be a beard of longer fur on the face, however, and a trail of long fur behind the body. Grooming of these guinea pigs should be carried out in a similar way to grooming Peruvians.*

the Abyssinian breed, as are Brindles with red and black coloration mixed in their coats. If black, rather than red, hairs predominate, then such individuals are described as being heavily brindled, but if the reverse applies, they are known as lightly brindled. It takes time for the coat of an Abyssinian to develop fully, so this breed is not often exhibited until 18 months old.

Rexes

The Rex form of the guinea pig is often described as the Teddy in North America because of its cuddly appearance. Young Rex guinea pigs have wavy coats when young, which then start to look wooly. The hair is coarse to the touch and does not lie flat, possessing a distinctive, springy texture. The Rex characteristic can be combined with any color as well as other mutations, including the Satin.

Long-haired Varieties

Long-haired guinea pigs are not commonly seen outside show circles, simply because their coat care is very demanding. Don't think of getting one of these guinea pigs unless you are prepared to groom your pet on a daily basis. The Peruvian is the oldest of these particular breeds, and its coat has become much more profuse as the result of domestication, although newborn Peruvians have relatively short coats. At this stage, it is easier to see that their long hair originates from just two rosettes present on the head and rump.

When young Peruvians are about three months old, their hair should be trained with wrappers attached to the coat, rather like curlers. Three wrappers are needed at first: one for the tail end, called the sweep, and one for each side of the body—with more being required as the coat grows. The wrappers consist of lengths of paper about 6in (15cm) wide. A piece of balsa wood measuring 2 x 1in (5 x 2.5cm) is enclosed under a fold of paper at the top end, which is then taped down. The paper is folded inward on both sides of the wood, and then the paper is folded up lengthwise in concertina style. The paper is then unfolded and placed under the hair and then folded back up again, being held in place with a rubber band. Peruvians are always exhibited on a hessian-covered stand, raised 6in (15cm) off the ground, with their long hair trailing down the side. Show training from an early age is important, to encourage the guinea pig to stay still while judging is taking place.

Other long-haired combinations now exist, such as the Sheltie—which can be easily distinguished from the Peruvian because there is no rosette of long fur on the head.

Combining the Rex characteristic and the long coat of the Peruvian has now resulted in the Alpaca breed, which has a long, curly coat. The equivalent Rex form in the Sheltie is known as the Texel. The crested long-haired form of the Sheltie, which has a central parting, is called the Coronet, while the Rex-coated variant is called the Merino. These varieties are all quite scarce.

Hamsters

LITTLE COULD THE MEDICAL RESEARCHER WHO TRAPPED SOME hamsters on the sides of Mount Aleppo in Syria in 1930 have imagined that he was obtaining the ancestors of virtually all of the Golden hamsters kept today. Since other color varieties have now occurred in domestic strains of these rodents, they are better known today as Syrian hamsters.

Back in the laboratory, this original group were soon breeding very successfully, and within a year more than 150 had been produced at the Hebrew University in Jerusalem. Soon afterward, a pair was smuggled into Britain, where they were kept for research, and later a few pairs were presented to London Zoo. The prolific nature of these rodents meant that by 1937 the first Syrian hamsters became available for pet enthusiasts, with others being sent to the United States from Britain.

The rapid growth of interest in the Syrian hamster as a pet saw these rodents being exhibited for the first time in 1948. Their popularity was further enhanced by their readiness to breed, and hamster-keeping received considerable publicity when the world's first hamster farm was set up in England, soon to be followed by one in Alabama. These and similar establishments helped to meet the worldwide demand for these rodents.

More recently, dwarf Russian hamsters (*Phodopus* species) have also become very popular, and these are also now bred in an ever-expanding range of colors. There are actually over 24 different species of hamster around the world, but the only other hamster that has attracted the interest of pet-keepers and exhibitors to date is the Chinese species (*Cricetulus griseus*). These particular hamsters were first seen in Britain over 70 years ago but, in common with the dwarf forms, they have only been widely kept since the 1970s.

▶ *The prominent eyes of the Syrian hamster reflect the fact that these rodents live mainly in the dark environment of underground burrows. They have a keen sense of smell and good hearing as well.*

Hamster Lifestyles

HAMSTERS FORM A SUBFAMILY WITHIN THE myomorph (mouselike) division of rodents. They are found only in the Old World, with a distribution ranging from parts of Europe eastward through the Middle East, including Syria, and into Russia and China. The largest member of the group is the European common hamster (*Cricetus cricetus*), which can grow to just over 11in (28cm) and may weigh up to 2lb (0.9kg). In contrast, the dwarf Russian is the smallest, often being no bigger than 2.5in (6.5cm) overall, with a body weight of just 1.75oz (50g).

The name of these rodents comes from the German word *hamstern*, meaning "to hoard,"

◀ *Hamsters instinctively hide away, because in the wild this gives them their best protection against predators. They can easily squeeze into tiny spaces in the home, too, as this picture demonstrates.*

and reflects the fact that all hamsters possess cheek pouches which they stuff with large quantities of food in order to carry it back to their burrows to eat later (see page 7). Hamsters are naturally shy, remaining under ground for much of the day and emerging under cover of darkness to seek their food. This tendency is still apparent in domesticated strains, with hamsters sleeping during the day and waking up at dusk, then remaining active through the night. This in part explains the reputation that hamsters sometimes have for biting—they are being woken for handling during their natural sleep period.

Sharp teeth enable hamsters to crack the tough outer casing of seeds, nuts, and similar foods which form the main part of their diet. They also use their front paws to assist in this task, picking up morsels of food with them. Hamsters are also very fastidious about grooming themselves and use their paws for this purpose as well.

In common with many other nocturnal rodents, hamsters rely less on their sense of sight and more on their senses of hearing and smell. Their prominent whiskers help them to determine whether they can slip through an opening

Fact File

Names: Syrian or Golden Hamster; Chinese Hamster; Dwarf Hamsters.

Scientific names: *Mesocricetus auratus; Cricetulus griseus; Phodopus* species.

Weight: Syrian hamster 4.5–6.5oz (128–184g); dwarf hamsters 1–1.5oz (28–43g); Chinese hamster 1.5–1.75oz (43–50g), with females being heavier than males.

Compatibility: Not generally amenable with others of their kind and must be housed individually, with matings being carefully supervised. Dwarf hamsters are the most social.

Appeal: Attractive appearance. Popular with older children or teenagers. Hamsters tend to bite, so they are less suitable for younger children. Very popular in exhibition circles.

Diet: Cereal-based seed mixture augmented with fresh food in small amounts, preferably given on a daily basis. Complete diets also available.

Health problems: Can be vulnerable to tumors—especially dwarf hamsters—and to injuries caused by falls as the result of careless handling. Also various dietary problems.

Breeding tips: Females must always be introduced to the male's quarters, rather than vice-versa, to reduce the likelihood of fighting.

Pregnancy: Syrian hamster 16–18 days; 21 days in other species.

Typical litter size: Syrian hamster 8–10 young; 3–7 young in other species.

Weaning: Typically about 22 days in all species.

Lifespan: 2–3 years

▲ *The Chinese hamster differs from other pet hamsters by having a relatively long tail, which can measure just over 0.75in (2cm) in length.*

● *Do pet hamsters have an unpleasant odor associated with them?*

No. Like other rodents originating from arid parts of the world, their kidneys produce a concentrated urine, which does not have a pungent odor. Occasionally, however, a hamster may urinate through the sides of its cage. Therefore it is advisable to stand the cage on an old towel, which can be washed as necessary, or on sheets of newspaper.

● *How can I tell the approximate age of the adult hamster I wish to buy?*

It is virtually impossible to age hamsters once they are fully grown, but as they reach the end of their lives their coats often thin out, and bald areas become apparent.

● *Can I buy a hamster from a pet store, or should I find a breeder?*

You should be able to obtain a young hamster suitable as a pet from either source, but if you are seeking to develop an exhibition strain, then it will be better to seek out a breeder who specializes in the variety which appeals to you. This gives a better opportunity to breed youngsters that will hopefully prove to be successful at shows.

easily, and they will always seek to escape by burrowing, rather than remaining above ground. They tend not to be great climbers, as reflected by their almost non-existent tails.

Solitary Rodents

Hamsters are prolific when breeding, but their lifespans are short. They live for less than three years on average. As a result, it is very important to start out with a genuine youngster of between three and four weeks of age. It is also much easier to tame a hamster successfully at this age. If you are looking for pets that live together in harmony, however, hamsters are not a good choice. In contrast to many other rodents, hamsters are decidedly antisocial, and after weaning, the young need to be housed separately. Even subsequent introductions for breeding purposes should only be carried out under supervision, because hamsters can prove to be very aggressive toward each other and will fight viciously if confined together. On occasions, it may be possible to house dwarf hamsters together after weaning, but even so, outbreaks of aggression can frequently arise without warning.

▶ *The lack of a tail means that hamsters can encounter difficulties when trying to balance off the ground. However, they do have strong forepaws which they use for climbing and also for holding food.*

Housing for Hamsters

Traditionally, hamsters were housed in metal cages fitted with a wire mesh top, but today plastic also features in the design of most hamster cages—although there is usually still wire mesh on the top. Plastic has a number of advantages. First, it is seamless, so the hamster is far less likely to injure itself by becoming caught by a toe, for example. Plastic is also easy to clean and disinfect and will not rust. Unfortunately, its major drawback is that it will prove to be less durable, bearing in mind that hamsters, in spite of their small size, have very strong teeth. This means that a hamster can rapidly damage a plastic cage. It can even escape from one by gnawing through the plastic. Once the rodent has discovered a weak point, it will often not take long for it to create a sufficient gap to squeeze through.

▼ A typical hamster cage. The top part can be easily separated from the base for cleaning, while the access doors allow the hamster to be caught when needed.

When choosing a cage, therefore, always check that the mesh top fits snugly into the plastic base. You should also ensure that it is securely anchored by stout clips. If the clips are weak they may snap over time and, unless they can be replaced, you will have to obtain a new cage. Cages held together with metal hooks are a much better choice, since these will remain effective provided they do not become bent.

Another point of weakness in some cages is the door fastening. It is often worth fitting a small padlock here as an additional precaution, to prevent any possible escape. One of the problems with hamsters is that they become active at dusk, and so they can disappear overnight and will be hard to track down the following morning.

Dwarf hamsters may sometimes be able to escape through the bars of a standard hamster cage as a result of their small size, especially when young. As a result, it is generally safer to house them in a spacious, all-acrylic tank fitted with a ventilated hood. The other alternative will be to use a converted glass aquarium, again with a ventilated hood, but this will be much harder to maneuver because of its weight.

Housing Systems

Tubular housing systems have become very popular for hamsters over recent years, mimicking the natural burrows and chambers that they occupy in the wild. It is possible to begin with a starter kit and then add further sections in due course. Ensure that these are assembled correctly, however, because again any weakness here is likely to be exploited by the hamster's sharp teeth. Cleanliness can sometimes be a problem with housing of this type, although hamsters will generally use one area as a latrine, which simplifies the cleaning process.

Even so, you will probably need to dismantle all of the sections to wash them occasionally. Therefore it is worth investing in a small ventilated acrylic carrier in which the hamster can be housed securely while its quarters are being cleaned. You may need to alter the design of the tunnels or tubular systems as your hamster grows older, since it may encounter more difficulty in climbing through the sections. It is also not unheard of for hamsters to become stuck in the narrower tunnels, because they often put on weight as they age.

Positioning a Hamster's Quarters

● Place the unit on a level shelf, table, or chest so that it is off the ground.

● Be sure that it is out of drafts and not adjacent to a radiator.

● Avoid positioning the cage in front of a window, especially in hot weather.

● Do not choose a locality adjacent to a television or stereo, since this is likely to disturb your pet.

● Ensure that children can reach the hamster easily, without any risk of knocking the unit onto the floor.

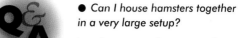

● Can I house hamsters together in a very large setup?

... No, there are really no normal circumstances in which it is recommended that these rodents be kept together. This is particularly true in the case of the Syrian and Chinese species. Hamsters are solitary creatures in the wild, with each having its own burrow, and trying to compel them to share accommodation is likely to have a fatal outcome.

● What sort of bedding should I buy?

Various types of bedding are available, and one of the best kinds for use as a general floor covering in the hamster's quarters is coarse wood shavings sold specifically for pet rodents. Bedding will also be needed so that the hamster can make a separate nest. It is very important to choose only safe, proprietary bedding of the type sold at pet stores for this purpose. The fibers from other materials, such as cotton, may be swallowed, causing a fatal intestinal blockage.

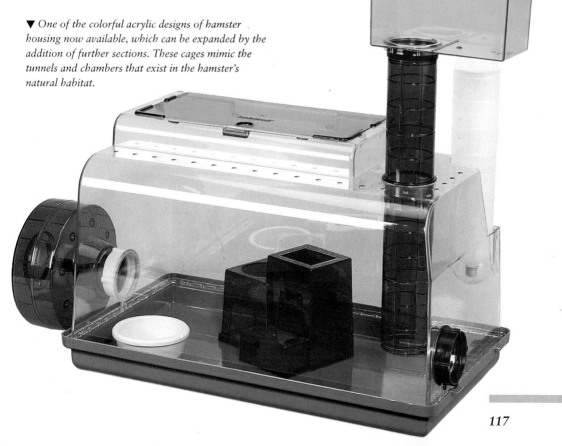

▼ *One of the colorful acrylic designs of hamster housing now available, which can be expanded by the addition of further sections. These cages mimic the tunnels and chambers that exist in the hamster's natural habitat.*

Feeding Hamsters

▲ *Hamsters will eat fresh foods, as well as dry seeds. A variety of vegetables can be offered to them, including peeled carrot and celery. These should be cut into pieces so your hamster can nibble them without difficulty.*

HAMSTERS CAN APPEAR TO HAVE VERY BIG appetites, despite their relatively small size. This is because they store extra food in their cheek pouches when they eat, just as they would in the wild. Trying to persuade your hamster to eat a balanced diet can sometimes be difficult, too, because it will simply eat its favorite items and hide other food out of sight.

Most pet stores offer hamster mixes of various types. An ideal diet consists of seeds augmented on a regular basis with fresh foods such as pieces of dessert apple and sometimes even mealworms. While a typical hamster mix will be suitable for larger species such as Syrian and Chinese hamsters, it may be necessary to modify the diet of dwarf Russian hamsters, since some of the ingredients may be too large for these particularly small hamsters to carry back

and eat in their nests. Small cereal seeds such as millets and plain canary seed (which feature in Budgerigar seed mixtures) are ideal because of their small size, and they can be added to a standard mix.

Hamsters should not have access to large quantities of oil-based seeds, such as sunflower and peanuts (or groundnuts). These contain a high percentage of fat in the form of oil and are a prime cause of obesity in hamsters, which can shorten their lives. By contrast, grains like millets are comprised mainly of carbohydrate rather than fat, and the hamster's metabolism is well adapted to dealing with this type of food.

Some items can help prevent the teeth from becoming overgrown. Various chews and treats are available, while other hard foods like dog biscuit can be offered. Non-chemically treated pumice is also useful. Freshly cut branches from non-poisonous trees such as apple and hazel are also popular with hamsters, because they can nibble the bark. Be sure that the trees have not recently been sprayed with harmful chemicals.

▼ *A typical hamster mix consisting mainly of seeds including oats, sunflower, and flaked corn, augmented with other items such as dried fruit.*

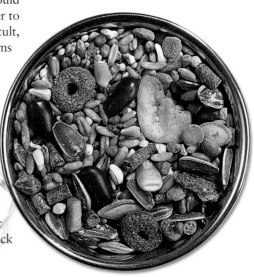

● *My friend gives her dwarf Russian hamsters both hay and mealworms. Are these items necessary?*

Because they come from a part of the world where the weather conditions are harsh, and food is often in short supply, these hamsters will eat a varied diet. Hay adds valuable fiber to their food intake, while the mealworms provide additional protein, which can be beneficial when you are hoping to breed these hamsters—although there is no real evidence to show that a raised level of dietary protein helps to increase their litter size.

● *Are there any fruits or vegetables which I should avoid feeding to my hamster?*

Do not offer any which are highly acidic, such as citrus fruits like orange, or kiwi fruits. Avocado is also best avoided, along with green lettuce—although red-leaved varieties of lettuce can be given. Always restrict the amount, however, in case your hamster decides to gorge itself and suffers a severe digestive upset because of the sudden change in its diet.

● *Do I need to use a supplement if I feed my hamster on pellets?*

No, simply because these foods should contain a correct balance of all the nutrients needed by the hamster. Some fresh food and hay may be beneficial, however, to increase the fiber content of the diet.

▼ *These biscuit-like materials are available from pet stores. They allow your pet to gnaw and so help to keep the teeth in trim.*

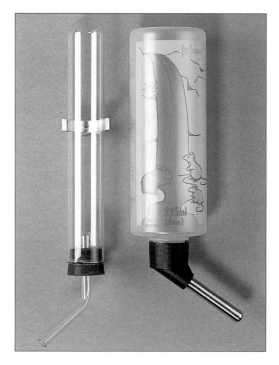

▲ *Although they do not drink much water, hamsters should be offered a fresh supply each day. This should be provided in a bottle fitted with a stainless steel spout or a strong plastic spout, as shown here.*

Water Requirements

Originating from rather dry parts of the world, hamsters obtain some of their water naturally through eating vegetation, and fresh food of this type should be offered daily in small amounts.

Another advantage of offering fresh foods is that a powdered vitamin and mineral supplement can be sprinkled over the moist surfaces, adhering readily. Various products of this type are available, and they help compensate for any nutritional shortcomings in the hamster's diet. Choose one formulated especially for small mammals, and do not exceed the recommended dose. Some vitamins can have toxic side-effects in the longer term if given in excess.

Bottles designed to attach to the side of a cage are supplied with a metal clip for this purpose, but there are also other types of bottle intended for use with plastic housing systems. Small bottles which are suspended in a sling from the roof can be used where a hamster is being kept in a converted aquarium.

Routine Care of Hamsters

● *Will my cat learn to leave the hamster alone?*

... Unless your cat is very docile, this is unlikely, and you will have to ensure that they are kept separate at all times. Never allow the cat into the room when you are cleaning your hamster's quarters, or at any time when the hamster is out of its quarters.

● *Are some hamsters easier to tame than others?*

Syrian and Chinese hamsters are both quite bold and therefore easy to tame, although differences occur between individuals. Dwarf Russian hamsters are a little more timid. Roborovski's dwarf Russian hamsters are generally more nervous than Campbell's, and so the latter are more popular pets.

● *What arrangements should I make to ensure my hamster is looked after while I am on vacation?*

Find a friend or neighbor who will visit daily to check all is well and provide your pet with fresh water and food. Leave sufficient food for the hamster, and provide clear, written instructions about its care, including the name of a veterinarian who can be contacted in an emergency. If you decide to take your hamster with you, make sure there is no problem in having the animal at your destination. A short journey by car, with the hamster in its cage located securely on the floor behind the seats, is safer than using public transport.

HANDLING A HAMSTER IS USUALLY QUITE A straightforward task, but it will take time to win your pet's confidence—especially when you are dealing with a new individual. Always aim to coax the hamster onto your hand rather than picking it up and restraining it, because if the hamster feels threatened it is likely to bite you. You can help break down your pet's fear and win its trust by offering food from your fingers.

Escapes from Cages

Of all the small animals kept as pets, a hamster is likely to prove the hardest to recapture if it escapes from its cage. Unlike a gerbil, for example, hamsters show a particular desire to escape from view, especially during the daytime. And since they are most likely to have escaped overnight, they could easily have moved to another part of the house. This is why the door of the room in which a hamster is kept should always be closed at night.

If you have the misfortune to lose a hamster in your home, start by looking carefully in drawers and behind chests—the sort of places in which the hamster could have curled up and gone to sleep during the daytime. However, make sure you move furniture with great care. Should this

Setting a Trap

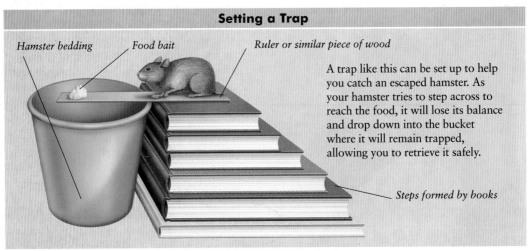

Hamster bedding *Food bait* *Ruler or similar piece of wood*

A trap like this can be set up to help you catch an escaped hamster. As your hamster tries to step across to reach the food, it will lose its balance and drop down into the bucket where it will remain trapped, allowing you to retrieve it safely.

Steps formed by books

▲ *A hamster should be provided with a snug retreat in its quarters, where it can burrow away and sleep during the day. A variety of different designs of suitable nest, some in the form of small houses, are available.*

search fail to locate your pet, sit quietly in the room as darkness falls, listening for any scuffling sounds which might betray its presence.

Cleaning the Cage

Each evening, when the hamster has left its nest, you should check here for any uneaten fresh food and remove it, because it is likely to turn moldy quite rapidly, endangering the hamster's health. Any particularly soiled areas of the hamster's quarters should be cleaned every day or so (a large spoon is ideal for this), and the whole cage should be swept out thoroughly once a week. Since hamsters are not especially messy, this will simply entail tipping the soiled litter into a bag, which can then be safely disposed.

Once a month, the hamster's quarters should be washed out thoroughly, using one of the special disinfectants formulated for use with small mammals. Follow the instructions for using the disinfectant carefully to avoid any health risks to your pet. Avoid using very hot water for washing the hamster's surroundings because this may distort the plastic component of the housing unit, making it almost impossible to reassemble the cage properly again afterward.

Toys and Other Equipment

Exercise is very important for hamsters, and they will appreciate having a play wheel in their quarters for this purpose. There are a number of designs available; some are free-standing, whereas others attach to the side of a cage. Select a closed wheel if possible, because these prevent any risk of the hamster slipping through the rungs and possibly injuring itself as a consequence. Unfortunately, these wheels often prove to be rather noisy when in use, and it may not always be possible to overcome the problem entirely by lubricating the axle. This is worth considering if the hamster is being housed in a bedroom. Sometimes you can adjust the wheel mechanism and thereby reduce the noise, however. These wheels are favored by pregnant females, although all hamsters will use them, sometimes "walking" 5 miles (8km) in a night!

▼ *A hamster in an exercise ball. These can provide temporary accommodation when cleaning out your hamster's quarters, but do not leave your pet in one for more than 15 minutes and keep out of direct sunlight.*

Breeding Hamsters

ONE OF THE CHARACTERISTICS OF HAMSTERS is their free-breeding nature. These rodents not only mature quickly but also have short gestation periods and produce relatively large litters of fast-growing young. As an example, the gestation period of the Syrian hamster ranks among the shortest of all mammals; it lasts just 16 days, with females producing up to 14 offspring and having as many as ten litters a year.

Nevertheless, mating needs to be carried out very carefully to avoid the risk of serious injury, especially to the male hamster which is smaller than his intended mate. It is possible to sex hamsters by viewing them from the side. The male has a step-like area above the tail, whereas that of the female is rounded in profile. Confirmation of a hamster's gender can be obtained by examining its anogenital area, with the orifices here being significantly closer together in the female.

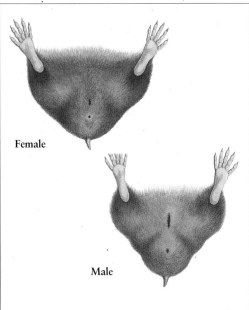

Female

Male

▲ *The anogenital orifices are further apart in the male hamster, which also has a more elongated rear and a visible scrotal swelling.*

The Honeymoon Mating System

● Remove the plastic divider from the acrylic cage and allow both the male and the female access here on their own.

● Replace the divider and place the male on one side of it and the female on the other.

● Remove the divider so mating can take place.

● Separate the hamsters afterward, removing the male back to his quarters.

The Breeding Cycle and Birth

The estrus cycle of the Syrian hamster typically lasts between four and seven days, and it will soon become apparent when a female is ready to mate, because when touched in the vicinity of the lower back, she will stand still and lift her tail to facilitate mating. Whenever mating is to take place, it is important to introduce the larger female to the male, rather than placing him in her quarters. Mating usually occurs within half an hour if the female is receptive at this stage, after which she can be transferred back to her quarters. It may be possible to leave a pair of dwarf hamsters together for longer—even sometimes through the breeding period if no quarreling is occurring.

A few days before birth occurs, the female hamster will enlarge her normal nest and should be provided with more bedding material for this purpose. It may be better to transfer her to an acrylic tank at this stage, to avoid the risk of the young hamsters becoming trapped by the cage bars once they leave the nest. The tiny young are blind and helpless at birth. It is important not to disturb the nest to check on them, however,

▲ *Young hamsters grow quickly, as shown by these youngsters which are about two weeks old. Their eyes are open, and their coloration is clearly apparent. Check they cannot slip out through the sides of the cage.*

because this is likely to upset the female which may respond by attacking or even cannibalizing her offspring. Their fur starts to emerge when they are about five days old, and soon afterward they will start to eat solid food in the nest. The eyes of the young hamsters will be open by the time they are two weeks old, and at this stage they will start venturing out of the nest. Their mother continues to suckle them until they are at least three weeks old, but once they are fully independent they should be moved to separate accommodation on their own.

Q&A

● **How long will it take for my Syrian hamster to be fully grown?**

... This process will take between four and six months, but bear in mind that hamsters can breed much earlier in life, which is partly why it is important to separate members of a litter soon after weaning.

● **I suspect all is not going well in the hamster nest. Is there any way that I can peek in here without endangering the young?**

Try rubbing the blunt end of a pencil in the nest litter, and then using this to lift up the bedding very carefully when the female hamster is out of the nest. If you need to remove a dead hamster pup, use a pair of blunt-ended forceps treated in the same way as before. Thankfully, though, problems of this type are rare.

● **I was very worried when I saw my female Syrian hamster with one of the pups in her mouth, but she appears not to have harmed it. Is this behavior usual?**

A female will pick up and retrieve her offspring in this way, usually when they have ventured out of the nest. Although it may sometimes appear quite violent, no injury is generally caused by this action. Hamsters can be quite gentle despite having sharp teeth, and sometimes use a similar light grip when toying with a finger, for example.

◀ *Hamsters are most social when they are young. They sleep in this curled-up position to help conserve their body heat.*

Illnesses in Hamsters

LIKE OTHER RODENTS, HAMSTERS CAN BE prone to digestive disturbances, which may be the result of a sudden change in diet, although in other cases, the cause is infectious. Young hamsters are especially vulnerable to the disease often described as wet tail, which gets its name because of the staining around the vent area caused by diarrhea. Affected individuals are also likely to be hunched up, show no interest in their surroundings, and lose their appetite.

Stress is suspected of being a major trigger for this illness, and newly acquired hamsters should be allowed to settle in their new quarters without excessive handling for the first week or so. Treatment is difficult, with a veterinarian relying on fluid therapy to counter the potentially fatal dehydration associated with this illness, and specific antibiotics to treat the underlying infection. If a hamster dies from this illness, its quarters must be thoroughly cleaned and disinfected before another is acquired.

▼ *Fruit and greenstuff are beneficial to your hamster's health, although too much can cause diarrhea. This should resolve itself, but cases of diarrhea in hamsters can be serious because of the resulting dehydration.*

▲ *Keep a check on the amount of water your hamster is drinking. Increased thirst is often a sign of diabetes, which is relatively common in older hamsters. You may also notice white cataracts on your pet's eyes.*

Dietary Problems

At the other extreme, hamsters can also suffer from constipation, particularly if they are provided with unsuitable bedding such as cotton, which leads to an obstruction in the intestinal tract. An affected individual will be seen straining with its back arched. Similar symptoms may occur in young hamsters that have not adapted to drinking from a bottle. It is always worth placing the tip of a bottle in a hamster's mouth and squeezing gently to express a little water for this reason. When constipation occurs, offering greenstuff may be beneficial, along with a couple of drops of olive oil given directly into the hamster's mouth through a dropper, three times a day.

On occasions, the hamster's cheek pouches can become blocked. Do not give foods such as oats, which have a sharp husk, since these can lodge in the walls of the pouch, causing an irritation. There is also the possibility of an accompanying infection. The typical signs in both cases include swelling of the affected area, saliva running out of the mouth, and a loss of appetite. Seek veterinary advice as soon as possible, because successful treatment is quite feasible.

Hamsters are also prone to dental decay, because of their diet. The amount of snacks and sweet treats should be restricted for this reason. The only effective treatment will be for your veterinarian to remove the affected tooth, which if left may lead to a painful abscess. It is also particularly important that hamsters are not fed chocolate. This is likely to be fatal for them, since it contains a chemical known as theobromine which affects the respiratory system.

Another dietary problem that can occur is a calcium deficiency induced particularly by a diet containing excessive amounts of sunflower seed. The resulting weakness in the hamster's skeletal structure means that it is then more susceptible to fractures, either from falls or from snagging its legs in an open-tread play wheel. Prevention of this problem is straightforward, with a mineral block or even a broken piece of cuttlebone as supplied to pet birds helping to compensate for any calcium deficiency in a seed-based diet.

As hamsters age, the coat becomes much thinner. This is quite usual, and there is really nothing that can be done to overcome the problem.

Q&A...

● **What is behind the rumor about hamsters coming back from the dead?**

When the temperature falls, hamsters will often respond by becoming torpid. This means that all their body processes, including their rate of breathing, become slower than normal. The hamster does not respond to external stimuli, nor does it appear to be breathing—thus giving the impression that it has died. But if transferred to warmer surroundings, the hamster reawakens from this state, appearing to have come back to life again.

● **Can you give me information about LCMV? Why is it a risk to people?**

LCMV stands for lymphocytic chorio-meningitis virus, which is a widespread infection in wild mice. Hamsters up to the age of three months old can become infected by being bitten, with the virus then appearing in their urine, feces, and saliva. Should a person come into contact with the virus, they are most likely to develop an influenza-like illness. However, it is certainly not a common problem, especially if you only have one hamster rather than a large collection.

● **Are there any other health problems to consider when owning a hamster?**

Although these rodents generally remain quite healthy, especially once established in their quarters, they are vulnerable to injuries as a result of careless handling. Falls can be fatal for them, and so it is very important to discourage children who are unaccustomed to handling hamsters to walk around holding their pet. Instead, persuade the child to sit on a sofa or chair when playing with the animal. In the event of a fall, the best course of action is to place the hamster back in its quarters—assuming it is not showing obvious signs of injury—and allow it to recover quietly here. If the hamster subsequently appears to have difficulty walking, it may have sustained a fracture and so veterinary advice must be sought as soon as possible. It may be possible to apply a splint to the break, allowing the hamster to make a good recovery in due course.

◄ *Pets such as cats should be discouraged from getting this close to your hamster's cage. Apart from the alarm this may cause the hamster, it could be injured by an inquisitive paw probing through the bars. There is also the possibility of fleas being transmitted to your hamster.*

Hamster Species and Varieties

THE NUMBER OF COLOR VARIETIES HAS EXPANDED in the Syrian hamster and in Campbell's dwarf Russian hamster, but at present they are still scarce in the Chinese hamster.

SYRIAN HAMSTER

The Syrian or Golden hamster is now bred in an ever-expanding range of colors and coat types. The natural form is technically described as a White-bellied Agouti. There is black tipping to the golden hairs on the body and distinctive black stripes present across the cheeks. The undercoat and ears are grayish.

The Dark Golden has much more pronounced black tipping on the coat, with the basic color being a much richer reddish shade. This increase in pigmentation is reflected by the ear color, which is black rather than gray, and by the outlines of black circles around the eyes. At the other extreme, the overall color intensity is reduced in the Light Golden, which has no black tips to the individual hairs. Selective breeding of Goldens has created the Sepia, which has a light tawny-beige coat and black eyes.

Whites and Creams

In the White, there are again three different color variants, each defined by its degree of pigmentation. The Albino characteristically has pink ears and eyes. The Dark-eared White (also misleadingly called the Black-eared Albino) is distinguished by the color of its ears when mature, although young have pink ears which only start to darken from the age of three months onward. Eye color is the defining feature of the Black-eyed White, with the ears again being pink.

The Cream is another popular variant. The coat of these hamsters must be entirely cream, with no white hairs in the coat. The actual shade of cream differs somewhat between individuals but, generally, a darker shade bordering on apricot is favored in these particular hamsters.

A paler, pinkish-cream body color and dark red eyes distinguish the Ruby-eyed Cream from the black-eyed form. This difference in eye coloration may only be apparent in a good light, although young hamsters of the ruby-eyed variety have lighter reddish eyes. The Red-eyed Cream can be separated from the other two cream varieties by its pinkish, rather than gray,

◀ *The Black-eyed Cream was one of the first color varieties to be bred, back in 1951. The young have much paler ears than the adults, but these become blackish as they mature.*

ears and the unmistakable red coloration of its eyes. The coat color in this variety can vary from a dark shade of cream, with an apricot tone, through to a much lighter cream.

Similar Pale-coated Varieties

Other similar, pale-colored varieties are now well established. The Yellow resembles the Black-eyed Cream, although it can be distinguished by its slightly darker yellow coloration. The Honey is similar to the Yellow, but the ears are a paler color and the eyes are red, not black.

In the Blonde, the fur is creamy-blonde in color, with ivory-white crescents on the face and matching belly fur. The eyes are red, and the muzzle usually has an orange tint.

The most brightly colored hamster variety is the Cinnamon. A rarer variant is the Cinnamon Fawn, in which the orange color is more pastel and the pale areas are a very light shade of cream. The Rust or Guinea Gold variety on the other hand is darker than the Cinnamon, displaying a more orangish-brown color on the fur and with blackish eyes.

● *Are there any genetic problems of which I need to be aware when breeding these different varieties?*

The main consideration is that male hamsters with ruby eyes, such as the Ruby-eyed Cream, are usually sterile. This therefore means that they are of no value for breeding purposes. Females of such varieties must be crossed with males that carry the ruby-eyed factor in their genetic makeup, but do not actually display this feature themselves.

● *Is it true that male Cinnamon Fawns are normally sterile, although they are pink eyed?*

Yes, this is because they have been evolved from crosses between Cinnamons and Ruby-eyed Fawns, with the sterility problem deriving from their fawn ancestry. Not surprisingly, therefore, ruby-eyed forms of the Syrian hamster are relatively scarce due to the difficulty in breeding them.

▼ *The most brightly colored of all hamster varieties is the Cinnamon, with its pure, rich, orange fur. The crescents on the face are ivory, as are the underparts. The ears are brownish.*

● Is there much difference in temperament between the different varieties of Syrian hamster?

Many breeders would argue that Creams, or colors of cream origin such as the Sable, are more docile, but much depends on how you handle and tame your hamster, as well as the age at which you obtained it.

● Do I need any special accommodation when exhibiting my hamster, or can I use its usual quarters?

You will need to invest in a special show cage. Your national hamster club will be able to give you details about the design and where such cages can be obtained. The advantage of using standardized cages is that judges will not be distracted by the hamster's surroundings. Always ensure that the cage is clean and that the paintwork is not chipped.

▲ A Black and White Angora hamster at one month old. The coat at this stage is still relatively short. This is a difficult variety to breed with balanced white and colored bands in the offspring.

▶ A Black Syrian. The first black hamsters were bred by introducing the umbrous or "sooty" gene into Black-eyed Cream bloodlines, rather than being the result of a mutation.

Grays

There are also a number of gray varieties associated with the Syrian hamster. The Dark Gray has a dark, pearl-gray coat, with its coloration being emphasized by the black guard hairs. The cheek flashes are black, as are both the ears and the eyes. Paler in color, the Light Gray can also be easily distinguished on the basis of its slate-blue, rather than slate-gray, underfur. The outer coat is buttermilk in color and heavily ticked with black, creating the impression of gray.

The Silver Gray is of a more silvery shade, as its name suggests, with black eyes and ears. The underparts are very pale, bordering on white, while the cheek flashes are blackish, thanks to the heavy ticking on the fur here. The Smoke Pearl also has pale gray fur, with a decidedly creamy tone extending right down to the roots. Unlike the Silver Gray, however, these hamsters have very dark gray, rather than black, ears.

A soft, pale shade of gray with a brownish tone characterizes the beige color variant. There is no ticking in this variety. The eyes are black, whereas the ears are a very dark shade of beige, corresponding to the color of the cheek flashes and chestband. A lack of ticking is also a feature of the Lilac, which has a warm gray undercoat.

▲ *In most cases, the long hair of the Angora is evident toward the rear of the body, with the hair elsewhere being quite short. Longer hairs can measure 1in (2.5cm) in length, but can occasionally be three times as long.*

The eyes in this variety are ruby, with the ears being pinkish gray.

Eye coloration serves to distinguish the red-eyed and black-eyed forms of the Ivory, with the ears of the red-eyed variety also being significantly paler in coloration. The basic fur color of these hamsters is grayish-cream.

Blacks

The original Black, now known as the Sable, can be distinguished by its black top coat, with ivory-gray beneath. Similar, lighter-colored circles are present around both eyes, but unfortunately the cream ancestry has led to other undesirable patches of color breaking through in the coat, often reflected by white areas on or near the chin. Breeders then combined these hamsters with the Rust, to create the Chocolate. The name of these original black hamsters was changed to the Sable in 1990 when a genuine black form of the Syrian hamster emerged.

Coat Variants

It has proved possible to improve the sheen on the coat of the Syrian hamster thanks to the emergence of the Satin mutation in 1969, which also serves to darken the color slightly. Satins should never be paired together, however, because they produce offspring with a relatively thin coat. They must always be mated with normal-coated varieties which means that, on average, about half of the resulting offspring will be satin coated.

The long-coated Angora hamster, better known as the Teddy in North America, needs regular grooming with a toothbrush to prevent matting of the coat, which is at its most profuse in the male. Angoras can be bred in any color variety, but Selfs are favored simply because markings are made less distinctive by the length of their coat.

The Rex mutation of the Syrian hamster arose in 1970. Rexes have a short, wavy coat, with their whiskers also being curled. Rex forms of any color variety can be created, as can long-coated Rexes. It is important that Rex hamsters have a dense coat—any thinning of their hair is a serious fault in this variety.

Patterned Varieties

A number of patterned varieties of the Syrian hamster have also been bred. They include the Tortoiseshell, in which the coat is a combination of cream and white mixed with another color in equal proportions. A wide range of such varieties can be created as a result. Darker, contrasting colors are often preferred.

The piebald or variegated varieties are similar to the Banded but their colored and white areas of fur occur randomly, which means there can be considerable difference in appearance between individuals. In the Spotted, the areas of white are not present in the form of blotches, but as discrete spots which should be evident over most of the body, dominating the colored areas of fur.

DWARF RUSSIAN AND CHINESE HAMSTERS

Spotted patterning is currently the best-known mutation in the Chinese hamster, although a white variety has been bred as well. The natural color of these hamsters is brown, with a dark stripe running down the center of their back, contrasting with their pale whitish underparts. Males have a prominent scrotum.

Color varieties are now much more common in dwarf Russian hamsters, especially the Campbell's form (*Phodopus sungorus campbelli*). Instantly recognizable by their small size, these hamsters display a darker stripe down their backs, offset against the pale, brown-gray fur. The underside of the body is almost whitish.

In the Argente form, this color is effectively diluted to a more sandy shade. The eyes are pink, and the back stripe appears grayish. The Albino is also popular, with the fur of these hamsters being entirely white, while the ears are pink and the eyes are red. Superficially similar in appearance is the Dilute Platinum, which is whitish but has black eyes. The darker platinum

● **Is it possible to breed Campbell's and Winter whites together successfully?**

It is possible because they are so closely related, but it is not recommended because this dilutes their unique characteristics. In addition, the fertility of their progeny tends to be lower.

● **Why is it not recommended to pair mottled Campbell's together?**

This is because of a potentially harmful gene which may affect the eyes of these hamsters, reducing their size or even resulting in some offspring being born without eyes—a condition known as anopthalmia. They should therefore be mated with other varieties. This gene is not confined to Campbell's, however—it has also been identified in the Syrian hamster.

▼ *A Cinnamon Banded Satin Syrian hamster. A band of white fur should encircle the center of the body, creating two distinct areas of color. The Satin feature imparts a greater sheen to the coat.*

form displays white ticking offset against the dark fur, so the overall effect creates a color not dissimilar to that of the precious metal from which it derives its name. Among other colors now being developed are a black variety, and the Opal—which has bluish-gray, rather than black, color in its coat. Patterned varieties of all these colors are also being developed, with such hamsters described as mottled. A glossy Satin mutation has also arisen, as in the Syrian hamster.

The closely related Winter white dwarf Russian hamster (*P. s. sungorus*) is less commonly kept. Its body shape is less rounded, and its face appears to be slightly longer, but it retains many of the features seen in Campbell's, notably the fur present on the feet and the very small tail. As its common name suggests, the Winter white dwarf Russian hamster changes significantly in appearance at the onset of winter. It molts the grayish-brown coat and is transformed to a pure-white color which provides it with excellent camouflage when snow is on the ground. Smudging tracing the line of the dark stripe down the back will still be visible, however.

The Sapphire was the first color variant to be recorded in this subspecies and arose in Britain in 1988. These hamsters display bluish-gray coloration, with markings such as the black stripe normally seen on the back being transformed to blue. The Pearl, with a white coat evenly tipped with black, is the only other mutation in these dwarf hamsters which is now well established. It is a very attractive variety.

Roborovski's dwarf Russian hamster (*Phodopus roborovskii*), originating from Mongolia, is less commonly kept, thanks partly to its more nervous nature. These hamsters have golden-brown upperparts, with no dorsal stripe down their backs, while the underparts are white. The coat has a very soft texture and is slightly longer than that of other dwarf hamsters. Because of this feature it does not appear as sleek, but this is not a sign of ill-health.

▼ *Roborovski's dwarf Russian hamster. These are small, agile rodents, which move faster than Syrian hamsters, so they can be harder to handle. No color variants have yet been recorded in this species.*

Gerbils

IT SEEMS CURIOUS THAT RODENTS FROM REMOTE PARTS OF THE world have become widely available as pets. However, as with the Syrian hamster, the popularity of the Mongolian gerbil today is the result of scientific research. The first description of these gerbils was by the French missionary Père David, who encountered the species in Mongolia in 1897 and sent specimens to the Paris Natural History Museum. Their scientific name, *Meriones unguiculatus*, means "the warrior with fingernails"—a reference to their claws, although why they were considered to be fighters is unclear, since they are docile and social. Indeed, these were the traits that led to them becoming pets.

The origins of today's strains of Mongolian gerbils can be traced to 1935, when a small number were trapped in the Amur River Valley and taken to Japan for medical research. The gerbils reproduced readily, and in 1954 a number were sent to the United States. The first specimens reached Britain ten years later. They also bred readily, and soon surplus stock passed into the hands of pet-owners, who were captivated by these rodents. Since then, an increasing number of color mutations have emerged in captive stocks, and this has led to the development of growing interest in exhibiting gerbils. Prescribed judging standards have been drawn up for the different varieties, both in terms of their coloration and markings where appropriate, as well as their physical appearance or "type."

Other species of gerbil, or jird as members of this group of rodents are also known, have also been introduced to the pet market, but none has achieved the popularity of the Mongolian gerbil. Some are significantly larger in size, a fact which must be reflected in their accommodation, and some are less social than the Mongolian gerbil and may need to be housed individually as a result.

▶ *The names "jird" and "gerbil" are both used for members of the genus* Meriones. *This is Shaw's jird, which is closely related to the Mongolian gerbil. It, too, makes an attractive and lively pet.*

Gerbil Lifestyles

THE GERBILS FORM A SUBFAMILY WITHIN THE myomorph (or mouselike) family of the rodent order. There are just over 80 different species, found in parts of the Middle East, Africa, and Asia. They inhabit relatively arid countryside, with some species occurring in desert areas.

Mongolian gerbils, like other related species, burrow to escape the blazing heat of summer as well as the frozen winters which are likely to be encountered in their habitat. They are highly social, living in family groups. Their burrows, typically extending 18in (46cm) or so under ground, consist of a central tunnel with chambers running off it and include food stores to sustain them when the ground is covered in snow.

Body Adaptations

When out of the burrow, the gerbils' agouti coloration helps them blend in with the sandy background of their native habitat. The underparts, which are white, reflect the heat from the ground and thus help to reduce their body temperature.

▶ *Gerbils are adapted for survival in the arid, often hot environment of the desert. Their bodies display a range of features that help them cope with life in their habitat.*

Q & A ...

● *Are gerbils from some regions more social than those from others?*

Some correlation exists, with those found in semi-arid areas, such as the Mongolian gerbil, being more social than those found in true desert surroundings. This may be a reflection of the availability of food, which is likely to be scarcer in a desert region.

● *Which gerbils make the best pets?*

Because of their more social natures, Mongolian gerbils probably make the best pets. Their size also makes them easier to handle and house than some related species such as jirds and jerboas. In recent years, interest in the Mongolian gerbil has increased due to the development of new color varieties and their exhibition potential.

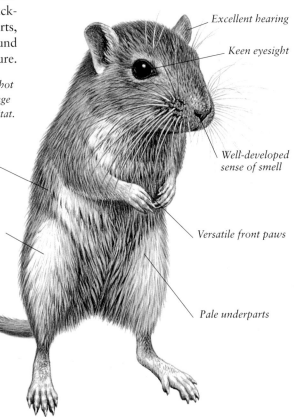

Excellent hearing

Keen eyesight

Well-developed sense of smell

Versatile front paws

Pale underparts

Agouti upperparts

Fragile tail tip

Powerful hind limbs

Long counterbalancing tail

Fact File

Name:	Mongolian Gerbil
Scientific name:	*Meriones unguiculatus*
Weight:	2.5–3.5oz (70–100g), with males usually heavier than females.
Compatibility:	Highly social, and so should be kept in groups comprised of individuals of the same sex if breeding is not required.
Appeal:	Lively, friendly, and odor-free. Relatively low maintenance requirements.
Diet:	Provide a gerbil food seed mix, available from a pet store, or possibly a complete, pelletized diet. Avoid offering sunflower seed in large quantities.
Health problems:	Can be at risk from epileptic seizures. The tip of the tail can be damaged very easily.
Breeding tips:	Separate the male when a litter is due, because females can mate successfully again almost immediately after giving birth.
Pregnancy:	24 days
Typical litter size:	4–6 young
Weaning:	21–25 days
Lifespan:	4–5 years

The furred tail, which can be over 4in (10cm) in length, helps provide a counterbalance when the gerbil jumps. It ends in a distinctive darker tip. This acts as a decoy for would-be predators, which attack this part of the body. Although the tail may be damaged under these circumstances—or even shed, since it is very fragile—it allows the gerbil to escape more or less intact. Unfortunately, unlike the situation with some lizards, the missing part of the tail will not subsequently regrow, although the skin may heal.

The gerbils' fore legs are much shorter than their hind legs, enabling them to sit up and use their front paws like hands for holding food. This position also gives them a good view of potential danger. When a possible threat is detected, a warning may be given by one member of the group using its hind legs to drum on the ground. The hind legs also enable gerbils to jump great distances. Gerbils have large eyes and a keen sense of vision. Their hearing is also acute, particularly in the case of desert-dwelling species. This is achieved by an enlargement of the chambers in the ears known as the tympanic bullae. As a result, gerbils can even detect the wingbeats of approaching avian predators like owls, allowing them to escape to their burrows.

Gerbils rely mainly on their sense of smell to recognize members of the family group. Scent from a gland located on the underside of the body is transferred to the fur and thence to others in the group by direct contact.

Occurring in areas where access to water is limited, gerbils have adapted by conserving as much water in their bodies as possible. Their kidneys are extremely efficient at concentrating their urinary output, to the extent that these rodents produce very little urine. They may drink drops of condensation which form in their burrows overnight, as well as water obtained from plant material which features in their diet.

Prolific Breeders

Gerbils have a high rate of reproduction. Studies of wild Mongolian gerbils have revealed that females may rear three litters in succession through the year, each of which may consist of up to 12 youngsters. These offspring remain within the family group, even once they are independent. At maturity, it appears that females will leave the group briefly to mate with other males, however, which serves to prevent in-breeding.

▼ *As domestication has occurred, an increasing number of color variants (like this blue variety) have emerged in captive stocks. Many of these are now being bred for exhibition purposes, as well as making popular pets.*

Housing for Gerbils

THE SOCIABLE NATURE OF MONGOLIAN GERBILS means that these lively rodents should not be kept on their own, and this in turn affects the size of enclosure they require. Their desire to dig and tunnel also means that they cannot be kept satisfactorily in most wire-topped cages, because their shallow bases allow the cage lining to spill out onto surrounding furniture. Gerbils are currently poorly catered to in terms of commercially available housing, especially since hamster cages are generally too small and insufficiently deep to accommodate them satisfactorily.

Most gerbil enthusiasts therefore use a converted aquarium to house their pets, covering the top with a secure mesh lid—which may need to be made specially for this purpose. As a general guide, a standard aquarium measuring 18in (46cm) in length by 12in (30cm) in width and height will accommodate a pair satisfactorily. The lid should consist of good-quality wire mesh stapled to a frame made from timber 1in (2.5cm) square. The wire mesh will need to be attached using special netting staples, being placed every

0.5in (12mm) around the timber frame. The frame should fit neatly over the sides of the tank. It is important not to skimp on the use of these staples, especially if you have a cat, because they will give your gerbils more security and support

▼ *The gerbils' quarters should be fitted with a secure lid to prevent them from leaping out or from cats getting in. You may need to make a lid yourself by stapling wire mesh to a wooden frame, as described in the text.*

◀ *A typical gerbil setup in a converted fish tank. Note the hood, which contains a sliding panel and fits over the sides of the tank. The water bottle is fixed securely at a convenient height, and there are plenty of hiding places for the gerbils to explore.*

▲ *Gerbils are inquisitive creatures and should be provided with a selection of retreats in their quarters. Although you can use items such as cardboard tubes, more attractive and durable options can be purchased.*

the cat's weight should it decide to climb on top of their quarters. Extra strength will also be provided by folding the mesh over the sides of the frame and attaching it here, rather than leaving it flush with the top of the timber.

Lining the Cage

A relatively deep lining of wood shavings is required in the gerbils' quarters, to allow them to burrow. Some breeders use peat-based substrates for their gerbils, but these are not ideal, partly because the peat tends to stain their fur. In addition, if the peat is moistened to stop it from becoming dusty, the moisture can be harmful to the gerbils.

You can include some items in the gerbil's quarters to assist their burrowing activities. Bedding can be provided in a corner of a cage, with hay being favored for this purpose. The gerbils may nibble this into pieces of suitable length to form their nest, and they may also eat some to supplement the fiber intake of their diet. It is very important only to provide top-quality hay. The hay should not be damp or musty, nor should it contain thistles, which have prickly leaves.

Q&A ...

● **What housing should I choose for other species of gerbil?**

They can be kept in a similar setup to that used for Mongolian gerbils, although the aquarium should be larger, and also taller (18in/46cm high), to minimize the risk of them jumping out when the hood is lifted off.

● **Should I choose a glass or acrylic aquarium?**

Glass aquaria tend to be much more readily available at present, but they are quite heavy—especially the larger sizes—and it may require two people to lift one of these units safely. Acrylic tanks are much lighter, but they will still break if dropped and can scratch easily.

● **Will a larger rat cage suffice for a pair of Mongolian gerbils?**

Commercial breeders often use laboratory-type rat cages for this purpose, because the bases are much deeper than those of other cages. Unfortunately, their design is not especially attractive and does not allow you to see the gerbils clearly. Standard pet rat cages may be suitable although, as with hamster cages, their shallow base is often a major drawback.

Cage Furnishings

Listed below are the main items that should be included in your gerbil's cage.

Floor covering Wood shavings (left) to a depth of at least 2in (5cm) are recommended.

Retreats Flower pots broken in half and cardboard tubes from the center of kitchen towels are ideal, being partly buried in the floor covering.

Items for gnawing Special chewing blocks can be bought from pet stores, or fresh twigs can be cut from trees such as apple.

Bedding Good-quality, dust-free hay is favored. Safe, paper hamster bedding can also be used for nesting purposes.

Food and water containers Earthenware or stainless steel bowls are recommended for food. Water should be supplied from a water bottle.

Toys Little is required in the way of toys, since gerbils keep each other amused. Exercise wheels must be of the closed-tread variety.

Feeding Gerbils

LIKE MANY OTHER SMALL RODENTS FROM ARID parts of the world, gerbils subsist in the wild on a variety of seeds and other plant matter, with a few species also preying on insects. Feeding pet gerbils is therefore very straightforward, using one of the commercially available diets. These contain a variety of ingredients but should be based largely on cereals rather than oil seeds. Wheat, barley, and crushed oats all figure prominently in most gerbils' diets, but for variety you can add some Budgerigar seed containing millets and plain canary seed.

Flaked maize (which resembles cornflakes) is present in some mixes, as are flaked peas. Whole maize may also be included but is a very hard seed in its dry form, making it difficult for a gerbil to eat easily. A better alternative is kibbled or

▼ Gerbils will thrive on a fairly basic diet of various seeds, which they hold in their front paws to crack them and extract the kernel within. A constant supply of fresh drinking water should also be provided.

cracked maize, which is broken into pieces. Although gerbils enjoy sunflower seeds, these should only be offered sparingly because of their high oil content. Not only can an excess lead to obesity but it may also trigger skin ailments. This caution also applies to peanuts, which should not comprise more than 5 percent of the mix.

It is also important to provide gerbils with a choice of fresh foods on a regular basis. Dandelion leaves and flowers are appreciated by many gerbils and so are vegetables such as carrots (cut into small pieces), cabbage, and red lettuce. Always wash and, where necessary, peel the items, removing anything left uneaten at the end of the day. Try to provide just sufficient to meet your pets' needs, rather than giving them large quantities which they will not eat.

Complete diets for gerbils are now available, and these can be offered straight from the packet. Complete diets are carefully formulated to meet all the gerbil's nutritional requirements, and it is not recommended to use a vitamin and

mineral supplement with them because of the risk of overdosing. When a supplement is necessary, it may be better to use a powdered supplement which will adhere to fresh food rather than one which is administered through the drinking water, because gerbils drink relatively little. It is important to follow the dosage instructions carefully, to prevent giving excessive amounts which will be harmful in the longer term.

Gerbils have powerful teeth, and it is important to provide their food in earthenware bowls which they will not be able to destroy. These are available in various sizes. Use separate bowls for dry and fresh food.

Water Requirements

Drinking water should be provided in a bottle, to ensure that it does not become contaminated with bedding or food. Some acrylic cages have hoods which incorporate a screw-in water bottle. If your cage does not have such an arrangement, you will need to fix a drinking bottle to the mesh on the top of the cage with some wire.

It is very important that the bottle is suspended at a convenient height so that the gerbils can sit up comfortably and drink from it with no risk of it falling onto them, since this could prove fatal. Always fill the bottle to the brim, however, to create an adequate seal to prevent leaking. Also, keep the spout of the bottle away from contact with the bedding, to ensure water will not be drawn out by capillary action and soak the shavings. Gerbils only drink a small amount of water each day— usually no more than 0.3fl oz (10ml).

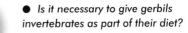

● **Is it necessary to give gerbils invertebrates as part of their diet?**

Some gerbils will eat insects, but they are not truly essential. Mealworms, widely sold by many pet stores for reptiles and various birds, can be offered in very small numbers on a daily basis. Try to encourage your pet to take them by hand, otherwise they may disappear into the bedding and emerge as meal beetles in due course.

● **How long can I keep gerbil pellets before they go stale?**

Choose pellets with the longest shelflife printed on the packet, and do not use them beyond the recommended date due to the risk of the vitamin content deteriorating after this time.

● **Do gerbils store food like hamsters?**

This behavior is not seen in the Mongolian gerbil or in other species commonly kept as pets, although it has sometimes been recorded from the wild.

● **I've heard it is beneficial to feed dog biscuits to gerbils occasionally. Is this true?**

Dog biscuits are often recommended for gerbils, mainly as a means of keeping their incisor teeth in trim. Even so, it is a good idea to break a biscuit of this type into pieces of a reasonable size, so that the gerbils can pick them up easily.

▼ *Other items can be offered to gerbils to provide variety in their diet and keep their teeth in trim. Mineral blocks (left) supplement the intake of vital nutrients such as calcium that may be lacking in seeds. Wood chews (below) are good for gnawing. Treats (below left) should be offered only occasionally.*

Routine Care of Gerbils

GERBILS ARE FRIENDLY CREATURES, BUT THEY are not as keen as some small animals on being picked up. They must also be handled with care, because the tip of the tail is especially delicate and may be shed easily. Do not try to pick up an unfamiliar gerbil simply by wrapping your hands around its body. You may end up being bitten using this approach, unless it is very tame. Young gerbils will soon become used to being handled, but these animals can collapse or suffer a fit if handled too much. If this happens, return the gerbil to its cage to recover.

▼ *Gerbils will soon become tame enough to sit on your open hand, especially if they are accustomed to being handled from an early age (below). Their inquisitive and active nature means that they will often run up your arm and rest on your shoulder (bottom). Only handle one gerbil at a time, so you can prevent escapes.*

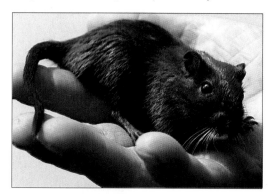

Cage Cleaning

One of the great advantages of gerbils as household pets is that they are very clean. There is also no unpleasant odor associated with them. They produce only small amounts of urine, and so their quarters need not be cleaned as frequently as those of pet mice, for example. Simply clean out obviously soiled areas as required, and strip down their quarters every two or three weeks on average if there are no young in the nest. It will be useful to have a spare acrylic container in which the gerbils can be housed to ensure that they do not escape during this period.

Dealing with Escapes

Should a gerbil manage to escape into the room, first close the door to ensure that it cannot move further afield. You can then concentrate your efforts on catching the gerbil. If it is very tame,

How to Handle a Gerbil

● Begin by offering titbits from your hand.

● After several days, try stroking the animal gently as it feeds.

● Restrain the gerbil by holding the base of its tail. This which will encourage it to lie on all fours.

● Now gently scoop up the rodent by placing your hand under its body, taking care not to allow it to dangle in the air.

● If the gerbil runs up your arm, gently transfer it back to your hand.

● Gently stroke the gerbil once it is resting in your hand. You may also want to offer it a titbit at this stage.

● Do not walk around holding a gerbil. Sit with your hand over a table, or alternatively a chair, so that if the gerbil falls for any reason, it is unlikely to be injured and will be less likely to escape.

you may be able to simply recapture it with your hand—but do not make a sudden grab at the animal, which might alarm or injure it. If this fails, you may need to either use a net, or encourage the gerbil to run into a container (such as bucket placed on its side) baited with food. Once the gerbil has ventured in, gently lift the bucket up so that the animal is trapped inside.

Large Collections

There may come a time when you want to expand your interest in gerbils and enlarge your collection. Most serious breeders and exhibitors house their stock in outbuildings, some of which are specially built and others which are in the form of a converted shed. Just as in the home, it is important that the gerbils are not placed within the direct rays of the sun, because they can rapidly succumb to heatstroke under these circumstances. The building should nevertheless be designed so that it is well lit in order that the occupants can be seen easily.

● *How often do I need to feed my gerbils?*

Gerbils normally require feeding once a day, and it is best to do this at a regular time, encouraging them also to take titbits from the hand as they feed. The drinking water should also be changed on a daily basis.

● *Should I get out both of my young gerbils at the same time?*

No, this is not advisable. Trying to keep control of one lively gerbil can be quite demanding, but if both decide to run off at the same time it may be very difficult to catch them before they go into hiding.

● *How should I heat an outbuilding during winter?*

Use a greenhouse-type convector heater in the form of a sealed tube, positioned fairly close to the floor. The thermostat should be set to provide a minimum heat output of about 50°F (10°C).

▼ *A shed can be adapted to provide accommodation for large collections of gerbils—or indeed many other small animals.*

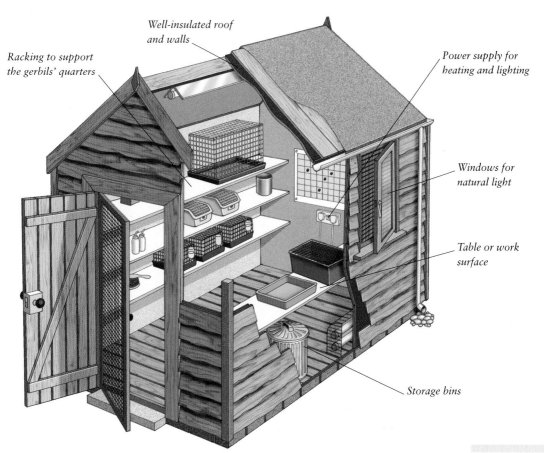

Well-insulated roof and walls

Racking to support the gerbils' quarters

Power supply for heating and lighting

Windows for natural light

Table or work surface

Storage bins

Breeding Gerbils

GERBILS ATTAIN SEXUAL MATURITY QUITE rapidly—by nine weeks of age—even though it will be another three weeks or so before they are fully grown. It is therefore very important to introduce them together before this age, not just for breeding purposes but also to ensure that gerbils of the same sex do not quarrel. This means buying your gerbils when they are between six and eight weeks old.

You can usually persuade older animals to accept each other by first introducing them on neutral territory which does not carry either animal's scent. However, with each new gerbil this task is more difficult, with a correspondingly increased risk of fighting.

Sexing these rodents is not especially difficult, particularly in the case of the Mongolian gerbil, since the male is noticeably larger when mature than the female. Before this time, however, as with other gerbil species, an examination of the vent area will be necessary to separate the sexes with certainty. Young male gerbils have a dark colored area at the base of the tail, which is the outline of the scrotal sac. As the gerbil grows older, the testes descend here from inside the abdomen, causing the area to swell.

Q&A...

● *My female gerbil has died, and I am left with two youngsters. Can I foster them?*

It is possible if you have another female with a litter born at the same stage, providing the young are under a week old. Any later, and they are likely to be rejected. You must first disguise the orphans' scent by rubbing them gently but thoroughly with bedding from the foster parent's quarters, before placing them in the nest alongside her young.

● *Should I give my female gerbil milk to drink now she has given birth?*

No, providing that she is receiving an adequate diet, this is not necessary and could cause a digestive upset because she will not be accustomed to it.

● *What sort of records should I keep in my gerbil stud?*

You need both a stock register and individual breeding cards for each pair. You should keep all information about the adult stock in your stock register, while noting pairings, dates of birth, and the number and color of the progeny on the breeding cards for each pair. This can then be transferred to your stock register, where other information such as show wins can also be recorded.

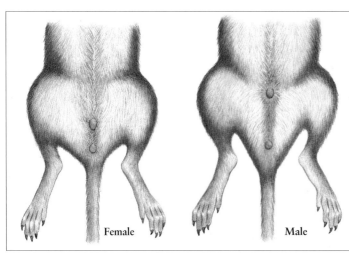

Female   Male

◀ *It is quite easy to distinguish between the sexes in gerbils. The distance between the anus and the vaginal opening in the female is very much shorter than the distance between the anus and penis in the male. Overall, males are larger than females.*

Introducing a Pair for Mating

Allowing Mongolian gerbils to grow up together before mating gives the best hope of ensuring breeding success, but there are often times in a breeding program where the aim is to use different partners. The gerbils should then be removed from their usual quarters and introduced on neutral territory, preferably in the evening when mating normally takes place. The first few moments of this stage are critical. If they cautiously sniff and then carry on exploring their new quarters, this is a good sign. However, if they launch into a fight, they will have to be separated without delay.

If they fight, place a piece of thin plywood between them, rather than trying to separate them by hand—for unless you are wearing stout gloves, you are likely to end up being badly bitten. Reintroducing the gerbils a few days later may lead to a better outcome, because females come into heat at intervals of four days throughout the year. If a pair fails to accept each other after several attempts, however, try brushing talcum powder into their coats. This will disguise their scent. When the female is ready to accept the male's advances, she will stand still so that mating can take place. Mating usually occurs several times in quick succession.

Pregnancy and Birth

It is only toward the end of the gestation period that the female displays outward signs of being pregnant. By this stage, an increase in the size of her abdomen becomes apparent. She will give birth to her litter approximately 24 days after mating occurred. A covering of fur starts to develop on the young gerbils' bodies when they are about six days old. After another ten days, their eyes open and they start to move around.

This is also the time when the young gerbils begin taking solid food by themselves and, although they are basically weaned by three weeks old, most breeders wait a further week before taking the young away from their parents. A female gerbil can mate successfully again within hours of giving birth. If you do not want her to have another litter, therefore, the female must be separated from the male at this stage.

▼ *This mother gerbil is instinctively carrying one of her young in her mouth, back to the safety of the nest. Gerbils are helpless at birth, but they develop rapidly.*

Illnesses in Gerbils

As with other rodents, gerbils can suffer from dietary-induced diarrhea if their diet is suddenly changed. There may also be more sinister causes of diarrhea, such as Tyzzer's disease, which results from an infection by the bacterium *Bacillus piliformis*. Tyzzer's disease can cause widespread mortality, particularly among the younger animals in a colony. This infection is usually brought into a collection via an animal already carrying the infection in a subclinical form, and then it spreads via the animal's droppings to other members of the group.

Gerbils suffering from diarrhea will appear hunched up and lose their appetite. Treatment

depends on identifying the likely cause of the problem, with a veterinarian often being able to assist by giving fluid therapy to prevent dehydration and antibiotics to counter an infection.

Fits
Mongolian gerbils are also especially susceptible to epilepsy. Seizures can afflict young gerbils from the age of two months onward and become most frequent when they are six months old. Repeated, prolonged handling can trigger an epileptic fit, and it has been suggested that this may be a means of deterring predators, which then leave the convulsing gerbil on the ground. The rodent will normally recover uneventfully if left quietly. Studies suggest that this problem may be linked with particular strains, with inbreeding of closely related animals worsening the situation in their offspring.

Other Common Problems
Another problem which may have genetic origins is the the high incidence of tumors within the female's reproductive tract. These usually

◀ *Dental problems are relatively common in gerbils, as in all rodents. Here a veterinarian is carrying out an examination of the incisors at the front of the mouth.*

develop in individuals approaching the end of their reproductive life, around two years of age.

Other health problems associated with old age in gerbils are diabetes mellitus, to which obese gerbils are particularly vulnerable, and progressive kidney failure. The signs in both cases are similar at first, with an affected gerbil starting to drink much more than usual. There is also accompanying weight loss. Euthanasia will ultimately be needed to prevent suffering.

Gerbils are also at risk of picking up respiratory infections such as common colds from humans. Rather than the virus itself, it is an associated streptococcal bacterium that represents the danger to them. The cold can spread from an infected gerbil to others in the colony, with similar symptoms being apparent. In most cases, they will show signs of recovery in a few days, although they are vulnerable to blocked noses. A decongestant ointment, smeared on paper towelling and suspended out of the gerbils' reach inside their quarters, may help in such cases.

Physical Injuries

Injuries from fighting are rare among established members of a colony but, if they do occur, the weaker gerbil will need to be transferred to separate accommodation. Dab any obvious injury with an antiseptic cream to minimize the risk of an infection developing. Fighting in a group is most common when there is overcrowding, and so it may be necessary to divide the group up.

Out of their quarters, gerbils may sometimes sustain a fracture of the leg as the result of a fall, although this can also be the result of providing an unsuitable play wheel in their accommodation. High levels of sunflower seed—in excess of 10 percent of the food mix—will increase the likelihood of fractures, since they will result in a subclinical calcium deficiency. Simple bone fractures can be fixed by your veterinarian, who will apply a splint around the limb. The fracture should then heal rapidly. The dressing must be kept on the leg for two weeks.

▶ *Gerbils can sometimes suffer injuries in their cages. Play wheels with open treads can be particularly dangerous, because a gerbil can trap its legs or tail in them. A totally closed design is safest.*

Q&A...

● *I've lost a number of my gerbils with Tyzzer's disease. What can I do to prevent further outbreaks?*

Recurrences are not uncommon, partly because the bacterium can survive in the gerbil's quarters for up to a year and forms spores which are resistant to many disinfectants. The best way of trying to eliminate the infection is to wash and then soak the gerbil's housing and food bowls thoroughly in a strong solution of bleach, to kill off any spores before they cause harm.

● *My gerbil has a reddish discharge around its eyes, but I can't see any actual injury. What should I do?*

The cause is likely to be stress, which may be the result of overcrowding or possibly an irritation of the eyes caused by unsuitable bedding, causing the eyes to "weep." Gerbils actually produce red tears, due to the presence of a pigment in them known as porphyrin, and this produces the red color around the eyes. In severe cases the excess tears will cause a sore nose, too. Seek advice from your veterinarian.

● *The tip of my gerbil's tail seems to have been injured. What should I do?*

You can try dabbing the affected tip with some antiseptic ointment, but usually, if most of the skin here is lost, the tip will die back and ultimately sloughs off, leaving the gerbil with a slightly shorter tail than before.

Gerbil Species and Varieties

THE MONGOLIAN GERBIL IS BY FAR THE MOST commonly kept species, and it is now being bred in an ever-expanding range of color varieties. These can be divided into four categories. First, there are gerbils which have white spots or patches—often described as marked. Then there is the Self group, comprised of gerbils which have matching fur over their entire bodies. The third group, the Non-self varieties, have a different color, usually white, on their underparts. Finally, the Colorpoint category is the most recent grouping to emerge, with such gerbils having body extremities which are darker in color than the rest of their bodies, resembling cat breeds such as the Siamese in this respect.

The natural color of the Mongolian gerbil is agouti—being yellowish-brown or reddish-brown, offset with contrasting black bands of ticking running down the individual hairs. This creates a grayish-brown color, with the belly fur being white. Such individuals are now often described as Golden Agoutis, to distinguish them from other agouti variants which have been developed.

MARKED VARIETIES

The first mutation recorded in the Mongolian gerbil was the White Spot. It emerged during the late 1960s in Canada. Such individuals have white spots of fur—ideally three in total present

● *I want to breed White Spot gerbils for exhibition purposes, but cannot seem to standardize their patterning. Any suggestions?*

This is almost impossible to achieve and, as a result, breeding this variety can be frustrating. Even well-marked adults may not have similar offspring, and the Golden Agouti seems the least predictable of all. Ideally, you should aim for large, round, even-sized spots, which are unbroken by traces of colored hair.

● *I have five pairs of dove-colored gerbils but none has ever produced a litter consisting only of young of this color. Why is this?*

The Dove is a color which does not breed true, so you therefore usually end up with litters comprised of dove, lilac, and pink-eyed white offspring. Since the combination of the genes is random, there is a slight possibility that you could occasionally end up with all dove offspring, but this cannot be guaranteed.

▼ *A Black Patched Mongolian gerbil. The extent of the white markings serve to distinguish this variety from the White Spot. It has proved possible to introduce this characteristic from the Golden Agouti to other varieties.*

▶ *The Lilac has become a popular color variety. These gerbils have distinctive bluish-gray coats with a rosy hue, and pink eyes. They were derived from Black and Argente Golden gerbils.*

on the nose, forehead, and the back of the neck—in amongst their colored fur. The feet should also be white in a well-marked specimen, as should the tip of the tail. Patched gerbils can be distinguished by the larger areas of white on the body.

SELF VARIETIES

The Pink-eyed White was the first of the Self varieties to be created, although it is not a pure white. Such gerbils may have odd dark hairs on their tails. They represent a dilute form of the Dark-tailed white. It is actually equivalent to the Himalayan pattern seen in rabbits and other small rodents, but in this case only the hair on the tail is affected. These gerbils appear white at birth, but develop their dark fur from about ten weeks onward.

The Ruby-eyed White is a more recent creation, bred from the Gray Agouti and the Lilac—a dilute form of the Black. It closely resembles the Pink-eyed White but can be distinguished by its deeper eye coloration.

Dilution of the Lilac's coloration has been achieved by crossings between gerbils of this color and Pink-eyed Whites. This in turn has led to the creation of the Dove, which resembles the Lilac but is a significantly lighter shade of gray, with pink eyes. The Sapphire is the most recent addition to these color variants, being of an intermediate shade between the Dove and the Lilac, with a bluish hue to its fur and ruby-colored eyes.

▶ *The Argente Golden is known under a variety of names, including both Golden and Cinnamon, although the most accurate description of these particular gerbils is White-bellied Golden.*

The Black is another member of the Self group, which first appeared in a litter of Mongolian gerbils born in Texas. These gerbils should have shiny black coats, which changes to matt on their underparts. Occasional white markings are seen in some individuals and are regarded as a serious show fault. The eyes, as well as the claws, are also black.

The Argente Golden is an attractive, warm, golden shade, having no hint of darker markings on its upperparts, with the underparts of the body being white. The eyes are pink, and this lack of pigmentation is also apparent on the ears, which are also pink.

NON-SELF VARIETIES

Not all color forms of the Mongolian gerbil have attracted obvious interest at the outset, as typified by the case of the Gray Agouti, also sometimes known as the Chinchilla. Unfortunately, the original example died without breeding, but the color re-emerged in laboratory stock in 1980. These gerbils were then crossed with Pink-eyed White stock, yielding Golden Agouti offspring, which in turn, when mated together, produced further examples of the Gray Agouti. With the golden coloration absent from their coats, they are basically white in color with black ticking.

While agouti gerbils always have ticking present on their coats, this feature develops later in the Dark-eyed Honey or Algerian color form. The young of this variety have a yellow-colored coat, with dark extremities persisting until the animals are roughly two months old. Their appearance is then transformed by gray ticking, with the belly remaining white. The eyes are black, as are the nails.

Foxes

In Germany, breeders have successfully combined the Silver Agouti and Dark-eyed Honey stock to create the variety now known as the Polar Fox. White coloration replaces the yellow associated with the Dark-eyed Honey in this case. Several other color variants feature within the fox grouping. The Yellow Fox looks rather like the Dark-eyed Honey but can be identified at a glance by the ruby, instead of black, color of its eyes. It has also been called the Ruby-eyed Honey and the Red-eyed Algerian Fox. The Blue Fox or Silver Nutmeg resembles the Polar Fox, but has silvery-blue, rather than black, ticking over its entire body.

The variety sometimes known as the Red Fox is very similar to the Argente Golden, except that it is a Self variant, lacking the white underparts, and generally of a more orange than golden shade. It is also referred to as the Argente Nutmeg. There is also a separate nutmeg variant, which is golden at first, and then starts to develop dark ticking by about eight weeks of

◄ *A Gray Agouti. The first recorded gerbil of this color was spotted by an enthusiast in a London, England, pet store, where its uniqueness had not been previously recognized. The individual went on to win top awards.*

▼ *Consistency of color is not a feature associated with the Dark-eyed Honey, since their color changes with age. At first, they are quite brightly colored, but ticking appears in the coat when they are about two months old.*

age. This is a Self form, ideally displaying a reddish, rather than a yellowish-brown, fur color over its entire body.

Schimmels

The Schimmel is another new variant, which initially resembles the Dark-eyed Honey. These gerbils lose the golden shade in their coats as they become mature at nine weeks old, and subsequently they are predominantly white in color, with orange to tan ticking present over their bodies. The eyes are black, although there is now also a red-eyed strain of the Schimmel as well.

The Silver Schimmel lacks the golden shade in its coat, which is replaced by white, and its overall body color is a deep shade of slate. The Champagne is the name given to the distinctive spotted form of the Schimmel. Young gerbils in this case have an orange coat, broken by white spots, which fades significantly in color as they mature, so they almost look completely white as adults. The Cream or Ivory Cream is another pale variety. The upperparts are a pale shade of cream, without any ticking, offset against ruby-colored eyes and white underparts. An even paler, light ivory-cream form exists, distinguishable on the basis of its very pale, light gray color.

COLORPOINTS

A whole new category has been created within the color range of the Mongolian gerbil by the emergence of the pointed varieties. These display darker points, compared with their body color. The Siamese, named after the cat breed, is one of the most distinctive forms. It has a cream-colored body and brown fur covering the tail, legs, ears, and nose. Mirroring the situation existing in the cat world, the Burmese forms of the gerbil have a darker body coloration than the Siamese, so the contrast with the points is less marked. Tonkinese gerbils are of an intermediate shade between these two extremes.

Q&A

● *How can I tell a Colorpoint Slate and a Burmese apart?*

... When compared, the Colorpoint Slate is of a slightly grayer shade, with blackish points. Bear in mind, though, that there is also a paler version of this variety, so do not be misled into confusing the Light Colorpoint Slate with the darker form.

● *What about the ruby-eyed forms of these varieties?*

They are considered to be visually indistinguishable, along with the Ruby-eyed Siamese. Each has a pure white body color, ruby eyes, and pink nails, but it can be possible to determine their identity on the basis of the color of their offspring.

▼ *The Colorpoint gerbil grouping is still being developed at present, offering considerable potential for breeders. Since these gerbils are still quite scarce, standardization is less apparent than in more established varieties. Undesirable markings may therefore be seen in some cases.*

Gerbil Species and Varieties

OTHER GERBIL SPECIES

A number of other gerbils and similar rodents are kept as pets, although they tend to be favored more by specialist breeders. Stocks of most of these animals are derived from either zoological collections or laboratories.

Jirds

Shaw's jird (*Meriones shawi*) is a close relative of the Mongolian gerbil, but occurs much further west, in the arid areas of North Africa and Egypt. Their coloration is similar, too. Pairs must be introduced on neutral territory for mating purposes, with up to five young then being born after an interval of 25 days.

Other Gerbils

The same requirements for mating apply to the Jerusalem gerbil (*M. crassus*), which is nearly twice the size of its Mongolian relative, being one of the largest members of the genus. These gerbils must also be kept individually and, since they show a greater tendency to bite than other species, they need to be handled with more care.

The small Pallid gerbil (*Gerbillus perpallidus*) originates from the same part of the world as Shaw's jird. It has identical requirements to the Mongolian gerbil, and is equally social by nature. In terms of coloration, the upperparts of the Pallid gerbil are of a more golden color, with the white from the underparts extending up to, and encircling, the eyes. The ears are relatively large, and the black eyes appear very prominent. The Egyptian gerbil (*G. gerbillus*) is another member of this genus which is sometimes available. It, too, has only a sparse covering of fur on the tail with no tuft at the tip, and a redder coat than the Pallid gerbil. Egyptian gerbils can become very tame, especially if obtained young.

One of the most bizarre of all gerbils is the Fat-tailed or Duprasi's gerbil (*Pachyuromys duprasi*), which originates from the northern area of the Sahara Desert in Africa. It is their broad, pink, hairless tail which immediately attracts attention. This actually has an important role to play in ensuring their survival in the harsh environment where they occur, providing a store of fat which can be metabolized into

▼ *Shaw's jird is slightly larger than the Mongolian gerbil. Females of this species are very aggressive, and they cannot be housed safely in groups, unlike their Mongolian relatives—although their basic care is similar.*

energy and water if required. The coat is longer and less sleek than that of other species, with their body profile being more rounded.

As with many other desert rodents, Fat-tailed gerbils are solitary by nature, and need to be accommodated individually. They are less active than other gerbils, sleeping for longer periods and tending to be nocturnal. Mating should take place on neutral territory, and must be supervised to prevent fighting. Usually four youngsters are born after a period of 19 days. They should then be transferred to separate housing once they are fully weaned, by four weeks old.

Jerboas

Jerboas are closely related to gerbils, with a body averaging about 4in (10cm) in length. They also originate from desert areas, with a distribution extending from parts of northern Africa eastward to China. They are sometimes offered as pets. Jerboas can be quite nervous and respond to danger by using their very powerful hind legs to jump, covering distances of up to 10ft (3m) in a single bound—which makes them very difficult to catch should one escape into a room. They are therefore rodents to look at, rather than handle on a regular basis. Breeding is most likely during the spring and early summer, with pregnancy lasting for nearly 40 days. The young are then independent six weeks later.

▲ *A Greater Egyptian jerboa. Jerboas' requirements are more specialized than those of the Mongolian gerbil. A converted aquarium will make suitable housing for a jerboa, but beware escape bids when lifting off the lid.*

● *I would like to acquire some Fat-tailed gerbils, but the local pet store can't help me. What can I do?*

Start by contacting your national gerbil society, and ask them if they know of any breeders who have them. Although these more unusual species are not generally seen at shows, they are to be found with enthusiasts. Looking through the advertizement columns of some of the pet-keeping magazines may also be useful, as can a search on the Internet.

● *Is it possible to keep jerboas in an outdoor enclosure?*

No. This is partly because they need to be kept warm, but also because—as with gerbils—they will dig burrows and so could easily escape from this type of environment, by tunneling their way out.

● *Can I house my Jerusalem gerbils in the same way as Mongolian gerbils?*

Jerusalem gerbils are larger than other species and can be more destructive toward a plastic-bottomed cage. It is advisable, therefore, to accommodate them in a converted, covered, glass aquarium. This is likely to prove more spacious for them, too.

Mice and Rats

TODAY'S DOMESTICATED MICE AND RATS ARE FAR REMOVED FROM their wild relatives, having been selectively bred over many hundreds of generations. The start of the domestication process dates back to the 1800s, when rats in particular were in danger of overrunning the streets of Britain's rapidly expanding cities, threatening to cause epidemics of disease. Large numbers of rat-catchers were employed to curb this menace, and they supplemented their incomes by selling live rats to public houses. Here, in specially erected pits, terriers and other dogs would dispatch the rats, with customers waging bets on the time it would take.

Occasionally, rat-catchers found unusually colored rats, and these were also sold, but for display rather than for the rat pit. Jack Black, Queen Victoria's official rat-catcher, went even further—he is reputed to have bred large numbers of pied rats, selling them as far afield as France. He also records having white rats, black rats, and other more exotic colors including fawns and tortoiseshell and white individuals.

It was also in the late nineteenth century that mice started to become popular as pets and exhibition subjects. Even so, mice were first kept thousands of years earlier in various parts of the world, with white mice being a common sight in Greek temples as long ago as 25 B.C. They were also domesticated in China at a similar stage in history.

Much of the impetus for the modern-day Mouse Fancy came from the British enthusiast Walter Maxey, whose name is commemorated in the Maxey show cage still used for mice today. He helped to pioneer not only the exhibition of Fancy mice, which were evolved from laboratory strains, but also helped encourage the Rat Fancy by ensuring that classes for rats were provided at shows organized by the National Mouse Club. In this respect, he was assisted by the dedication of the remarkable Miss Mary Douglas, who did much to popularize the keeping of rats in the early years of the 20th century.

▶ *Fewer color varieties of Fancy rat have been evolved to date, compared with mice. Both mice and rats can become very tame if handled regularly from weaning onward, although mice tend to be more nervous.*

Mouse and Rat Lifestyles

THE DOMESTIC STRAINS OF THE FANCY MOUSE are all derived from the House mouse (*Mus musculus*), which is widely distributed around the world—even occurring in the Antarctic, thanks to inadvertent human assistance. Mice were introduced there, and to other places such as Australia, by ships bringing supplies. The mice then established themselves successfully in their new environment, aided partly by their very rapid rate of reproduction. (This feature has also assisted the development of color varieties in these rodents.)

It is the Brown rat (*Rattus norvegicus*) which is the ancestor of all today's Fancy rats. This species started to displace its relative the Black rat (*Rattus rattus*) from much of its former range in Europe during the 1700s, with the latter having become very rare by the late 1800s. Even so, in the early days of the Rat Fancy, some color forms of the Black rat were being kept and exhibited, including an unusual greenish-colored variant. Other colors that existed during the 1920s were fawns and black-eyed whites. Black rats proved to be less friendly than Brown rats, and would also bite their owners quite readily, which meant they were less popular.

Q&A...

● *Apart from their size, is there much difference between mice and rats as pets?*

Rats tend to be bold and quite friendly, whereas mice are usually shyer and spend more of their time hidden in their bedding. The smaller size of mice means that they are easier to handle, and they have been bred in a much wider range of colors. The lifespan of individual mice at average two years is shorter than that of rats at three to four years.

● *My pet store only has white rats for sale. How can I obtain one of the more unusual color varieties?*

Contact your national Rat Fancy organization, which will be able to supply you with the names of breeders in your area. It is also worthwhile visiting shows, because breeders often exhibit their stock at these events. A search on the Internet is also likely to yield the addresses of suppliers.

● *Is it true that mice are color blind?*

Yes. This is due to the absence of cone cells in the retina of their eyes. (Cones are responsible for color vision.) Mice only have rods in their retina, which means they have a monochrome view of the world, although they still can see much better in the dark than we can, as befits their lifestyle.

▼ *The House mouse (left) and the Brown rat (below) are the ancestors of today's fancy varieties. In spite of their close relationship, mice are likely to be attacked by rats, and they must never be housed together.*

▲ *This mouse has chewed through an electric cable with its sharp teeth, illustrating the need to ensure that your own pets do not escape.*

Fact File

Names: Fancy Mouse; Fancy Rat

Scientific names: *Mus musculus*; *Rattus norvegicus*

Weight: Mice 1.1oz (30g); rats 10.5–17.6oz (300–500g), with males being heavier than females.

Compatibility: Mice especially are social by nature and can be kept in groups comprised of individuals of the same sex if breeding is not required, although bucks (males) are liable to fight. Rats are compatible in single-sex pairs or trios, in spacious housing.

Appeal: Intelligent, lively, and can be tamed quite easily. Not difficult to care for in the home.

Diet: Seed mixes or a complete, pelletized diet.

Health problems: Probably most vulnerable to respiratory infections, often indicated by sneezing and a runny nose in the early stages. Older animals often develop tumors.

Breeding tips: Do not allow the male to remain with the female when a litter is due, because they will be able to mate successfully within hours of the birth.

Pregnancy: Mice 19–21 days; rats 21–23 days.

Typical litter size: 9–11 young

Weaning: Mice 16–21 days; rats 21–23 days.

Lifespan: Mice 2 years; rats 3–4 years.

Close Neighbors

One of the characteristics that has contributed to the success of both the House mouse and the Brown rat is their adaptability. They can exploit a range of habitats and food sources, and can breed prolifically when conditions are right. Furthermore, the incisor teeth of rats and mice are immensely strong—so much so that rats can even gnaw through concrete. This destructive ability means they can live in close proximity to humans, invading buildings and accessing food stores with relative ease. Mice and rats have keen senses of both smell and hearing, although their eyesight is more specialized for low light conditions. They tend to be nocturnal in their habits or favor dark localities where they can remain out of sight. Their prominent whiskers help them to find their away around in these surroundings.

Mouse and Rat Behavior

The high reproductive rates of rats and mice have direct implications for the pet-owner, who may end up with literally hundreds of offspring over the course of a year or so from just a single pair. The lifespan of mice in particular is relatively short, however, and so it is important to start out with a young animal when seeking a pet, rather than an adult of uncertain age.

One of the unfortunate aspects of keeping mice and rats is the unpleasant odor associated with them, particularly males. This emanates from their urine and so is unavoidable. You can reduce the problem by regularly cleaning their quarters and by restricting your choice to females only if you do not wish them to breed.

Living in parts of the world where food is usually plentiful, these rodents have not developed the hoarding instincts associated with some members of this group, such as hamsters. They will eat a wide variety of foods, but they are essentially vegetarian. They are able to use their front legs to grasp food, and they can also climb well. Their long, scaly tails are vital for this task, helping them to keep their balance.

Housing for Mice and Rats

THERE ARE A NUMBER OF SUITABLE CAGES available for these rodents, although alternatively you can use a converted aquarium for them. If you choose a cage, it is better to invest in a double-story or a treble-story design, since this provides more scope for your pet to climb around its quarters. Separate climbing facilities will need to be provided if an aquarium is used. A cage with horizontal bars also offers a mouse or rat better opportunities to clamber about on the sides of its quarters than one with vertical bars. In most multiple-story cages a ladder is used to provide access to the higher levels.

Ease of cleaning is a particularly important consideration when choosing accommodation for these rodents, because of the unpleasant odor which can be associated with them. Cages that have a hard, epoxy-resin coating on the metalwork and a plastic base are recommended for this reason, being very easy to clean. You will also need to invest in an acrylic carrying container in which the rodents can be housed without risk of escaping while their quarters are being cleaned.

Check the way in which the two cage sections attach together and, if plastic clips are used, find out whether these can be purchased separately, since they can become fatigued and may even snap. The strength of the door latch is also very important, not only because these rodents can climb, but also because they can force their way through a poorly closed door and escape. Reinforcing the door with a small padlock can be a worthwhile precaution.

Cage Accessories

Although rats and mice are inquisitive and quite playful, they should never be provided with an open-weave play wheel in their quarters, because this could easily trap their long tails.

▲ *Mice and rats both appreciate toys in their quarters, but these will need to be replaced if they become soiled with urine. Wooden toys may also become badly gnawed.*

◄ *This design of tiered cage—which provides opportunities to climb—is suitable for mice and rats, although rats will need a large version.*

Wheels are generally too small to be used by rats, but there are a number of similar toys which can be provided for them. Cardboard tubes with an interior of suitable diameter can be converted into tunnels for these rodents and are easily replaced when they are gnawed away or soiled.

A sleeping area can be included on the floor as well, and lined with special rodent bedding. Try to avoid wooden sleeping quarters, however, because they can absorb urine which will leave a lingering odor as a result, no matter how frequently you change the cage lining.

The type of bedding on the floor of the quarters is very important, because rats and mice are prone to respiratory infections and eye irritations. Sawdust should not be used under any circumstances, because of its fine, dusty nature. Shavings sold for bedding purposes in pet stores have been used for many years, and have a high degree of absorbency, but there have been some concerns expressed in recent years over possible toxicity.

Both cedar and pine shavings have a distinctive odor associated with them, which is the result of chemicals called aromatic hydrocarbons. These are inhaled by the mice and rats and enter the blood, with the result that they must be broken down by the liver. Over time, the liver may show signs of enlargement as a result of this chronic stress, and the rodent's immune system may be adversely affected.

Q&A...

● *Will mice and rats benefit from being given wooden chews?*

These are certainly recommended, helping to keep their sharp incisor teeth in trim, and hopefully deterring them from gnawing at the plastic base of their quarters, and through the bars of the cage. Such chews are available in pet stores, while dried crusts of wholemeal bread baked in the oven can also be valuable for this purpose. They should be allowed to cool down before being given to the rodents.

● *Should mice and rats be given hay?*

Yes. This is important, being used both for bedding purposes and also eaten. But you must make absolutely sure that it is of prime quality and is therefore as dust-free as possible. Also beware of any dry thistles, whose sharp spikes could injure your pet.

● *What are mouse boxes?*

This is the type of housing favored by some breeders. It consists of boxlike accommodation with a hinged lid and a very fine mesh at the front. These boxes are partitioned into two sections, with a retreat at the back. The occupants are largely hidden from view under these circumstances, and so not recommended for general pet-owners.

▼▶ *Shavings have traditionally been used as bedding for mice and rats, thanks to their absorbent nature, but corn cob bedding (right) is one of the newer options available from pet stores, and recycled, paper-based cat litters are also now being used for floor covering in cages.*

Feeding Mice and Rats

IN COMMON WITH MOST OTHER SMALL PET mammals, specially formulated seed-based diets are widely available for both mice and rats, although it is not difficult to prepare a suitable mix yourself from cereal grains such as wheat and barley mixed with groats (dehulled oats). Corn is also a constituent of such diets, either in cracked or flaked form or in ground form. Avoid offering large amounts of either sunflower or peanuts, however. The high oil content of these seeds can cause skin problems—mainly in rats—as well as resulting in obesity. Small colored biscuits feature in many commercially prepared mixes, but you can also use dog biscuits, especially for rats which find these easier to handle. As with hardened bread, these help to prevent their teeth from becoming overgrown.

While this type of food mix serves as a basic diet, both mice and rats will benefit from being offered a wide range of foodstuffs. Fresh meadow hay can help raise the fiber intake of their diet, and other fresh foods can also be given in moderation. Pieces of carrot, celery, and cabbage stalks provide the opportunity for nibbling, and a vitamin and mineral supplement can be easily sprinkled over them as well.

▼ *A variety of feeding options are available for mice and rats. Seed-based mixtures (left) have traditionally been used, but now complete and pelletized diets are becoming more popular (right).*

Tips on Using Complete Foods

● Complete, pelletized diets can be purchased as an alternative to seed mixtures for mice and rats.

● Do not add a supplement to complete foods, since complete foods contain all that is needed in terms of vitamins and minerals.

● Complete foods must be used before the recommended "use by" date on the packaging, to ensure that the vitamin content in particular has not declined seriously.

● Keep the food in a sealed container and, as always, ensure that it remains dry.

● If you have a collection of mice or rats outdoors, it is wise to store their food in metal bins, where it will not attract their wild relatives which may introduce disease to your stock.

Cheese is an item indelibly linked with mice and rats, but although it can be used as an occasional treat, it should not be offered on a regular basis. Avoid using soft cheeses of any kind—cheddar is a good choice. You can also offer hard-boiled egg as a further means of boosting the protein level of the diet, and this can be especially valuable during the breeding period. Fancy mice and rats do not require livefood, but this should be offered to spiny mice and Nile rats (see pages 169 and 171) in the form of mealworms. Even so, not all such rodents will eat them. It is important not to offer mealworms in large numbers, because they can slip away and turn into adult beetles which could escape into the room.

Other foods can be offered for variety, but do not feed to excess, because they are

likely to result in digestive disturbances. A little rice, boiled potato, and other vegetables such as corn can be offered, once they have cooled after cooking. All perishable foods of this type should be provided in separate food containers from the dry food mix, since they will need to be removed within a day, before they turn moldy. The amount of food which these rodents consume is quite small—a mouse, for example, only eats about 0.25oz (7g) of food each day.

Water Requirements

A bottle-type drinker with a stainless steel spout (see page 119) should be provided as a source of fresh drinking water. This must be suspended securely at a suitable height so that the rodents can drink without difficulty. Always fill the bottle to the top, to avoid leakages once it is fixed in position. Neither rats nor mice drink large volumes of water, but their fluid intake can vary, depending on their diet and their environment.

▼ *Mice and rats will both eat a variety of foods, ranging from various seeds to fruit and vegetables. This rat is chewing into a corn on the cob. Fresh foods of this type should be offered, in small amounts, on a daily basis.*

● *A friend of mine gives her rat bones to gnaw. Should I do this?*

... Some rats enjoy gnawing at bones, but avoid offering types—such as chicken bones—that splinter easily when chewed and could therefore cause injury. Rats will nibble at the pieces of meat on bones and exercise their incisors on the bone itself. Remove the bone before the meat starts to turn moldy. A safe alternative to offering bones is to provide specially made chews like the ones shown here.

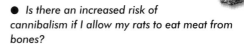

● *Is there an increased risk of cannibalism if I allow my rats to eat meat from bones?*

This is a popular myth, and there is no truth whatsoever in it. Nibbling meat will help to raise the protein level of the rats' diet and is an activity they sometimes pursue in the wild. What is often described as cannibalism is usually the direct result of fighting, caused by a disturbance in the rodents' social structure.

Routine Care of Mice and Rats

IT IS USUALLY POSSIBLE TO HANDLE MICE AND rats with little risk of being bitten. However, bear in mind that they have sharp incisors and relatively poor eyesight. Therefore if you are feeding your pet by hand, be sure to choose foodstuffs which you can hold in such a way that you are unlikely to be nipped accidentally. When picking them up, avoid grabbing mice or rats around their bodies, because this may result in them responding aggressively. Instead, start by letting them sniff your hand, and then seek to scoop them up from beneath. They will soon become used to your scent and will realize that they will not be harmed when being picked up.

Obviously, it will take several weeks for your new pet to become tame, and especially during this period, you will need to restrain it when it is in your hand. This can be achieved by placing

● *Do old newspapers make suitable bedding for mice and rats?*

No, it is not recommended that these are used in their quarters. This is because the inks on the paper may be dissolved by the rodents' urine and stain the fur—especially in the case of rats and mice with pale coats.

● *Is it true that television can disturb mice and rats?*

There is some evidence for this, therefore do not put your pet's quarters near a television screen, or indeed stereo speakers. Mice and rats are generally happier in fairly quiet surroundings.

▼ *The stages in picking up and restraining a mouse or rat, as described in the text. Always try to gain the animal's confidence before attempting to handle it.*

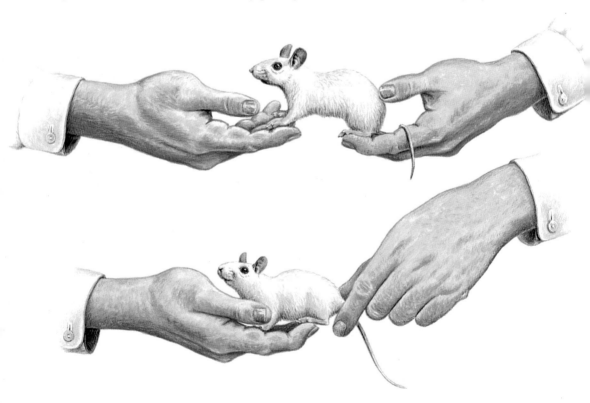

the thumb and first finger of the left hand close to the base of the rodent's tail. Never grab the tail by its tip, however, since this is not only likely to cause injury but will also prove to be a less satisfactory way of restraining your pet. Once tamed, many owners of rats like to encourage their pets to perch on their shoulders, but only be tempted to try this at first when you are sitting down, in case your pet falls off and injures itself.

Cage Cleaning

You will need to remove your pets from their quarters at least once a week, so that the bedding can be changed. The soiled bedding can be tipped into a trash bag, after which you may want to wash off the plastic base of the cage using one of the special disinfectants available for this purpose. You can also scrub the bars of the cage with a brush, although this should ideally be done outdoors, since the water will inevitably spray around off the bars. Rinse off the entire cage to remove any traces of disinfectant and dry everything thoroughly before reassembling.

Apart from cleaning the cage, this procedure will also remove any traces of the odor associated with these pets. If you want to introduce a new companion to an existing pet, the time to do this is immediately after washing the cage thoroughly, when neither will have a territorial advantage arising from its scent.

Grooming

Mice and rats generally need relatively little grooming—simply stroking their fur with your hand usually proves adequate. They are actually clean animals, as is apparent from the way in which they wash themselves regularly. However, prior to a show, some exhibitors will give their pet rats a bath to ensure that they look their best on the big day.

Rats can prove to be quite good swimmers, and do not display an instinctive fear of water, although they should still be introduced to their bath carefully. A clean, plastic basin will be ideal for this purpose. Start by filling this to a shallow depth—just sufficient to reach the top of the rodent's legs. Use a little mild baby shampoo to clean the coat, adding this to the tepid water before carefully placing your pet in the bowl. Keeping the rat's head dry to begin with, wash the rest of the body by working from the rear toward the head. Now wash the head, but be sure to keep the shampoo out of the eyes and ears. Then lift your pet out of the bowl, tip away the contents and refill to the same level as before with tepid water. Now rinse the shampoo out of its coat. Finally, towel dry the animal, after which it should be kept in a warm spot until its coat has dried thoroughly.

◀ *Despite their reputations, both mice and rats are avid groomers, using their front paws for this purpose. You can also gently comb them from time to time if the coat is particularly soiled.*

Breeding Mice and Rats

THE ENORMOUS REPRODUCTIVE CAPACITY OF these rodents means that pairings should only be carried out after careful thought, always ensuring that you can find good homes for all the offspring that you cannot keep yourself. If you want to avoid unwanted offspring in the first place, simply choose your stock carefully to ensure that you only have animals of the same sex. It is, however, possible to house a pair of the opposite sex together, provided you have the male neutered at eight weeks old. But bear in mind that he will almost certainly be sexually mature before this age, and so will need to be housed separately from any females until he has undergone this surgery. In any event, it is usually

Signs of Mating and Pregnancy

Whitish, waxy copulatory plugs are produced by females after mating and deposited in their quarters. Finding one of these confirms mating has taken place.

Mammary glands of female mice and rats start to swell from about two weeks onward.

Weight increase will be apparent throughout the pregnancy.

Nest building by female mice or rats occurs about a week before young are due.

▼▶ *Mice and rats can be sexed easily, and in a similar way. The distance between the anal and genital openings is greater in males than in females. The scrotal sac of males becomes apparent in mature individuals.*

Mouse

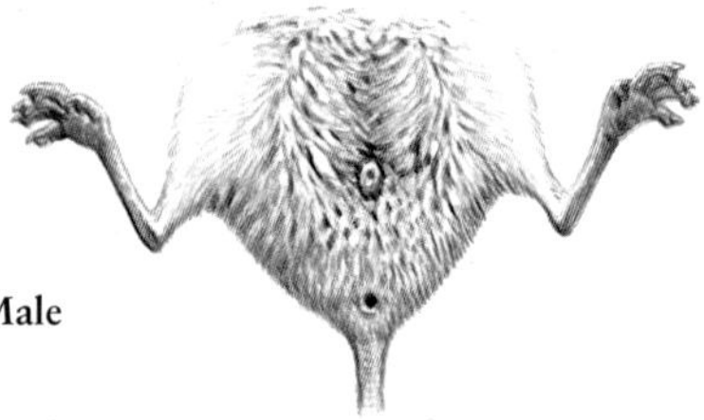

Male

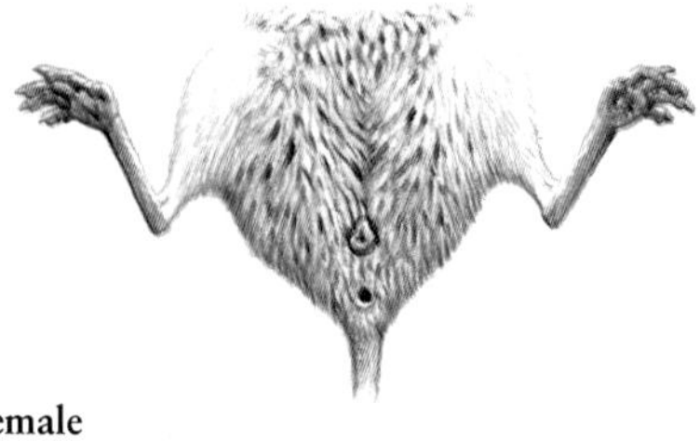

Female

Rat

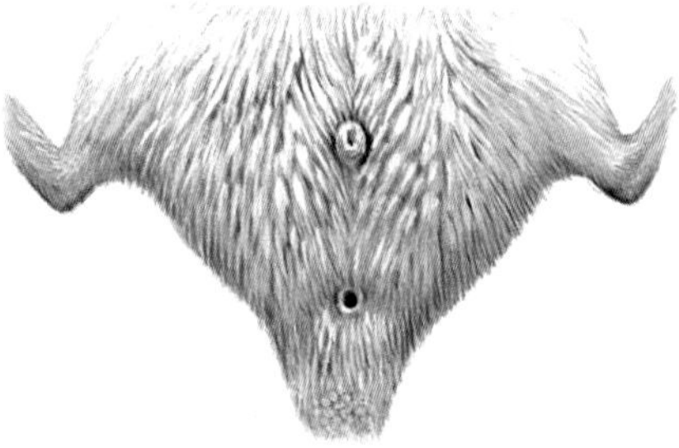

Male

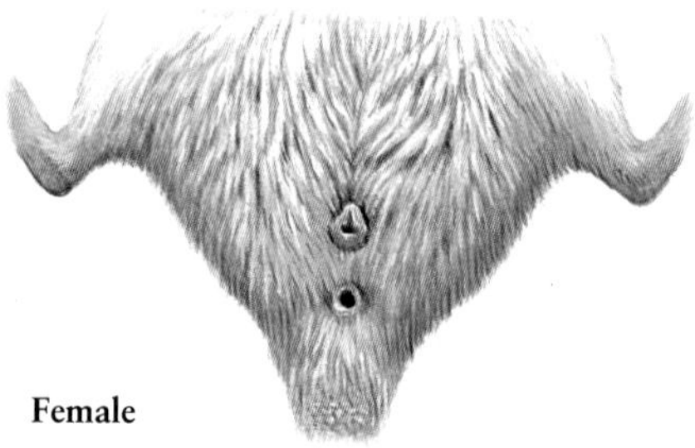

Female

not recommended that you allow rats to breed until they have reached this age, although mice can be mated safely from about the age of seven weeks onward.

Breeding mice or rats is not difficult, although it is generally better to allow them to do so in temporary accommodation. This avoids the strong possibility that other females in the group will become pregnant. Both rats and mice have short estrus cycles lasting four to five days, with mating most likely to occur overnight. About a week before the young are due, it is best to remove the male from the cage, leaving the female on her own. Otherwise, the pair will mate immediately after the young are born, when the female will be fertile again.

Newborn Mice and Rats

Do not disturb the nest once the young are born, since this may cause their mother to desert or even attack them. The young are completely helpless at birth—being naked, blind, and deaf at this stage—but their development is quite rapid. The female will require more to eat and drink now, in order to meet the nutritional needs of her growing family. Young rats start to develop their fur from the age of ten days, with their eyes opening by the following week. They then start to venture out from the nest, sometimes being carried back by their mother if they stray too far.

Newborn mice develop in a similar way, with the young of both groups usually being weaned when they are between three and four weeks of age. It is often recommended to transfer the pregnant female to an acrylic or glass tank, because very young mice may be able to slip through the sides of a cage when they first leave their nest.

By this stage it will be possible to sex the youngsters without too much difficulty, and they should be kept in groups of the same gender to prevent in-breeding, since some may mature at a relatively early stage. You can, of course, leave the young females with their mother, if her cage is suitably spacious. Should the mother become pregnant again, however, it will probably be better to remove all her previous young before she gives birth.

● *My friend was badly bitten by his female rat when he tried to pick up her pups. Was this just a coincidence?*

Almost certainly not—female rats can be very protective of their young and may view your attempted handling as a threat to them and so bite in a defensive manner. Always, therefore, pacify the mother first by giving her some reassuring attention before touching the youngsters.

● *Is it true that if you keep a group of female mice together, they start to come into estrus at the same time?*

This does occur in the absence of a male and is known as the Whitten effect. What happens is that the females stop their regular cycles, and when a male is introduced to the group, all the females are likely to come into estrus within three days.

● *Why does litter size vary quite widely among my breeding females?*

The age of the does is very significant, with young females breeding at less than 13 weeks producing relatively small litters. At the end of their reproductive lives, from 14 months onward, the number of young per litter will also be reduced. Furthermore, some strains and colors are less prolific than others. Diet may also play a part, with those kept on a relatively poor one having fewer offspring.

▼ *Once born, young mice and rats develop quickly. These Berkshire rats are just a week old, and it is possible to make out their coloration quite easily.*

Illnesses in Mice and Rats

ALTHOUGH WILD MICE AND RATS MAY CARRY many diseases to which they seem immune, their domesticated relatives can succumb to a number of illnesses quite readily. Part of the reason for this may be related to their environment. In particular, if housed in dirty surroundings, the build-up of ammonia from urine will attack the delicate lining of the rodents' respiratory tracts, leaving them vulnerable to infections. A wide variety of microbes can then affect the respiratory system, although the symptoms are generally similar. A nasal discharge and repeated sneezing are often seen in such cases and, if untreated, this type of illness can progress to pneumonia. This is reflected by labored breathing. In addition, the coat will feel rough and will not lie sleekly.

Poor coat condition can be an outward sign of a number of illnesses, in fact. Diarrhea is another symptom. Many illnesses can spread quickly through a group of these rodents, so seeking veterinary assistance with minimal delay gives the best hope of establishing the correct cause and providing successful treatment.

Fur and Skin Conditions

Hair loss is not uncommon in mice and rats and may have a dietary origin. For instance, it may be triggered by a high level of fat—which in turn may be related to excess amounts of oil seeds, such as sunflower, in their diet. In this case, changing the diet will resolve the problem simply. However, if the symptoms persist, the cause could be due to ringworm infection. Ringworm is a fungal disease and is especially important because it can be spread to people from animals.

Ringworm causes loss of fur in a circular pattern, with similarly shaped red blotches appearing on the skin of infected humans. The infection is easily spread, with the fungal spores remaining viable on equipment such as grooming brushes

▼ *Mice and rats can be affected by external parasites such as mites and lice. Intense irritation of the skin and localized hair loss are typical signs. Seek veterinary advice, especially with regard to treatment. Mite infestations, like the case shown here, can be treated in various ways, including medicated baths.*

and food bowls. Should you suspect that your pet is infected, seek veterinary advice.

If there is no such obvious cause of hair loss, however, then watch your pets carefully. It may well be that one of the other members in the group—usually the dominant individual—is nibbling the hair. Overgrooming of this type may reflect a lack of fiber in the rodents' diet, so offer hay and root vegetables such as pieces of carrot. If this fails to cure the problem, you will need to remove either or both the individuals involved from the group—such behavior may also be indicative of overcrowding. This condition tends to be more common in mice than rats.

Swellings and Tumors

Look for early signs of swellings on the surface of the body by examining your pets regularly. Mice and rats can suffer from abscesses, often resulting from bites, as well as tumors of various types. Females are especially vulnerable to mammary tumors. As a general guide, abscesses develop very quickly, often at the site of an obvious injury and, as they swell in size, they feel relatively hot to the touch. Always seek veterinary advice without delay so appropriate treatment can be carried out where possible.

In the case of an abscess, it may simply be a matter of waiting for it to come to a head, whereas the likelihood of removing a tumor successfully by surgery will be greatly increased if this is done at an early stage. If you find that your pet's abdomen starts to droop noticeably, this can be a sign of a tumor affecting the body organs—although a change of this type is quite normal in a pregnant female.

Renal Problems

A condition often prevalent in older animals is chronic renal failure—although it can occur in younger individuals. Symptoms include thirst and higher urinary output, as well as loss of condition and abdominal swelling. It is often linked with a high protein diet. This causes progressive damage to the kidneys. Once signs are apparent the condition is serious, but it may be possible to stabilize it, especially by changing the diet. Offer a lower protein food, as well as some boiled rice mixed with a vitamin and mineral supplement.

▼ *Ear infections can often be linked to bedding. Persistent scratching is a typical symptom, and rapid treatment is essential to prevent the infection from spreading further down the ear canal.*

Q&A

● **Is it true that mice can suffer from osteoarthritis?**

... This condition is not uncommon in older individuals, and the symptoms can be relieved quite successfully by using an anti-inflammatory drug such as aspirin under veterinary advice. Dosing can be carried out most easily by using a soluble product which can be dissolved in the mouse's drinking water.

● **My friend's rat has started weeping what seem to be bloodlike tears. How does this happen?**

There are several possible causes of red tears in rats, but these are not the result of a hemorrhage caused by an eye injury. Instead, the red pigments are produced in the Harderian glands in the eyes and are usually shed as the result of a respiratory infection. Red staining may be seen over the paws as well, when the rat wipes its face. Treatment depends on the cause of the problem.

● **Some breeders were discussing an unpleasant condition called ringtail. What causes this?**

If young rats are kept in very dry surroundings, their tails become constricted and swell, before being sloughed off at the point where the swelling occurred. This is a problem which occurs when the relative humidity falls below 50 percent—an unlikely situation in the home, although central heating can lower the humidity considerably.

Mouse Species and Varieties

MORE THAN EIGHT HUNDRED VARIETIES OF Fancy mouse have now been developed—more than for any of the other small animals kept as pets. This is largely a consequence of their rapid rate of reproduction.

SELFS

The first of these to emerge was the Pink-eyed White, which is a true albino first bred more than 2,000 years ago. Although young individuals have pure white fur, it is not unusual for their coat to develop a slight yellowish hue from the age of about six months onward.

The Self Black also has a long history, being first recorded from Japan about 1600. Its coat has a consistent, gleaming black sheen, with no trace of lighter fur visible among the black hairs. In the 1700s, the dilute form now called the Self Dove was documented. These mice are dove-gray in color, with pink eyes. The Self Blue is a darker shade of slate-gray, although again, individuals differ in their depth of coloration.

The Self Chocolate is another long-standing variety. It was originally documented in Japan over 400 years ago, but died out, with today's strains dating back to the 1870s. Dark, even coloration, corresponding to that of plain chocolate, is sought after in exhibition stock. The dilute form of this color is the Self Champagne, characterized by its pink eyes and by its champagne-brown coloration—which has a decidedly pinkish hue.

One of the most striking varieties today is the Self Red, especially when this is combined with the Satin mutation (which increases the natural gloss of the coat). The Self Fawn should ideally be a deep shade of tan but, more commonly, it is orangish in color. Combined with the Chinchilla mutation, Self Fawns then played a central part in the development of the Pink-eyed Cream. (There is also a Black-eyed Cream, created by a breeding program involving Chinchilla and Self Lilac stock.)

Another popular Self variety whose ancestry can be traced back to these breeding experiments is the Pink-eyed Self Silver. The undercoat is an icy-blue shade, with the overall color matching that of a silver coin. Black-eyed Self Silvers are much rarer. These can easily be confused with Self Lilacs, with paler examples of this color having a silvery coat.

OTHER SILVER FORMS

There can also be confusion between Silvers and Silver Grays, particularly in young mice. It becomes easier to tell them apart after a month

▶ Pink-eyed white mice are among the most popular varieties being bred today. Their ears are pink, too, reflecting the lack of black melanin pigment in their coats. This is also the reason why their eyes are not black.

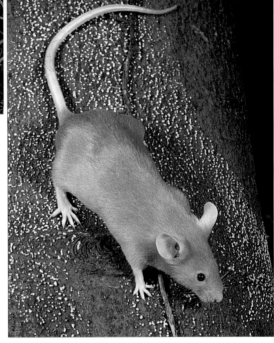

▲ *A Satin Self Red. The Satin characteristic imparts a definite gloss to the coat of these mice. One particular exhibition fault commonly associated with the Self Red is ears which are smaller than usual.*

▶ *A Self Fawn. These mice are so called because their coloration resembles the tan coat of a young deer. The Self Fawn is the result of breeding programs involving a subspecies of the House mouse which has red eyes.*

old, when the white and black bands running down the hairs of the Silver Gray create a distinctive appearance. There are three recognizable shades, ranging from light, through medium, to dark. Individuals should be an even shade of color, however, with lighter coloration being a common flaw associated with this variety. Silver Fawn and Silver Brown varieties were once common but have now become scarce.

The Pearl bears a close resemblance to the Silver Gray. It was originally called the Chinchilla. The Pearl can be distinguished by its off-white undercoat. The tips of the hairs are black or gray in color, depending on the individual, with the result that some Pearls are darker than others. The true Chinchilla form of the Fancy mouse has a fur color resembling that of the South American rodent of the same name (see page 172); it appears bluish-gray in color, thanks partly to the black tipping on the individual hairs, with those on the underparts being tipped with white.

Q&A...

● **Is it true that some varieties of Fancy mouse are more prone to obesity than others?**

This does appear to be the case, and it may be a reflection of differences in metabolism between various strains. Self Reds, Self Fawns, and related bloodlines are especially prone to this problem, so avoid offering them large amounts of sunflower seed and similar oil seeds. They also tend to have smaller litters.

● **I have a litter of Self Black mice with decidedly grayish fur. Is this usual?**

All Self Black mice are this color at birth, so it is nothing to worry about—their coats will start to develop their characteristic color at about a month old.

● **What is the rarest of all the mouse varieties?**

... This is probably the Tri-color. This color variety has never been established, although odd individuals showing three distinct colors in their coats have been recorded from time to time.

● **Can you give me some advice about keeping spiny mice?**

These rodents (*Acomys* species), distinguished by their relatively spiky fur, originate from fairly arid parts of the world and range from North Africa to Asia. They are best kept in converted aquaria because of their small size. Take particular care when handling them because of their fragile tails. They require a similar diet to Fancy mice but should also be offered small amounts of mealworms, available from pet stores. Females have a long pregnancy, lasting around 40 days on average, and only produce two or three offspring per litter. These are born fully developed. The young can be weaned after a further two weeks and will be mature at eight weeks old.

▲ *Members of the Fox group have clearly defined white underparts. This distinguishes them from the Tan group, in which the underparts are tan in color. This is a Chocolate Fox.*

OTHER COLOR VARIETIES

There are various color varieties in mice which correspond to those seen in other types of small animal. The Silver Fox mouse is a typical example, resembling the equivalent rabbit breed (see page 70) in its patterning. There are black, chocolate, and blue forms. The silvery coloration results from the white ticking running down the sides of the body to the feet. The underparts, by contrast, are pure white. A combination of the Chinchilla and Black Tan mutations has led to the development of these colors.

▼ *In the Tans there is a straight line around the sides of the body demarcating the colored upperparts from the tan coloration present on the underparts of the body. This is a Champagne and Tan.*

PATTERNED VARIETIES

In the Tans there must be very clear delineation between the colored fur on the top of the body and the tan underparts. Tan combinations of all the Self colors now exist.

Fancy mice displaying a range of white markings have also been created. The Even-marked is an old variety, recognizable by having ears of the same color. In Broken-marked individuals, however, these should display matching white and colored areas over their bodies, with a contrasting ear color. There is also a Dutch variety, with markings matching the corresponding rabbit breed (see page 67). A more unusual variant is the Rump White, which combines colored fur with white on the rump, hind feet, and tail.

The Himalayan mutation is well established, being first recorded from a strain of American laboratory mice during the 1920s. The fur on the body is white, with the young soon developing their characteristic darker point coloration. Varieties such as black and chocolate are often bred, but there are other colors as well. The Siamese, with markings like those of the cat breed, is characterized by having beige fur on the body, offset against the darker coloration of the points on the nose, ears, feet, and tail.

The Chinchilla mutation has proved to be one of the most significant in the history of the Mouse Fancy, having contributed to the development of many varieties. The "normal" form of the domesticated House mouse is known as the Golden Agouti, thanks to the more golden shade apparent in the coat. By combining this feature with the Chinchilla mutation, and thus removing this color, the Silver Agouti has been bred. It has silvery-gray coloration replacing the warm, bronze tones.

The Argente is a paler, pink-eyed version of the Golden Agouti, with the corresponding mutation in the Chinchilla variant being described as the Argente Creme. Another variety displaying ticking is the Cinnamon—recognizable by its chocolate, rather than black, banding on the individual hairs.

Some color varieties are quite rare. Among these is the Marten Sable, created by combining Chinchilla and Sable bloodlines. Such mice have white underparts, compared with the golden tan coloration associated with the Sable itself. Sables can be bred quite easily by pairings involving Black Tans and Self Reds.

COAT VARIANTS

Apart from variations in coloration and patterning, there are several mutations now established which directly affect the state of the fur, including two varieties of Rex. The Astrex is the oldest, first described in 1936. Both the whiskers and the fur over the entire body are curly, but after the age of two months it becomes progressively harder to distinguish between Astrex and normal mice. This change does not occur in the Rex mutation itself, however, which arose in the 1970s and results in a thinner coat. Long-haired mice were first bred in 1966. Their ears are slightly smaller than normal.

▼ *A group of spiny mice. They are so called because of the shape of their hairs, which resemble spines in appearance, although they are not spiky to the touch. This feature is less apparent in the young, however.*

Rat Species and Varieties

AS THE DOMESTICATION OF RATS HAS TAKEN place, it has been those varieties furthest removed in coloration from the wild rat that have become most popular with pet-keepers.

SELFS

The most widely kept variety today is probably the Albino, characterized by its white fur and pink eyes. The Black-eyed White, first bred in the early 1980s, is much rarer. Both eye colors also exist in the Cream, which is a scarce variety. The more common Self Champagne is similar in color, but with a rosy hue to its beige coat, offset against pink eyes.

The Self Chocolate occurred relatively early in the history of the Rat Fancy, being first recorded about 1915, but has only started to become popular again since the 1980s. As with other Selfs, these rats should display an even shade of coloration throughout their coats. The Self Black is another dark variety, being jet-black in color, with no trace of any other color in its coat.

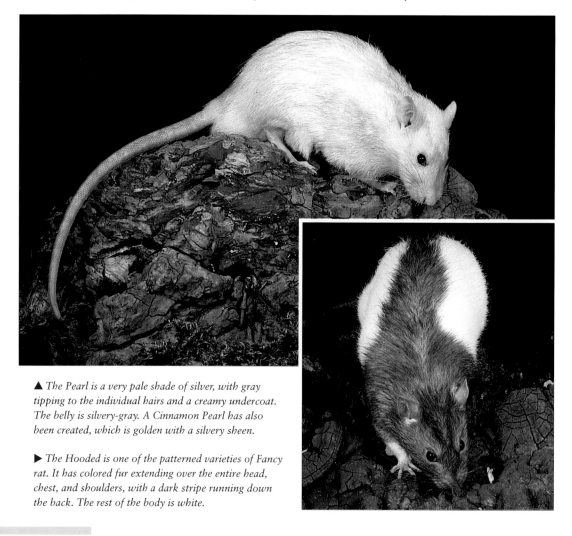

▲ *The Pearl is a very pale shade of silver, with gray tipping to the individual hairs and a creamy undercoat. The belly is silvery-gray. A Cinnamon Pearl has also been created, which is golden with a silvery sheen.*

▶ *The Hooded is one of the patterned varieties of Fancy rat. It has colored fur extending over the entire head, chest, and shoulders, with a dark stripe running down the back. The rest of the body is white.*

There are a number of other varieties of Fancy rat which correspond to similar mutations seen in mice, including the pointed Himalayan and Siamese forms, characterized by their darker extremities. Not all color variants of mice have parallels in the rat, however, as shown by the Self Mink. It is believed that this is probably the same mutation originally described as the Self Blue, which became extinct in the 1900s. Such rats are a light coffee color with a distinctive bluish sheen. The dilute version of this color is known as the Self Lilac, although there is considerable variation between individuals, with some a significantly paler shade of light gray than others.

The Self Mink has also been used to create the Pearl. There is also a Cinnamon Pearl and the Cinnamon itself, which is russet brown with chocolate, rather than silver, guard hairs.

Silver varieties have become popular in recent years. The silver hairs effectively dilute the color and create a sparkling appearance in the coat. The Silver Fawn, better known in North America as the Orange Fawn or Amber, is a particularly attractive variant. The eyes are red, with the underparts being clear white, offset against the warm, orange-fawn fur elsewhere.

PATTERNED VARIETIES

A number of distinctly marked varieties are also recognized in Fancy rats. The Capped is distinguished from the Hooded by having a more restricted area of colored fur on the head, which is not permitted to extend beyond the ears, and there may be a white blaze between the eyes. This particular feature is always present in variegated rats, which should display even areas of colored and white fur over the body.

The Irish variety takes its name from a subspecies of the Black rat identified in Ireland in 1837, thanks to a similarity in patterning. There is a distinctive white area in the shape of an equilateral triangle on the chest, ideally extending between the front feet. The American Irish (in contrast to the English variety) has a different pattern, which more closely resembles the Berkshire, with less white fur. The appearance of the Berkshire rat is based on the pig breed of this name, with a white spot on the forehead helping to identify these rats, along with symmetrical

white areas of fur extending up the fore and hind legs to the ankles, and on part of the tail as well.

New varieties of Fancy rat are still being developed. They include Husky rats, with light gray on their bodies and white underparts.

COAT VARIANTS

Coat variants are also becoming more common, especially Satins and Rexes. Hairless rats, known as Sphinxes, were first recorded from the United States in the 1930s but are not especially popular. Manx rats with short tails also evolved in the 1940s. They can suffer skeletal problems affecting the hindquarters and are not widely kept.

▼ *Nile rats are more difficult to keep than Fancy rats because of their large size and more destructive natures. They grow to 28in (71cm) and can weigh 3.3lb (1.5kg).*

● **What are Dumbo rats?**

These are named after the popular Walt Disney elephant character, being distinguished by their large, rounded, low-set ears. They were first bred in the United States in 1991 from ordinary Fancy rat stock and have since proved to be more placid and friendly than normal domesticated rats, which has helped to ensure their popularity.

● **Apart from variants of the Brown rat, are there any other species of rat available?**

Three other rat species are becoming more widely bred, but they are most suited to experienced owners, partly because they can be more aggressive and may bite if disturbed. They are the Nile rat (*Arvicanthus niloticus*), the African giant pouched rat (*Cricetomys gambianus*), and the Cotton rat (*Sigmodon hispidus*).

Chinchillas

THE WIDESPREAD POPULARITY OF THE CHINCHILLA AS A HOUSEHOLD pet today is largely due to the efforts of a mining engineer called M. F. Chapman. By the 1920s, when Chapman was working in South America, these rodents had already been hunted to the edge of extinction by trappers keen to trade their thick, soft fur. Previous attempts at breeding chinchillas in captivity had failed, but Chapman was determined to succeed—for he appreciated the huge commercial rewards that would follow if he could set up a successful breeding farm for chinchillas in the United States.

The plight of the chinchilla by this stage was such that in spite of hiring a team to seek out wild chinchillas for him, they only managed to locate 11 individuals after a search extending over three years. In time, Chapman was able to take these chinchillas back to California where he had established his farm. Under his care this initial group proved quite prolific, and he was able to supply others seeking to establish chinchilla farms.

Perhaps surprisingly, it was not until the 1960s that chinchillas started to be kept as pets, although this was partly due to their cost. Even today, when they are much more widely available, they still rank among the more costly of pet rodents. This is largely because they are not prolific breeders. There is also a scarcity of some of the new colors that have emerged in recent years, which means that prices for these particular chinchillas are rather inflated. This high cost has given chinchillas quite an exclusive image, nevertheless, which has been reinforced by their natural cleanliness. Chinchillas also have more specialized dietary and general care requirements than other rodents kept as household pets, but their growing popularity means that it is not difficult to purchase all the items needed to look after them.

At present, chinchillas are not commonly exhibited, but the signs are that this situation is now changing, as color varieties become more numerous and widely available. It is likely that you will still need to contact a breeder if you are seeking a particular color.

▶ *A Standard chinchilla. Color varieties are now becoming more commonly available, but often only this variety—corresponding to the wild color form—is available from pet stores.*

Chinchilla Lifestyles

CHINCHILLAS LIVE IN THE ANDEAN REGION OF South America—a rather inhospitable environment where temperatures plummet at night, and food is in short supply. There are two separate species of chinchilla: *Chinchilla brevicaudata* has the widest distribution, being found in the Andean areas of Peru, Bolivia, Chile, and Argentina. The domesticated varieties of the chinchilla have been bred from *Chinchilla lanigera*. This species occurs only in northern Chile and can be recognized by the fact that it has a longer tail and larger ears.

Since there is very little natural cover in the high altitude areas inhabited by chinchillas, they rely heavily on their senses to warn them of possible predators. Their large ears are highly sensitive to sounds and can turn to locate the source of a noise with great accuracy. On the ground, foxes pose a major danger to these rodents, while birds of prey can swoop on a chinchilla in the open. The agouti coloration of the wild form of the chinchilla—shades of gray with whitish underparts—helps to provide some camouflage

Fact File

Name:	Long-tailed Chinchilla
Scientific name:	*Chinchilla lanigera*
Weight:	1–1.5lb (0.5–0.7kg)

Compatibility: Single-sex pairs usually compatible, especially if from the same litter or introduced together while still young. True breeding pairs can also be housed together. Introducing adult male chinchillas together can be much more difficult.

Appeal: Lively, with a cuddly appearance complemented by very soft fur. Clean, with no unpleasant odor associated with them.

Diet: Require specific pelletized food and good-quality meadow hay.

Health problems: Probably most at risk from digestive upsets and dental problems.

Breeding tips: Take care when breeding new colors. Genetic problems can emerge with some pairings.

Typical litter size:	1–4 young
Pregnancy:	About 111 days
Weaning:	About 56 days
Lifespan:	10–15 years

▼ *A pair of Fawn chinchillas, demonstrating the social nature of these rodents. The Fawn is one of the color varieties developed as the result of domestication.*

against this threat by concealing their presence on the ground.

In the wild, chinchillas live in small caves and rocky outcrops where they can retreat from danger, spending much of the daytime here before emerging under cover of darkness in search of food. The eyes of chinchillas are relatively large and help them to see in these surroundings. Even in the home, chinchillas will spend much of the day asleep. They emerge as dusk falls, making them ideal companions if you are out at work all day. They are naturally quiet, and their calls will not upset neighbors if you live in an apartment.

Like all rodents, chinchillas possess a sharp pair of incisor teeth at the front of each jaw. They are exclusively vegetarian in their eating habits, feeding primarily on grasses and the bark of shrubs growing in their native habitat. Other items such as the fruits of cacti also feature in their diet, with one of their particular favorites being those of the quisco cactus, called guillaves.

Chinchillas are naturally social creatures and live in small groups in the wild. They may communicate with each other using a very soft call, sometimes uttering a coughing sound if they are angry. They also possess a louder, higher-pitched call which alerts others in the vicinity to a direct threat of danger. Their sense of smell enables them to detect members of their group at close quarters by sniffing them, which also serves as a greeting. Outbreaks of fighting are not common, although males may quarrel on occasions.

Unique Fur

For many owners, one of the most appealing features of the chinchilla is its soft, dense fur. This provides excellent protection from the bitter cold in its natural habitat. As many as 80 hairs may sprout from a single hair follicle, instead of just the single hair which is normally the case in most mammals. The coat of chinchillas is so dense that they do not suffer from fleas or other parasitic infestations here. The covering of fur extends right down to the tip of the tail, while the prominent whiskers on the face are specialized hairs providing sensory information about the environment close to them. They help these rodents to find their way around, even in conditions of total darkness.

▲ *Accommodation for chinchillas should always include some opportunities for climbing. A large piece of natural timber is ideal for this purpose.*

Q&A...

● **Chinchillas look so cuddly. Do they like being stroked and petted?**

Unfortunately, they are less amenable to being handled in this way than other members of the caviomorph group such as the guinea pig. This is not to say they are unfriendly, though—a young individual can be tamed quite successfully.

● **Are chinchillas very active?**

Yes, and they can move very fast as well, typically being able to jump distances of up to 20in (50cm) in a single bound to escape a predator. As well as being very agile, chinchillas can also climb well.

● **Can I keep a chinchilla with a rabbit?**

Although they are unlikely to quarrel, this is definitely not to be recommended. Even if they were housed together in a suitably spacious enclosure, the specific dietary needs and lifestyles of chinchillas make such a pairing inappropriate.

Housing for Chinchillas

THE HEIGHT OF THE ACCOMMODATION IS AN important consideration for chinchillas, partly due to their relatively large size compared with other rodents and also because they climb readily. Incorporate at least one wooden platform in a chinchilla's quarters so it can climb up here. The platform may need to be replaced after a period, since it is likely to be gnawed. It is therefore vital to use only untreated timber for this purpose, rather than old planking that may have been painted previously. Sycamore is a good choice, but pine may be harmful if ingested by

▼ As well as a nesting box, other retreats should be included on the floor of the cage. Pots, like the one shown here, or clay pipes with a diameter of about 6in (15cm) and a length of about 9in (23cm) are ideal.

these rodents. Attach platforms carefully to avoid the risk of them collapsing. It is also possible to purchase specially designed chinchilla cages which are supplied with platforms already.

As a guide, a chinchilla cage should be at least 24in (60cm) in height. Its length and width may be less, but should be as great as space permits. Indoor aviaries of similar design are another housing option for these rodents, although in this case it will be necessary to replace the accompanying plastic floor tray before it can be gnawed by them. Plastic can be fatal to chinchillas if consumed.

A metal base is a safe option, although you should always check that there are no sharp edges here or elsewhere in the cage where your pets could injure themselves. You should also

Tips on Floor Coverings for Chinchillas

● There is no need for a floor covering if the cage has a wire mesh floor. Urine and droppings will pass through the mesh, onto the tray beneath, and can be removed when the chinchilla is asleep.

● If your cage has a solid base, the metal tray should be lined with a shallow layer of coarse shavings sold specifically for pet bedding.

● Do not use shavings that may contain potentially dangerous wood preservatives, and cedar is specifically not recommended because of its harmful resins.

● Avoid using newspaper for a covering, because the inks may be harmful if ingested should the chinchilla chew the paper.

● *What is the recommended mesh size for a chinchilla's cage?*

... It is best not to exceed a mesh size of about 0.5in (12mm) square. This size should ensure that there is little risk of a chinchilla getting one of its paws caught in the mesh, and will also help keep it safe from the claws of pet cats which may be sharing your home.

● *A breeder was talking about setting up a polygamous housing unit. What is this?*

This is a commercial breeding setup comprising about three or four separate units, each housing a female chinchilla. Their accommodation is linked to that of a male by a series of tunnels. The male can move through the tunnels at will to reach the females, but the females are prevented from using the tunnels because they are fitted with a collar that obstructs their passage through them. This arrangement enables a single male to sire young by mating with a number of different females.

consider the size of the door opening in indoor aviaries, because you will need to be able to move your chinchilla in and out with ease, and the openings in some bird cages are quite small.

It is important to provide a suitable retreat in the chinchilla's quarters, in the form of a nesting box, where it can sleep. This is usually sited on, or within easy reach of, the platform. An ideal size is about 20in (50cm) long x 10in (25cm) in width and height, but may need to be smaller depending on the size of the chinchilla's quarters. There should be an entrance hole with a diameter of about 6in (15cm) at the front.

Climbing Branches

Relatively thick branches for climbing should be sited in the cage but, again, these must be cut from trees that have not been sprayed recently with chemicals. Chinchillas are likely to nibble at these to keep their teeth in trim, with thinner side shoots more likely to be favored for this purpose. Securely fix the branches in such a way that they do not clutter the inside of the cage. The main reason why a relatively large enclosure is recommended at the outset is so that the chinchillas can move around easily and display their natural agility, even with the cage furnishings in place. This is particularly important if it is not possible to allow the rodents out of their quarters on a regular basis.

▼ *Many typical rodent cages are unsuitable for chinchillas, not only in terms of their size but also because of their design. This is a properly constructed chinchilla cage. It has access doors at the top and the side, and the platforms can be fixed in a variety of positions. If you opt for a plastic-bottomed enclosure, be sure that the base unit cannot be dislodged or gnawed by the chinchillas.*

Feeding Chinchillas

ORIGINATING FROM A PART OF THE WORLD where food is in short supply, chinchillas have adapted to feed on meager rations containing a high-fiber intake. They are entirely vegetarian and must be provided with a very specific diet. This may seem rather monotonous, but changes to their regular rations can spell serious digestive disorders and even death. Chinchillas must be fed on specially formulated pellets if they are to be kept in good health. These can be purchased either from many pet stores or by mail order from specialist suppliers. The pellets are made from dried grass and other ingredients, and include adequate vitamins and minerals to meet the chinchilla's nutritional requirements.

Although it is cheaper to buy chinchilla pellets in bulk, they should not be used after their shelflife has passed, since their vitamin content will have deteriorated by then. The pellets must also be kept dry, because they will deteriorate rapidly if they become damp.

While pellets may appear to be costly, chinchillas only eat relatively small amounts of them—averaging about 1.2oz (35g) daily. This is the equivalent of between one and two tablespoons of pellets each day. However, it is advisable to check the feeding instructions carefully to ensure that you are feeding the correct quantity.

Other Food Items

The other major item which must feature in a chinchilla's diet is top-quality hay. It is vital that this is not dusty or moldy, nor should it have been contaminated by other rodents such as mice. Suitable hay can be obtained in bags from pet stores and needs to be stored in a dry place until required. Beware of bargain offers of hay—although if you have the space it can be much cheaper to purchase hay in the form of a bale. Hay should be offered in a bowl, rather than becoming mixed with the bedding on the floor of the cage. You can also provide small cubes of hay, which are tightly compressed, so the chinchillas will gnaw on them, keeping their teeth in trim.

Some fresh greenfood can also be beneficial, but this must be fed strictly in moderation. Offer it on a regular basis, rather than intermittently in larger amounts, because this will inevitably lead to digestive upsets. Chinchillas normally produce very hard, dry, fecal pellets. Any tendency toward diarrhea is potentially serious, even if it has been caused simply by eating unsuitable food, and veterinary advice should be sought.

▲ Special chinchilla pellets should form the basis of the diet for these rodents, rather than seeds. Their nutritional needs are very specific and must be adhered to carefully.

◀ Alfalfa cubes can be used to supplement a chinchilla's hay intake. As with pellets, provide these in a heavyweight bowl.

Treats sold for other small animals are not generally recommended for chinchillas, either. Unfortunately, chinchillas very rapidly acquire a taste for items such as sunflower seed and peanuts. These have a much higher oil content than their usual diet, and the chinchilla's metabolism is not geared to coping with such foods. The end result of offering this type of food can be liver damage, weight loss, and death.

Water Requirements

In the wild, chinchillas drink very little water, surviving instead on the water present in their food and by lapping at dew. However, fresh drinking water should always be offered to pet chinchillas. A small animal drinking bottle with a stainless steel spout is needed for this purpose. The bottle should be fitted with a bottle guard at the front, to avoid the risk of the chinchillas puncturing the plastic of the bottle with their sharp teeth. The bottle must also be fixed firmly in place.

▼ *Chinchillas use their front paws to hold food that cannot be swallowed easily. This allows them to nibble off pieces without difficulty. Fresh vegetable matter can feature in their diet in small quantities, but not fruit.*

● *I would like to obtain a bale of hay for my chinchillas, but I don't have a shed. Where else could I store it?*

Take a clean, plastic garbage bag and punch holes in this for ventilation purposes. When you cut the twine on the bale, you will find the hay falls apart in compressed sections. These should then be transferred into the sack. Tie off the top loosely and store the sack in a cupboard. You can then simply take out the amount needed for the chinchillas each day, keeping the top tied after use.

● *How can I tell if my chinchillas are in good physical condition?*

This can be hard to determine, thanks to their dense covering of fur. Apart from weighing chinchillas regularly, the simplest solution is to gently palpate the back and rib cage. The bones here should feel well covered. If they feel too prominent, this indicates weight loss. Obesity, on the other hand, is very uncommon in these rodents, assuming that they are receiving a proper diet.

● *Can I use other pelleted foods for my chinchillas?*

No, this is definitely not to be recommended, because their nutritional content is designed for different rodents. For example, the fat content of other pelleted foods is usually too high for chinchillas.

Routine Care of Chinchillas

ONE OF THE MOST IMPORTANT REQUIREMENTS of chinchillas is a regular dust bath to keep their fur in top condition. Specially designed baths are available for this purpose, although you can use a glass container if necessary—providing it is large enough for your chinchilla to move around so that the dust coats every part of its body. The container will need to be partially filled with special dust, which is similar to the volcanic ash that these rodents use for this purpose in their natural habitat. Chinchilla dust is readily obtainable from pet stores that sell chinchilla foods and other requisites. Do not be tempted to use sand as a substitute. Pour about 2in (5cm) of the dust into the container, allowing the rodent to roll around here for five minutes or so while the powder removes the grease from its coat.

On average, chinchillas require a dust bath every other day, but occasionally—particularly when the weather is warm—they may need a daily dust bath. Typical signs under these circumstances will be a coat that appears to break (move apart) more readily than usual, lies flat, or is more greasy than normal. Do not allow the chinchillas to bathe too frequently, however, because the powder can dry the skin, causing an irritation. If you see your chinchillas starting to scratch more often than usual, reduce the frequency of dust bathing and, hopefully, this will result in an improvement in the condition.

◀ ▼ A chinchilla dust bathing. The bath contains chinchilla dust (inset) to keep the coat in top condition. Make sure the container gives your pet room to roll around sufficiently for the dust to penetrate the fur.

How to Handle a Chinchilla

● Handling a chinchilla is not difficult and, especially if you start with a youngster about 10–12 weeks old, it will soon become accustomed to being picked up regularly.

● Chinchillas may bite if they become frightened and will shed their fur if handled carelessly.

● Never hold a chinchilla by its tail, since this is also quite fragile.

● Place one hand behind the chinchilla to prevent it from backing away and slide the other hand under the abdomen. Now you can lift it up using both hands.

● If you need to carry the chinchilla, the safest way to do so is with its body lying against your chest and its head pointing upward, supported by a hand at the rear of the body.

Adult chinchillas instinctively know how to use a dust bath, but you may need to encourage younger individuals to venture here initially.

Grooming a Chinchilla

Your chinchilla's coat will need grooming about twice a week on average, and you will need to restrain your pet in order to do this. Special combs are available for grooming. Start at the rear, and comb the back and sides of the body until these appear smooth. Grooming will make the coat more open, enabling the powder from a bath to penetrate further into the pelt. Regular grooming is particularly important during shedding periods, which occur every three months or so. At this stage, the new hair will be clearly apparent emerging through the coat. Usually, there will be a clear line of demarcation between the old and the new fur. This is known as the priming line—a term that originated from the fur trade, with the chinchilla's pelt being considered to be in prime condition when this reached the base of the tail.

▶ *When holding a chinchilla always provide adequate support to the hindquarters with one hand, while gently but firmly restraining the rest of the animal's body with your other hand, as shown here.*

Q&A...

● *Should I allow my chinchilla out to run around the room?*

Young chinchillas are very curious about the world around them and will scamper around madly if they are allowed out, although tame adults will settle more readily in these surroundings. Their jumping abilities mean that ornaments may be knocked over, however. Chinchillas may also gnaw electrical cords, so you will need to prepare the room accordingly. Chinchillas must obviously be kept apart from dogs and cats. It is also very difficult to house-train them, so you must be prepared to clear up after a chinchilla which has been out in a room.

● *Can I reuse the dusting powder?*

Provided that you remove any soiled areas carefully, this can be used over the course of a week or so. Each chinchilla cage should have its own bath and powder, to avoid any risk of transferring infections.

● *Can chinchillas get too hot in the home?*

Yes. Once the temperature reaches 75–80°F (24–27°C) your chinchilla may start showing signs of heat stress—breathing more heavily and trying to stretch out to cool its body. Move the chinchilla immediately to a cooler, but still draft-free, locality, if only on a temporary basis. A fan or cooling unit can be invaluable in such circumstances. Never place a cage in front of a window, because the sun's rays are likely to be intensified, even on a relatively mild day.

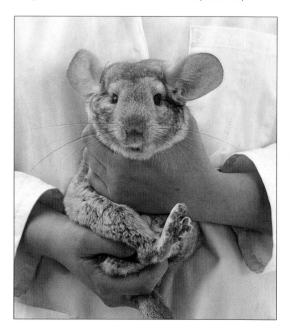

Breeding Chinchillas

CHINCHILLAS MAY START BREEDING WHEN THEY are around seven months old. If the pair are of a similar age, there is less likelihood of any conflict between them. (An older, mature male may attack a young female which does not respond to his advances.) House the chinchillas next to each other for a week or so before attempting to introduce them, and then transfer the male to the female's quarters. Hopefully, after an initial period of mutual sniffing, they will settle down. Nevertheless, you should remain close by until you are certain that they are not likely to fight.

There may be some playful sparring initially, but you will soon notice if they start fighting in earnest because the female will start spraying urine over her would-be partner. If this happens you may need to separate them. Wear a stout pair of gloves when you do so, because of the chance of being bitten. Keep the chinchillas apart for another week, and then try introducing them again in quiet surroundings. They may then accept each other.

It is usually possible to check when a female is ready to mate, because her vaginal opening changes in shape from a slit to an oval. Mating may take place at night, so you may be unaware of the event. Nevertheless, you should find a white, waxy deposit produced by the female—often described as the copulatory plug—on the floor of their quarters.

Pregnancy and Birth

The pair can stay together for much of the pregnancy, but it is better to remove the male just before the birth to avoid the pair mating immediately afterward, when the female may conceive again. Pregnancy typically lasts 111 days, and in the latter stages it is important to increase the amount of food offered to the female. She will start to grow in size in the last quarter, and you should try not to handle her more than is strictly necessary at this stage to avoid any possible damage to her developing offspring.

It is quite normal for a female to lose her

Female

Male

▲ It can be quite difficult to sex chinchillas correctly, especially when the animals are young. A common mistake is to identify the female's urinary opening, which protrudes slightly, as the penis of a male. The gap between this orifice and the anus is much shorter in a female compared with the male, however; this space measures approximately 0.5in (12mm) in a mature individual. In addition, there is a slit between the two openings in the female, which represents the entrance to the vagina. This becomes more prominent when a female chinchilla is in heat. In adults, distinguishing between the sexes from their overall appearance is also possible, since males are smaller overall, with proportionately larger heads.

▲ *A chinchilla suckling from its mother. Sometimes, especially with large litters, there may be a shortage of milk, and aggressive quarrels may break out between the young as they compete for food.*

appetite just before giving birth and sleep on her side. Avoid offering her a dust bath at this stage, because there is a risk that this could predispose her to a vaginal infection. The fully developed young, known as kits, are normally born at night, over the course of two or three hours.

The female chinchilla feeds her offspring in a standing position, and they will be seeking to feed an hour or so after being born. Weaning occurs when the young are between six and eight weeks of age. Excessive amounts of food can be fatal to recently weaned chinchillas, with too many pellets causing diarrhea. Start by giving them half the recommended daily allowance of pellets and hay until they are about five months old. Over the next month, gradually increase this amount to the full adult diet.

● **Is there any particular sign to indicate that the birth process is not proceeding normally?**

This phase normally passes without problems, and do not be concerned if the female cries out in the early stages of birth. It is also quite usual for her to eat the afterbirth, and this is not a sign of impending cannibalism. Should the birth process become protracted, however, extending to four hours, then you should seek veterinary advice without delay. It could well be that one of the litter has become stuck in the birth canal—often because it is abnormally large. A Caesarean section may be required under these circumstances.

● **Is hand-feeding necessary?**

Large litters, comprised of four offspring, are likely to need extra milk. Condensed milk and bottled (unchlorinated) water in a 1:1 ratio can be offered, using a dropper. The kits need to be fed every three or four hours at first. Allow them to drink at their own rate, and then disinfect and rinse the dropper afterward. Ensure the kits are relatively warm, since newborn chinchillas are vulnerable to hypothermia.

Illnesses in Chinchillas

● *Should my chinchilla's teeth and ears be yellowish?*

... This is the normal color of their teeth; white teeth in the chinchilla suggest a vitamin A deficiency. Yellow ears, however, reflect a shortage of vitamin E, and also of choline and methionine, which regulate liver function. In their absence, plant pigments containing carotene are deposited in the skin and body fat.

● *My chinchilla suffers from watery eyes. What should I do?*

Arrange for your veterinarian to check its teeth, because this is usually an early sign of a dental problem, caused by the roots of the teeth growing toward the eyes. A persistent ocular discharge can also be caused by dusting powder, or hay, entering the eye.

● *What is fatty liver disease?*

This is likely to be the result of feeding the chinchilla an unsuitable diet, including peanuts, sunflower seed, and similar items. These will shorten the animal's life expectancy. It can also be linked with a dietary deficiency of vitamin E and obesity. Changing the diet will overcome this problem.

▼ *Rolling and stretching out in this way is often a sign of bloat, resulting from a build-up of gas in the intestine. This condition requires veterinary assistance.*

THE DISTINCTIVE FUR OF THE CHINCHILLA CAN suffer either as the result of a poor diet, or as a result of rough handling. In addition, it is not unknown for chinchillas to chew their own fur. This may occur when they are housed together in pairs, or simply when one chinchilla is housed on its own. In the case of fur chewing, the areas most likely to be affected are the sides of the body and the shoulders, with the fur looking clearly damaged and the undercoat becoming more evident as a result. It can be quite difficult to determine the cause, but this behavior is more common in some bloodlines than others, suggesting that it can be inherited.

Environmental factors may also play a part, with fur chewing being more likely in chinchillas housed in overcrowded conditions or kept in surroundings which are too hot. Such behavior has also been linked with internal disorders such as liver problems, while dietary factors such as a shortage of fiber may also be implicated.

It can therefore be difficult to isolate the cause of fur chewing, which is why the advice of a veterinarian experienced in dealing with chinchillas should be sought. If the underlying problem can be corrected, however, the fur will regrow after shedding.

A specific problem that can arise as a result of the chinchilla's dense fur is the presence of a fur ring in males. In this condition the fur may become twisted tightly around the male's penis as a result of mating, and it should be checked accordingly. If you suspect a fur ring, contact your veterinarian, because you could injure your chinchilla by trying to cut the fur yourself.

Teeth

It is also important to keep a check on a chinchilla's teeth, to ensure they are not becoming overgrown. The incisor teeth at the front of the mouth grow relatively fast—up to 3in (7.5cm) or more in a year. If the teeth become too long, the chinchilla will not be able to eat properly and

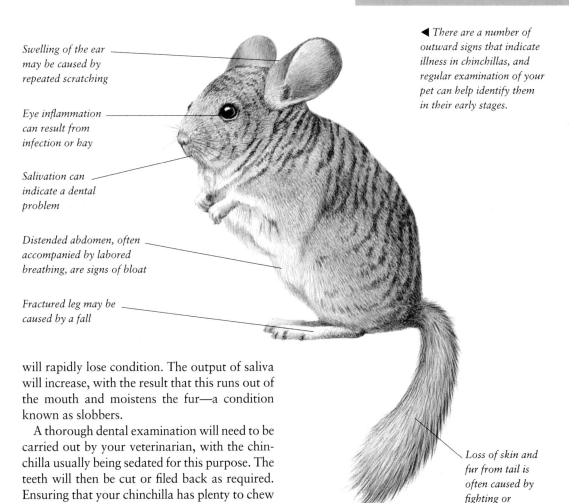

Swelling of the ear
may be caused by
repeated scratching

Eye inflammation
can result from
infection or hay

Salivation can
indicate a dental
problem

Distended abdomen, often
accompanied by labored
breathing, are signs of bloat

Fractured leg may be
caused by a fall

◀ *There are a number of
outward signs that indicate
illness in chinchillas, and
regular examination of your
pet can help identify them
in their early stages.*

Loss of skin and
fur from tail is
often caused by
fighting or
careless handling

will rapidly lose condition. The output of saliva will increase, with the result that this runs out of the mouth and moistens the fur—a condition known as slobbers.

A thorough dental examination will need to be carried out by your veterinarian, with the chinchilla usually being sedated for this purpose. The teeth will then be cut or filed back as required. Ensuring that your chinchilla has plenty to chew on, including a pumice block, may help prevent any recurrence. Since this problem can be inherited, it is recommended that you do not breed from affected individuals.

Dietary Problems

The dietary needs of chinchillas are highly specific, and changes to their diet are likely to result in a range of potentially serious digestive problems. Bloat is relatively common in young kits which are being hand-fed. This causes great discomfort to the young chinchilla, and will need urgent veterinary attention. Diluting the feeding mixture should help prevent a recurrence.

Unsuitable foods can also result in bloat, as well as having more serious effects on the body. Peanuts and other oil-rich seeds such as sunflower will soon affect the liver, causing fatty deposits in this organ.

When a chinchilla has diarrhea, it is virtually impossible to determine the cause accurately at first, although treatment will ultimately need to be given. Fluid replacement is the first course of action taken by a veterinarian and should help to counteract the severe dehydration which accompanies the condition. The results of subsequent laboratory tests will help to highlight the precise cause of the problem and, most importantly, whether it was caused by harmful microbes.

Cold, burnt toast may help to settle a digestive disturbance of this type, but since the natural rhythm of the digestive system has been disturbed, constipation often follows diarrhea. Green vegetables in moderation are then often recommended under these circumstances.

Chinchilla Color Varieties

THE NORMAL FORM OF THE CHINCHILLA IS described as the Standard; it displays a combination of bluish-gray tipped fur and a paler belly. The depth of coloration varies considerably between individuals, however, with some being much darker than others. This feature depends on the extent of the pigmentation running down each hair. Subdivisions within the Standard category are now being developed as chinchillas start to become more commonly exhibited, so that clear delineation is now often possible between Medium and Dark Standards. The tipping, sometimes described as veiling, extends over the entire body—apart from the pale belly—right down to the tip of the tail.

LIGHT-COLORED VARIETIES

Chinchilla color variants were first recorded in the 1950s, and their numbers have increased rapidly over recent years. The original white form, known as Wilson's White after the name of its breeder, can be distinguished from the Pink White by its dark ears and black eyes. All Whites

● *What are lethal factors?*

A number of chinchilla color varieties have lethal factors associated with them. This means that if you pair such colors together, no offspring are likely to result because the embryos will not develop. It is therefore important not to pair Whites together, but to mate them back to Standards, for example, which should also maintain the quality of the chinchilla's distinctive coat. Similarly, there is a lethal factor associated with both Black and Brown Velvets.

● *What influences the price of chinchilla colors?*

This depends on a number of factors, but chiefly the relative scarcity of the color form concerned. New colors are bound to be rarer and therefore more costly than well-established colors. The quality of the coat can also be a deciding factor in some cases.

▼ *A Pink White chinchilla, distinguished by the pink color of its ears and eyes. White forms of the chinchilla are now common, having first been bred in North Carolina during 1955.*

should have coats of a pure, snowy-white color.

Other paler colors include the Silver, with its silvery-gray coloration, and the Platinum, which has a bluish tone to its coat. Pied forms of the chinchilla have also been developed, in which the tipping is absent from some areas of the body. They are described as Mosaics.

The beige form of the chinchilla also exists in two varieties, although they represent the same mutation. Under normal circumstances, the genes responsible for an individual's characteristics—including color—are located on the chromosomes present in the nucleus of every living cell in the body. Sometimes both of the genes responsible for a color variety are the same. This state is described as homozygous. If, however, the genes responsible for a specific variety are different, then the combination is referred to as heterozygous.

Generally, it is not possible to distinguish visually between homozygous and heterozygous individuals, since one color is dominant over the other. But the beige mutation of the chinchilla is unusual in that a distinct difference in appearance between homozygous and heterozygous

▼ *A Black Velvet. Note the underparts are lighter than the remainder of the fur on the body. This distinguishes the Black Velvet from the uniformly colored Ebony.*

individuals exists. The homozygous Beige chinchilla is a very light shade of cream, with a pinkish hue. The eyes are also pink, with a white iris. The heterozygous Beige chinchilla is darker, varying in tone from cream to dark beige, depending on the individual. The underparts are significantly paler than the body, with the eyes being reddish in this variety. Light colored examples of the Beige are also known as Pearls, while those with darker coloration are called Pastels.

DARK-COLORED VARIETIES

The first black examples of the chinchilla emerged in 1956. They are often known as Black Velvets. Their coloration varies from matt to shiny black, while the underparts are paler. The Charcoal is an even shade of gray over its entire body although, in both these cases, the coloration may be less bright on the underparts.

A similar division exists in the case of the brown varieties, between the Brown itself, with its even coloration, and the Brown Velvet, in which the upperparts are darker than the fur on the belly. The Brown is also known as the Brown Ebony and has pink ears and matching eyes.

Violets are one of the latest additions to the list of chinchilla colors, distinguishable by their soft gray shading and white underparts. This variant originated in Zimbabwe.

Chipmunks and Other Small Animals

THE GROWING INTEREST IN SMALL ANIMALS AS PETS HAS LED TO AN increasing number of other species being kept and bred by enthusiasts over recent years. Although the requirements of some of these mammals are more demanding than those covered previously in this book, there are signs that several of the more easily maintained species could start to rival more established favorites in their popularity.

In North America, African pygmy hedgehogs have already gained a strong following as house pets, thriving and becoming tame in these surroundings. There are also signs that the degu, a relative of the chinchilla, is growing in popularity. Chipmunks have been quite widely kept for some time, but their behavior is such that they are really pets to be appreciated from a distance rather than handled. They also need spacious accommodation because of their active natures. Sugar gliders, too, should be housed in an aviary-type structure, whereas an enclosed paddock area will be needed for maras.

In general, many of the new, more exotic small animals now being kept as pets are descended from stock bred in zoological collections. A number of specialist breeders are also maintaining some of the more unusual species, and surplus stock may become available to pet-owners from this source.

One of the key factors determining whether or not a species becomes well established as a pet is the number of unrelated individuals available at the outset. Although the Syrian hamster shows that it is possible for a species to become domesticated from a small number of closely related individuals, this is an exception. There are various other rodents that have bred successfully in collections for a number of years, and then the fertility of the bloodlines drops dramatically due to persistent in-breeding, to the extent that, ultimately, the strain may be lost.

▶ *Chipmunks make lively companions. They spend a lot of time on the ground, as well as climbing about on branches, and this behavior must be reflected in their accommodation.*

Chipmunk Lifestyles

CHIPMUNKS ARE REPRESENTATIVES OF THE THIRD suborder within the rodent grouping, comprising the sciuromorph, or squirrel-like, category. This grouping has a very wide distribution across all the world's continents, although sciuromorphs are not found naturally in Australia. Chipmunks are very closely related to true tree-dwelling squirrels, as is apparent from their appearance. Both have highly flexible, bushy tails, as well as adept front paws which allow them to hold and manipulate their food easily.

This close similarity is also evident from their behavior. Chipmunks are active during the day and climb readily, scampering up and along branches, bounding from one to another, and displaying an excellent sense of balance. Even so, they are actually described by zoologists as ground squirrels. This is because they spend much of their time on the ground, even hoarding their food in underground burrows.

Although all but one of the 25 species of chipmunk occur in North America and do not differ significantly in their care requirements, it is the widely distributed Siberian species from Asia that is most commonly kept as a pet. In spite of its name, this particular chipmunk is found over a very wide area of eastern Asia, being present not just in Siberia but also Mongolia, northern and central China, and Korea. A number of distinctive subspecies are found through this range, with one of the most colorful having evolved on the Japanese island of Hokkaido.

Originating from temperate areas of the world, where the winters can be very cold, chipmunks have evolved various strategies for surviving under these conditions. Their coats become thicker and bushier in the winter, giving them better protection against the elements. Prior to the start of periods of snowfall, they build up food stores to sustain them over this period. Unlike true ground squirrels (*Spermophilus* species), chipmunks do not hibernate—although in severe weather they enter a

Fact File

Name:	Siberian Chipmunk
Scientific name:	*Eutamius sibericus*
Weight:	3.5–4.4oz (100–125g)
Compatibility:	Disagreements less likely if kept in true pairs or groups comprised of a single male with up to three females. Males housed together can fight viciously.
Appeal:	Attractive appearance. Lively and active during the daytime. Suitable for housing either indoors or outside in most areas.
Diet:	Mixture of seeds and nuts, as well as fruit and greenfood.
Health problems:	Can suffer from dental problems, particularly the incisors at the front of the mouth which become overgrown or damaged.
Breeding tips:	Ensure the female has sufficient material to line her nesting box, particularly if the chipmunks are housed outdoors.
Pregnancy:	4–5 weeks
Typical litter size:	Up to 8 young; average 4 per litter.
Weaning:	40–45 days
Lifespan:	Typically 5–6 years. Can be as long as 12 years.

state of torpidity, remaining asleep in their burrows for up to eight days without feeding.

Coat Coloration

The colorful coat markings associated with chipmunks help to provide them with camouflage when they are in the open. The stripes serve to break up the outline of their bodies, particularly in partially wooded areas. Feeding is a potentially dangerous time in the wild for chipmunks, and as with hamsters, they have extensive cheek pouches in which they can quickly store relatively large amounts of food. This is then carried back to the safety of their burrows either to eat there or to store as a larder.

Siberian chipmunks have been kept as pets since the 1950s, but it was not until the mid-

1980s that they started to become well known. The influence of the Hokkaido subspecies in today's domesticated strains can be seen in individuals which have more reddish or cinnamon hues in their coats. These chipmunks are also often slightly smaller compared with true mainland forms.

Two color mutations have also been developed. The dilute or white form is the most common. Their coats are much paler than normal, with beige stripes on their tails and deep, ruby-red eyes. In the nest, however, dilutes resemble young normals, until they are about 12 days old, by which time their paler fur will be clearly apparent. The rarer albino variant differs from the white form by having pure, snow-white fur and red eyes. These chipmunks also tend to be smaller. It is usually recommended that albinos are mated to other colors on a regular basis, both to improve their size and maintain their fertility. This approach can be beneficial when breeding dilutes as well.

▼ *Chipmunks are close relatives of true squirrels. Like squirrels, chipmunks can jump from branch to branch with great ease, assisted by their muscular back legs.*

Q&A...

● *What sort of behavior can I expect from a pet chipmunk?*

These rodents will not take to being cuddled like, for example, a rabbit will. Nor will they sit quietly for long periods, because they are very lively. Even so, it is quite possible to tame them sufficiently to feed from the hand and perhaps perch on your shoulder.

● *What should I look for when buying a chipmunk?*

The points you need to check are very similar to those which apply to other rodents. It is important that the incisor teeth are not overgrown and meet properly at the front of the mouth. The chipmunk should appear bright and lively; avoid dull individuals or any sitting with their fur fluffed up. The fur should show no thinning or blemishes, the nose must be free from any discharge, the eyes should be clear and bright with no trace of any opacity, and the ears must not be torn. The tail should be straight, with no trace of deviation which could suggest a past fracture.

● *What is the best age to obtain a chipmunk?*

If you are hoping to tame your pet, it is important to obtain a youngster between the ages of two and three months. Beware of purchasing older individuals unless you can be certain about their history, since they could have become aggressive.

Housing and Feeding Chipmunks

CHIPMUNKS MUST HAVE SPACIOUS QUARTERS, designed on the lines of an aviary-type structure. For indoor housing, special all-metal cages for chipmunks are available, or alternatively, a flight cage of the type sold for birds can be used. Whatever cage is chosen, it should be as large as possible to accommodate these lively rodents.

It is also possible to keep chipmunks successfully in outdoor enclosures, which should be built on the same lines as a small aviary. You can buy aviary panels, which simply need to be bolted together, or you can make your own. If you make your own, use timber at least 1.5in (4cm) square for the frames, and cover these with 16G (16-gauge) mesh. The strands of the mesh should measure 0.5in (12mm) square. This will exclude wild rodents such as mice which might enter and spread disease to the chipmunks.

The panels must be fixed on a brick or block-work base, extending at least 1ft (30cm) below ground level and attached to it by means of special brackets. The enclosure itself should be sited in a sheltered part of the garden, out of the direction of the prevailing wind if possible. Because chipmunks are keen burrowers, it is important that there is a secure base to their enclosure, made of concrete or paving slabs, to prevent them tunneling out and escaping. Cover the base with several inches of bark chippings, which will still allow the chipmunks to excavate.

Protection from the elements is important if the chipmunks are going to be kept outside throughout the year. A small shelter should be attached to their enclosure, and this also has the advantage of providing a dry locality in which you can place their food.

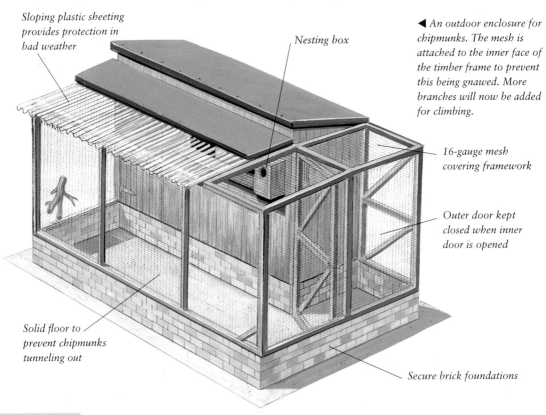

Sloping plastic sheeting provides protection in bad weather

Nesting box

◀ An outdoor enclosure for chipmunks. The mesh is attached to the inner face of the timber frame to prevent this being gnawed. More branches will now be added for climbing.

16-gauge mesh covering framework

Outer door kept closed when inner door is opened

Solid floor to prevent chipmunks tunneling out

Secure brick foundations

Chipmunk Nesting Boxes

● A choice of nesting boxes, each about 8in (20cm) square should be made available.

● Nesting boxes must be made of relatively thick timber, partly to withstand the chipmunks' teeth but also to keep the interior warmer if they are outside.

● Fix the nesting boxes securely to the framework with brackets, and ensure they are located under cover.

● Do not put the boxes on the floor, since their bases will inevitably become wet.

Fitting Out the Enclosure

Items such as hollow logs or clay tunnels to provide amusement and exercise can also be supplied on the floor of the enclosure. Branches should be provided to enable the chipmunks to climb easily around their quarters and enter the nesting box, and these should be cut from non-poisonous trees (such as apple) which have not recently been sprayed with chemicals. The branches should be relatively thick and must be fastened securely in place. The safest method of fixing these is to use short, right-angled brackets, fixing one end to an upright part of the framework and the other to the underside of the branch, thus supporting it from beneath.

Food for Chipmunks

Feeding chipmunks is straightforward. In common with many other herbivorous rodents, they have a large cecum in which beneficial bacteria help to break down the plant matter in their diet (see page 32). They consume their softer cecal pellets, so that they can then obtain the nutrients on the second passage through their intestinal tract.

It may be possible to obtain specially prepared chipmunk seed mixtures, but those produced for rats and mice are usually quite adequate. Avoid offering oats, because the sharp ends of this cereal seed can stick in their cheek pouches. Pine nuts can be added to their food mix.

● *I'm worried about a chipmunk escaping when I enter their enclosure. Any suggestions about what I can do to prevent this?*

Use a safety porch, which will enable you to go through the outer door, closing this behind you before opening the door to the chipmunks' enclosure. If one does slip past you, it will be confined in the safety porch, from where it can be easily persuaded back into its enclosure.

● *What additional protection should chipmunks have against the elements?*

It is a sensible precaution to fix some corrugated plastic sheeting over the roof section nearest to the shelter and also on the adjacent sides of the framework, so the chipmunks can remain outside without being exposed to the worst of the weather.

● *Should chipmunks be offered fresh foods?*

Items such as sweet apple, carrot, and greenfood should be offered to chipmunks on a regular basis, but do not give large quantities, mainly because a surplus is likely to be stored in the nest, where it may rapidly turn moldy, endangering their health.

◄ *Drinking water should be supplied in a bottle attached through the mesh of the enclosure. The bottle must be firmly supported and securely fixed so that the chipmunks cannot dislodge it.*

Mealworm

Giant mealworm

◄▲ *Chipmunk food should be offered in solid earthenware bowls. Avoid feeding too much sunflower seed, because of its high oil content. Mealworms, however, can provide a valuable source of protein.*

Breeding and Illnesses in Chipmunks

THERE WILL BE OCCASIONS WHEN YOU NEED TO catch and hold your chipmunks, particularly if you wish to sex them or examine them, or because you suspect a health problem. Although chipmunks can be persuaded to rest on your shoulder, they can be hard to catch since they dislike being handled. A deep net with a well-padded rim, as sold for catching birds, is also ideal for catching chipmunks. Move slowly and carefully to avoid scaring the chipmunk, and place the net over the animal when it is sitting on a suitable surface.

Then lift the chipmunk carefully out of the net, wearing a pair of strong gardening gloves to protect yourself against being bitten. Restrain a chipmunk by placing your fingers each side of the head, with its back lying in the palm of your hand. This will then allow you to look at most of its body. Always avoid grabbing a chipmunk by its tail, because this is likely to cause injury.

Q&A...

● I am keen to breed from my pair of chipmunks, but how should I introduce them?

House them in close proximity to each other and wait until the female is calling. Then transfer her into the male's quarters, removing her a few days later after mating has occurred.

● Should I check the nest when I suspect the young have been born?

No, this is not recommended, because you are likely to disturb the mother, particularly if you touch the lining in the box and introduce a strange scent here. She may either attack or abandon her young as a result. Only inspect the nest if you suspect something is wrong.

▼ *Chipmunks can be hand-fed at first using evaporated milk diluted with two parts boiled, cooled water. Make this fresh for each feed, and offer the mix through a syringe with no needle attached. Afterward, wash utensils thoroughly in baby bottle cleaner and rinse well.*

Mating and Birth

In common with other rodents, the difference in the length of the anogenital gap enables the sexes to be distinguished easily, whatever their age. It is longer in the male than in the female. The anogenital gap is visible when the animal is turned on its back. Only as males come into breeding condition will the testes become clearly apparent, occupying this space.

Mating occurs throughout the spring and summer. Female chipmunks come into heat about two weeks after the male's testes descend down into the scrotum again. It is quite easy to tell when a female is ready to mate, because she will utter a series of chirping calls to attract a male, with her period of estrus lasting about three days. Mating usually takes place on the second day.

Prior to giving birth to her litter, the female chipmunk will start to spend longer in her nesting box. The young are blind and helpless at birth. Although you are likely to hear them calling while they are in the nest, this is not generally a cause for concern. Their eyes will open by the time they are two weeks old, and their fur will be apparent by this stage. At about five weeks old they emerge from the nest for the first time, and they then resemble miniature adults.

It is possible to leave the family together for another two months, but the young can usually be taken away at seven weeks old. This will be essential if you hope to breed from the female again before the end of the breeding period. Generally, chipmunks only have one litter per year. Replace the nesting box with a clean one after the young have been removed.

Health Problems

Chipmunks living outside are more susceptible to parasites such as fleas and harvest mites, which are prevalent in the summertime and can build up in the confines of a nest. Persistent scratching, rather than regular grooming, combined with hair loss are typical indicators of a parasitic problem. Seek veterinary advice for the best method of treatment and to eliminate the risk of further infestations of this type.

There can be other causes of itching, however, with this problem sometimes being linked to an

▲ *When holding a chipmunk, be sure to restrain it securely in your hand to avoid being bitten. Chipmunks may prove harder to hold than most other pet rodents, simply because they are unaccustomed to this treatment.*

excess of flaked corn in the chipmunk's diet.

Overgrowth of the teeth is a problem that can be encountered if a chipmunk is being offered unsuitable food and is deprived of opportunities to gnaw branches. As a preventive measure, it is wise to provide a dog biscuit on a regular basis. This will help to wear down the teeth.

The sharp teeth of chipmunks can inflict painful bites if they squabble, and abscesses will develop should any wounds become infected. In the case of minor injuries treat these with an antiseptic, but if they subsequently swell up, seek veterinary advice. Antibiotic treatment may be necessary under these circumstances.

Injuries to the eyes can also be the result of fighting, although they may also be caused by unsuitable, sharp bedding. For this reason, always provide the chipmunks with special small animal bedding with which to line their nest. Treatment for injured eyes will require the application of an ophthalmic ointment or drops several times daily. If this is needed, it may be best to keep the chipmunk confined in a smaller cage for the duration of treatment, because catching it regularly could prove to be very stressful.

Other New World Rodents

Several other caviomorph rodents, apart from the guinea pig and chinchilla, are becoming increasingly popular as pets.

DEGU

Foremost among these at present is the degu which, like many of today's pet rodents, was first kept for medical research in the 1950s. Degus live in colonies in the Andean region of South America. They leap at fast speed over rocks to escape predators—for there is little natural cover in the part of the world they inhabit—although their agouti coloration assists in camouflage. The tail is covered in relatively coarse hair. The tip is delicate and easily injured, so they must never be restrained by this part of the body. If damaged, the injured portion of the tail will be shed and does not regrow. A point of difference with the chinchilla is that degus have sharp claws, which they will use for digging.

A large mesh enclosure indoors will provide suitable housing for a pair of these rodents, but take care to ensure that they will not be able to gnaw their way out with their sharp incisor teeth. Provide a range of clay pipes on the floor of their quarters, in which they can hide. The pipes can connect with a sleeping box. Branches for gnawing purposes are also needed. Alternatively, a pair of degus can be kept in a large, converted aquarium, with a well-ventilated lid.

Chinchilla pellets (see page 178) form the basis

Q&A...

● Are there other rodents from this part of the world which may become popular pets?

It is hard to predict, but there are a number of Cuban hutias (*Capromys pilorides*) descended from zoo stock now being bred in private collections. These are very appealing, tree-climbing rodents, with attractive, silvery-gray fur. Because they can measure up to 2ft (60cm) in length and can weigh as much as 15lb (7kg), they need a spacious indoor enclosure. Cuban hutias are primarily vegetarian in their feeding habits, browsing on leaves as well as bark stripped off branches, and various fruits. They are well adapted to life off the ground, with their tails being used for support as they climb around the branches. Females give birth to up to four young, born fully developed, after a gestation period of about 120 days.

Fact File

Names:	Degu; Mara (Patagonian Cavy/Patagonian Hare)
Scientific names:	*Octodon degus; Dolichotis patagonum*
Weight:	Degu 9–13oz (250–350g); mara 18–20lb (8–9kg).
Compatibility:	Quite social, but fighting will occur in overcrowded conditions.
Appeal:	Unusual and interesting animals.
Diet:	Degu based on chinchilla pellets; mara diet is greenfood, hay, and special pellets.
Health problems:	Dental problems relating to the incisors can occur.
Breeding tips:	Females with recently born young may be nervous, especially if they have not given birth before.
Pregnancy:	Both species about 90 days.
Typical litter size:	Degu 5 young; mara 1–3 young.
Weaning:	Degu 5 weeks; mara 8–12 weeks.
Lifespan:	Degu 5–6 years; mara 10–12 years.

◀ *Degus are diurnal (active by day). They are naturally inquisitive, and this means that within the home they are likely to become very tame if given regular attention.*

of the diet for these rodents, and a little green-food and fruit should also be offered, along with plenty of top-quality hay. Although some breeders use a seed-based diet, this is less satisfactory because it is likely to lead to obesity, with the added risk of the degus then developing diabetes mellitus as well. Degus may bathe in a similar way to chinchillas (see page 180), and should be provided with a dust bath for this purpose.

Sexing is straightforward, with the anogenital gap again being longer in males compared with females. It is usual to allow these rodents to breed from the age of six months onward. The pair can remain together throughout the subsequent pregnancy, with the young being born fully developed. They will start sampling solid food when two weeks old. Young degus can be tamed quite easily, since they will soon learn to feed from the hand. Their active nature means that they do not like to be restrained and petted, preferring to scamper around instead.

MARA

The mara is somewhat similar to the degu in appearance but significantly larger. In view of the space these rodents require, they are more commonly seen in zoos. However, if you have sufficient land and you can construct an escape-proof enclosure for them, then they can be fascinating to keep, especially as a group. As well as being able to run, or retreat into their burrow, maras can also jump well.

Barrels will be needed to provide shelter for maras housed indoors, along with some straw placed in piles on the ground. Their indoor quarters need to be kept relatively warm. A heat lamp can be used for this, but take care to ensure the electrical supply is kept well out of reach of their sharp teeth. It should also be born in mind that maras are nervous animals, particularly when moved to new quarters.

Maras are vegetarian, but it is important not to change their diet suddenly. This is particularly important if you are allowing them into an outdoor paddock for the first time, where they will have free access to grass. Provide them with fresh cut grass for about two weeks beforehand, and then increase the quantity on offer so their digestive system adapts accordingly. A special zoo diet as produced for ruminants can form the basis of their meals. You can also add hay, alfalfa, carrots, and other vegetables, as well as similar foods like chopped apples in moderation.

Breeding males can sometimes be aggressive toward their offspring, so it may be advisable to allow the females to rear young on their own. The young are born fully developed.

▼ *A young mara with its mother. These large members of the rodent clan are certainly not suitable for keeping in the home, and housing them outdoors is an expensive undertaking due to their specialized needs.*

Other Small Animals

OTHER SMALL ANIMALS, OR POCKET PETS AS they are better known in North America, are also growing in popularity. However, there may be legal restrictions on keeping and breeding them in some American states, so check current regulations with your local USDA office first.

AFRICAN PYGMY HEDGEHOG

The African pygmy hedgehog is a member of the insectivores, presently more widely kept in North America than Europe. These hedgehogs are descended from zoo stock and first started to attract attention among pet-seekers in the 1980s.

Although the original stock proved to be shy, today's domesticated strains are often described as "roll free." This means that the hedgehogs have lost their fear of people, to the extent that they will usually not roll up into a ball when they are handled. Housing is quite straightforward, with a covered indoor cage being suitable for them, although breeders often prefer to house pregnant females in indoor hutches which afford more privacy when they have young.

There are now special canned or dry hedgehog foods available for African pygmy hedgehogs.

▼ *Handling pygmy hedgehogs is not too difficult, since their spines are not especially rigid. It is still advisable to wear a thin pair of leather gloves as a form of protection.*

Fact File

Names:	African Pygmy Hedgehog; Sugar Glider
Scientific names:	*Atelerix albiventris; Petaurus breviceps*
Weight:	African pygmy hedgehog 1lb (0.45kg); sugar glider 3.4–5.7oz (95–160g). Males generally heavier.
Compatibility:	African pygmy hedgehog usually kept alone; sugar glider highly social.
Appeal:	African pygmy hedgehog cute and relatively easy to handle; sugar glider has unusual appearance and breeding habits.
Diet:	African pygmy hedgehog eats hedgehog food, invertebrates, hard-boiled eggs, and chopped fruit; sugar glider needs fruit, nectar, and invertebrates like mealworms or crickets.
Health problems:	Generally very healthy, but can be susceptible to diarrhea from unsuitable diet or dirty food containers.
Breeding tips:	Females with recently born young may be nervous, especially if they have not given birth before. Avoid handling or disturbing them accordingly.
Pregnancy:	African pygmy hedgehog 32–36 days; sugar glider 16 days gestation plus 70 days in the pouch.
Typical litter size:	African pygmy hedgehog 4–5 young; sugar glider 2 young.
Weaning:	African pygmy hedgehog 6 weeks; sugar glider 24–32 weeks.
Lifespan:	10–12 years

These are often stocked by larger pet stores, although dog and cat food can be provided as an alternative. Occasional hard-boiled eggs, cottage cheese, and invertebrates such as mealworms can also feature in their diet, but avoid milk, which is likely to lead to diarrhea. Drinking water must always be provided, preferably in a small, heavyweight bowl.

Examining the underside of the hedgehog's body enables it to be sexed easily. In males, the penis is directed forward, almost in the middle of the belly, whereas females have five pairs of teats evident here and their anogenital gap is much shorter than in males. Males also tend to be larger when adult. Pairing often consists of leaving the male and female together for two days, then separating them for ten days, reintroducing them for a similar period and then repeating this process after a further interval, since females do not ovulate on a consistent basis.

A nesting box should be provided on the floor of the female's quarters, in which she can have her young. This, like the floor of her quarters, should be lined with coarse wood shavings. It is vital not to disturb her now, because she may eat her offspring. The young are naked at birth, but the spines, which are modified hairs, soon appear. When the young are a month old, the nest can be removed—by which time they will be active and will soon start taking solid food.

SUGAR GLIDERS

The requirements of sugar gliders are more demanding, partly because they need much more spacious accommodation, in the form of an indoor aviary. These possums have been kept as pets for many years in their Australian homeland; they also occur in New Guinea. As their name suggests, sugar gliders have folds of skin around the sides of their bodies, which allow them to glide short distances from tree to tree. They are social and live harmoniously in groups.

In terms of housing, ease of cleanliness is a very important feature which must be carefully considered, due to their diet. Fruit—both fresh and dry—should constitute about three-quarters of their food intake. Lesser amounts of vegetable matter, a few nuts, and protein in the form of cat food and mealworms are eaten as well. They also require a nectar solution of the type given to aviary birds, and this must be provided in a sealed container due to its sticky nature.

It is important to match the amount of food being offered to sugar gliders to their appetites, in order to minimize wastage. Thanks to the perishable nature of their food, they will need to be fed twice daily. Feeding utensils should all be thoroughly washed with a detergent after use and then rinsed, and their quarters must also be wiped down regularly, because of the messy nature of their droppings.

Q&A...

● *Have any color varieties emerged in African pygmy hedgehogs yet?*

Yes, pale-colored hedgehogs have already been bred, in contrast to the normal agouti coloration. They include red-eyed whites (which are true albinos), as well as dark-eyed whites, cream, and piebald variants.

● *How should I make a nesting box for sugar gliders?*

Use melamine-covered chipboard for this purpose, since this is very easy to clean thoroughly simply by wiping it over with a damp cloth. Soft paper bedding, as sold for other small pets, can be used as a nest lining.

▼ *Sugar gliders are marsupials and, just like kangaroos, their young are very tiny and embryonic at birth. They must crawl into their mother's pouch, on the lower part of her body, where they will continue their development. The young will be mature by about a year old.*

Basic Genetics

Genetics is the study of the science of inheritance. Like most living things, small animals have sets of chromosomes in their cells which carry the genes determining all the characteristics of the individual—such as gender, coat color, or ear length in rabbits. The number of chromosomes varies between different species; mice, for example, have a total of 40 sets, whereas rats have 44 sets. (This difference effectively prevents cross-breeding between these rodents.) Members of the caviomorph group have even more chromosomes—for example, in the guinea pig there are 64 sets.

The sets of chromosomes are normally arranged in pairs. Sperm and egg cells only have half a set of chromosomes, but following fertilization of the female egg by the male sperm when reproduction occurs, the chromosomes of the sperm and egg unite to form complete pairs again. In this way, the offspring receive half their chromosomes from each parent.

Autosomal Recessive Mutations

A series of rules, called the rules of inheritance, operates during breeding. Central to these is the fact that the genes on one of the chromosomes—and representing the Normal form of an organism—can be genetically dominant over those present on the other when they pair together following fertilization. This situation occurs in the autosomal recessive mutation, which is the most common type of mutation demonstrating the rules of inheritance. It means that, for example, when a short-coated Syrian hamster is mated with a long-coated individual, all the offspring will have short coats. This is because the Normal, or short-coated gene, is dominant over its long-coated counterpart.

However, when a normal-coated and long-coated hamster are paired together, the gene responsible for long hair is also transferred to the offspring, despite the fact that they in turn all appear to be short-coated. The significance of this is that in matings where two recessive genes pair together, there is no dominant gene to mask their effect, and so the characteristic of the recessive

gene is then expressed instead. It is impossible to distinguish visually between a normal-coated or homozygous individual (in which both genes encode for this characteristic) and a heterozygous individual which has one short-coated gene and another for long hair, because only the short-coated gene is expressed in the animal's appearance or phenotype.

Five different pairings are possible involving this mutation. They are shown on the opposite page. Although these illustrations describe coat length in the Syrian hamster, the same underlying genetic principles can be applied to various other characteristics like coat color or other coat types, for example.

As with all genetic predictions, these figures are only averages, because genetic recombinations are random, and the results of individual pairings may sometimes differ from the predicted outcome. Nevertheless, if a normal-coated individual paired with a long-coated individual produces long-coated offspring, then you can be certain that the normal-coated parent is heterozygous. Under normal circumstances involving autosomal recessive mutations, the recessive characteristic will not re-emerge until the second generation—known as the F2 generation. (This corresponds to the second, third, and fourth pairings described in the diagrams opposite.)

Sex Linkage

Sometimes, the recessive characteristic—for example, a particular color—is present on the pair of sex chromosomes which determine the individual's gender. An example of this is the tortoiseshell mutation seen in the Syrian hamster. In this instance, the pattern of inheritance is slightly different, because in the male this pair of chromosomes are of unequal length. One chromosome, described as the Y chromosome, is shorter than the corresponding X chromosome.

As a result, males cannot be heterozygous or "split," and therefore cannot carry both genes, since only one is present on the unpaired portion of the X chromosome. Their genetic makeup will therefore match their appearance, because there is

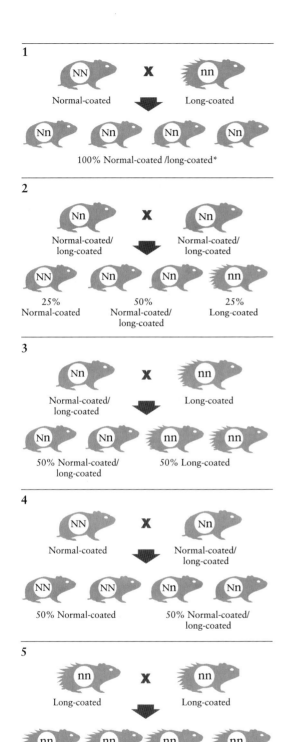

1

NN × nn
Normal-coated   Long-coated

Nn   Nn   Nn   Nn

100% Normal-coated /long-coated*

2

Nn × Nn
Normal-coated/   Normal-coated/
long-coated   long-coated

NN   Nn   Nn   nn

25%   50%   25%
Normal-coated   Normal-coated/   Long-coated
    long-coated

3

Nn × nn
Normal-coated/   Long-coated
long-coated

Nn   Nn   nn   nn

50% Normal-coated/   50% Long-coated
long-coated

4

NN × Nn
Normal-coated   Normal-coated/
    long-coated

NN   NN   Nn   Nn

50% Normal-coated   50% Normal-coated/
    long-coated

5

nn × nn
Long-coated   Long-coated

nn   nn   nn   nn

100% Long-coated

(*Whenever the genes for both characteristics are present, the recessive gene is indicated second.)

no opposing gene on the shorter, corresponding Y chromosome. Females, however, which have paired XX chromosomes, can appear either normal or yellow, or as the heterozygous combination known as tortoiseshell. The consequence of this is that male tortoiseshell hamsters are virtually unknown. They can only occur if there is a very rare chromosomal aberration leading to three chromosomes being present (XXY)—a condition described as trisomy.

Genetic Problems

In a few instances, lethal genes may also be involved during breeding. These are genes which have an adverse effect on the development of the young and may even render them non viable. This situation sometimes occurs in chinchillas. It is also seen in the dominant white mutation of mice and in the light gray form of the Syrian hamster, among others.

Problems are also likely to occur in pairings between White-bellied Syrian hamsters, and also between pairings of the Dalmatian guinea pig. These colors should always be outcrossed to Normal individuals rather than to others of the same color. Failure to do this could result in the birth of young with deformed or missing eyes.

Other Considerations

Characteristics such as Satin and Rex coat types, the crests on guinea pigs, and darker patterning are all determined by genes different from those controlling coloration, with the result that they can be associated with coats of different colors.

It is vital to maintain detailed stock records if you wish to breed particular colors, because this will enable you to trace the ancestry of the small animals concerned. Only with this information can you decide on the most appropriate pairings. Satin-coated animals should not be paired together in any case, because this leads to a rapid deterioration in the quality of the coat, which becomes thinner than usual in their offspring.

◄ *The five possible pairings, and the likely ratios of coat length in the offspring, when normal-coated and long-coated Syrian hamsters are mated together.*

Glossary

Agouti A coat pattern consisting of alternate dark and light banding running down individual hairs; common in many wild RODENTS.

Albino A MUTATION in which all color pigment is missing, resulting in white fur, pink skin, and red eyes.

Anogenital gap The region between the anal and genital openings.

Autosomal recessive mutation A MUTATION linked with the autosomes (CHROMOSOMES that have no influence over the animal's gender). The recessive nature of such mutations means that their characteristics will not emerge in the offspring if paired with a pure, NORMAL individual.

Bicolor Describes coat coloration in which two colors are evident, one of which is often white.

Boar A male guinea pig.

Breed A domesticated form of an animal with clearly defined, reproducible features which set it apart from its wild ancestor and other breeds.

Buck A male rabbit or mouse.

Cannibalism The tendency of some animals to eat their own kind. More prevalent in the mother, which may attack her newborn young, particularly if she is disturbed.

Caviomorph A member of one of the subgroups within the order Rodentia, whose members are characterized by relatively long gestation periods and the advanced development of their young at birth. Includes guinea pigs and chinchillas.

Cavy An alternative name for a guinea pig, derived from the animal's scientific name *Cavia*.

Cecum An enlargement of the digestive tract between the small and large intestines; vital for the breakdown of plant matter, since it contains protozoa and other microbes that can digest cellulose present in the cell walls of plants.

Chromosome One of the threadlike, normally paired structures present in the nucleus of all living cells. Chromosomes contain the GENES.

Closed ring A closed, circular, metal band placed over the hind foot of a rabbit; used for identification.

Cobby Of thickset appearance.

Cub A young rat.

Dilute coloration A paler-than-usual version of a color.

Diurnal Active during the day.

Doe A female rabbit or mouse.

Dominant characteristic A genetic characteristic that should emerge in a first generation pairing with a pure, NORMAL individual of the same SPECIES.

Fancy The selective breeding of animals for particular traits.

Fostering The transference of young to another LACTATING individual of the same species (or less commonly, another species), which acts as a surrogate parent.

Gene The part of the CHROMOSOME that carries the information responsible for determining the body's inherited characteristics.

Genotype The genetic makeup of an organism.

Hand-rearing Rearing of young away from their mother.

Heat The period when the female is ovulating and will accept a mate.

Heterozygous Describes the situation in which the particular GENES on opposing CHROMOSOMES do not correspond to each other, so that an individual can carry another characteristic in its GENOTYPE, which will not be evident from its appearance.

Himalayan patterning A temperature-sensitive MUTATION associated with certain MAMMALS, in which the extremities or POINTS are darker in color than the rest of the body.

Homozygous Describes the situation in which the particular GENES on the paired CHROMOSOMES match, so that the appearance of the individual matches its GENOTYPE.

Inbreeding Mating between very closely related animals, such as a parent and offspring.

Incisors The sharp-edged, paired teeth in the front of the mouth; of particular significance in the lifestyles of RODENTS and LAGOMORPHS.

Independent The time at which a young animal is feeding itself and can be separated from its mother.

Kit A young chinchilla.

Kitten A newly born rabbit.

Lactation The production of milk by the female for her offspring, under hormonal influences.

Lagomorph A member of the order Lagomorpha, which embraces rabbits, hares, and pikas.

Malocclusion A dental problem, usually associated with INCISOR teeth, in which the corresponding teeth in the upper and lower jaws do not meet correctly. This causes the teeth to grow abnormally, making eating a difficult task.

Mammal A warm-blooded creature with hair, which suckles its young.

Marsupial A member of the group of mammals whose young are born after a relatively short gestation period, and which then transfer to a pouch on the abdomen to suckle and complete their development. The best-known examples are wallabies and kangaroos.

Mastitis Inflammation of the mammary glands, arising during LACTATION, making it painful for the female to suckle her offspring.

Molt Shedding of hairs in the coat. This usually occurs regularly, on a seasonal basis.

Mutation A sudden, unexpected change in genetic character, which is reflected in the changed appearance of affected individuals.

Myomorph A member of the largest grouping within the order Rodentia—comprising over 25 percent of all the world's mammals—and incorporating mice, rats, gerbils, and hamsters.

Nocturnal Active at night.
Non-self An individual with more than one color evident in its coat.
Normal The usual coloration associated with a SPECIES.

Parasite An organism that lives on (ectoparasite) or in (endoparasite) another organism (the host) and depends on it for nutrition. Can cause serious illness.
Phenotype The observable traits displayed by an organism, such as its coloration, which are directly influenced by its GENOTYPE.
Pied Describes areas of both white and dark (usually black) fur evident in the coat of the same individual.

Points The extremities of the body, of particular importance in HIMALAYAN PATTERNING, generally comprising the face, ears, legs, feet, and tail.
Postpartum estrus The phenomenon seen in many small MAMMALS whereby the female comes into HEAT again within hours of giving birth.
Probiotic A product containing beneficial bacteria, especially useful in assisting recovery from disorders affecting the digestive tract.

Recessive characteristic A genetic characteristic that will not emerge in a first generation pairing with a pure, normal individual of the same species.
Refection Consumption of soft pellets produced in the CECUM, ensuring the nutritional value of the food can be absorbed into the body.
Rex A MUTATION causing a change in the appearance of the hairs, including WHISKERS, so they become curled.
Ringworm A fungal infection that typically results in circular areas of hair loss. Can be spread to humans.
Rodent A member of the order Rodentia—the largest mammalian grouping, consisting of over 1,700 species or more than 40 percent of the world's mammals.
Rosette An area of hair sprouting in a circular shape from a central point, associated with the Abyssinian guinea pig. Also describes an award given at shows.

Satin A MUTATION affecting the sheen of the coat, causing it to appear more glossy.
Sciuromorph A member of the subgrouping within the order Rodentia which includes the squirrel-like rodents, including the

chipmunks and the beavers.
Scurvy Skin damage resulting from a deficiency of vitamin C. Most commonly seen in guinea pigs.
Self A single-colored individual.
Sex-linked character A genetic character linked with the pair of sex CHROMOSOMES, responsible for determining the individual's gender.
Sheen A lustrous, glossy appearance.
Show standard A list of the key points deemed desirable in a particular VARIETY; used for judging purposes at shows.
Sow A female guinea pig.
Species Animals that show a close relationship to each other; normally occurring in the same area and being very similar in appearance.
Subspecies A taxonomic division below the level of SPECIES, indicating slight differences in appearance between different populations of an organism.

Tortoiseshell Describes an individual displaying red and black coat coloration; often female.
Tricolor Describes coat coloration in which three colors are evident, one of which is often white.
Type The desirable features of an animal for exhibition purposes.

Variety A subgroup within a BREED, usually distinguished by coloration and/or coat type.

Weaning The period during which a young animal switches from its mother's milk to feeding itself.
Whiskers The clusters of larger, thicker hairs on the head developed for sensory purposes, with extensive innervation at their roots.

Further Reading

Alderton, D. *A Petkeeper's Guide to Hamsters and Gerbils* (Interpet Publishing, Dorking, UK 1986)

Alderton, D. *A Petkeeper's Guide to Rabbits and Guinea Pigs* (Interpet Publishing, Dorking, UK 1986)

Alderton, D. *Rodents of the World* (Facts on File, New York, USA 1996)

Barrie, A. *Guide to Owning a Chinchilla* (TFH, Neptune, USA 1997)

Barrie, A. *The Proper Care of Gerbils* (TFH, Neptune, USA 1992)

Bliefeld, M. *Mice* (Barron's Educational Series, Inc., New York, USA 1985)

Brown, M. *Exhibition and Pet Rabbits* (Triplegate, Hindhead, UK 1982)

Bulla, G. *Fancy Rats* (Barron's Educational Series, Inc., New York, USA 1999)

Cooke, A. *Exhibition and Pet Mice* (Spur Publications, Hindhead, UK 1977)

Gendron, K. *The Rabbit Handbook* (Barron's Educational Series, Inc., New York, USA 1999)

Harkness, J. E. and Wagner, J. E. *The Biology and Medicine of Rabbits and Rodents* (Lea & Febiger, Philadelphia, USA 1983)

Henwood, C. *Chipmunks* (TFH, Neptune, USA 1989)

Himsel, C. *Rats* (Barron's Educational Series, Inc., New York, USA 1991)

Jones, A. *Encyclopedia of Pet Mice* (TFH, Neptune, USA 1979)

Kelsey-Wood, D. *African Pygmy Hedgehogs as Your New Pet* (TFH, Neptune, USA 1995)

Kotter, E. *Gerbils* (Barron's Educational Series, Inc., New York, USA 1999)

Leiper, B. *Gerbils and Jirds* (Basset Publications, Plymouth, UK 1980)

MacDonald, D. (ed.) *The Encyclopedia of Mammals, Vol. 2* (Facts on File, New York, USA 1984)

McKay, J. *The New Hamster Handbook* (Blandford Press, London, UK 1991)

Mays, M. *Your First Dwarf Hamster* (Kingdom Books, Waterlooville, UK 1998)

Mays, N. *The Proper Care of Fancy Rats* (TFH, Neptune, USA 1993)

Richardson, V. C. G. *Diseases of Domestic Guinea Pigs* (Blackwell Science, Oxford, UK 1992)

Richardson, V. C. G. *Diseases of Small Domestic Rodents* (Blackwell Science, Oxford, UK 1997)

Robinson, D. *Encyclopedia of Gerbils* (TFH, Neptune, USA 1980)

Robinson, D. *Exhibition and Pet Hamsters and Gerbils* (Saiga Publishing, Hindhead, UK 1979)

Roder-Thiede, M. *Chinchillas* (Barron's Educational Series, Inc., New York, USA 1999)

Sandford, J. C. *The Domestic Rabbit* (Blackwell Science, Oxford, UK 1996)

Turner, I. *Exhibition and Pet Cavies* (Spur Publications, Hindhead, UK 1977)

Vanderlip, S. *Degus* (Barron's Educational Series, Inc., New York, USA 2001)

Verhoef-Verhallen, E. *Encyclopedia of Rabbits and Rodents* (Rebo Productions, Lisse, The Netherlands 1997)

Von Frisch, O. *Hamsters* (Barron's Educational Series, Inc., New York, USA 1998)

Acknowledgments

David Alderton 38, 47, 53t, 94b, 114, 125; AOL 29b, 34–35, 37l, 37r, 96, 98, 101c, 116, 117, 118b, 119t, 119b, 121t, 137t, 137b, 139, 156l, 156r, 157 inset, 158, 159t, 177, 178, 180c, 193c, 193b; Heather Angel 10b, 140c, 145; Jane Burton 31, 50, 51, 52, 53b, 91, 103, 104, 144, 164, 169, 173, 174, 181, 184, 189, 194; Isabelle Français/Cogis 57; James de Bounevialle/Sylvia Cordaiy Photo Library 121b; J. Howard/Sylvia Cordaiy Photo Library 25; Chris Parker/Sylvia Cordaiy Photo Library 93; Eric Gaskin 56; Marc Henrie 12, 33, 40t, 40b, 43, 46–47, 49tr, 55, 58b, 61, 64, 68–69, 70, 74, 75b, 76, 77, 80, 84–85, 100, 106–107, 109, 135, 138, 147b, 148c; Juniors Bildarchiv/C. M. Bahr 8 inset; Juniors Bildarchiv/Nikita Kolmikow 101b; Juniors Bildarchiv/Regina Kuhn 3, 115b, 123b, 124b; Juniors Bildarchiv/St. Liebold 166; Juniors Bildarchiv/H. Schultz 197; Juniors Bildarchiv/Chr. Steimer 6, 8, 107, 118t, 143, 153, 157, 159b, 161, 175, 176, 180b, 183, 196; Juniors Bildarchiv/M. Wegler 7, 11, 13, 15, 20, 24–25, 26, 27, 28, 29t, 39, 41t, 41b, 49tl, 54, 65, 66, 67, 72, 88, 89r, 94t, 96 inset, 97, 99, 113, 179; Juniors Bildarchiv/J. & P. Wegner 124t; Juniors Bildarchiv/

Horst Welke 155; Cyril Laubscher 10t, 17, 34, 45l, 49b, 58t, 59, 60, 62, 63t, 63b, 65 inset, 67 inset, 68, 69, 71, 71 inset, 72 inset, 73, 75t, 78, 79, 80 inset, 81, 83, 85, 86, 86 inset, 87, 89l, 101t, 105, 106 inset, 108, 110c, 110b, 111, 115t, 123t, 126, 127, 128c, 128b, 129, 130, 131, 133, 136, 140b, 146, 147t, 148b, 149, 150, 151, 163, 165, 167t, 167c, 168t, 168b, 170c, 170b, 171, 186, 187, 198, 199; Andrew Henley/Natural Visions 16; Papilio Photographic 45r, 92; Pet House 18, 23; Kim Taylor 191; Bernard Welford 82. Artwork: Julian Baker; Andy Peck, Simon Turvey/Wildlife Art Ltd.

The publishers would like to thank especially the following: Rolf C. Hagen (UK) Ltd—call 01977 556622 for nearest stockist; Pet House, Southend-on-Sea, Essex; Breeders: Janet Bee, Reg Brooks, Barbara Brown-Campbell, Sharon Chapman, Jim Collins, Angela Cooke, Ian & Ann Davis, Sue Dooley, Mike & Lesley East, Amanda Egan, Alan Emson, Essex Breeding Centre, Alan Flarry, Luke French, Sue Garrett, Phil & Gail Gibbs, Helen Gimbert, Caroline Harlow, Ken Lettington, Stanley Maughan, Sue Pearce, Penny Pencliff, Paula Pyke, Rabbit World, Alan & Elaine Rogerson, Jackie Roswell, Geoff Russell, Pam & David Sydenham, Patricia Tilke, Bill Wicks.

Index

Page numbers in *italics* refer to illustrations